Dr. Harold Shinitzky

CW01497422

A Champion's Mindset©

A Champion's Mindset©: 15 Mental Conditioning Steps to Becoming a Champion Athlete

Printed by CreateSpace, An Amazon.com Company

- Available from www.Amazon.com and other retail outlets.

- Available on Kindle and other devices

ISBN-13: 978-1983440441

ISBN-10: 1983340442

Keywords: Sport psychology, Mental conditioning, Focus, Teamwork, Athlete, Mental toughness, Emotion management, Champion, Mindset, Corporate training, Peak performance, Executive coaching, A Champion's Mindset

A Champion's Mindset©:

15 Mental Conditioning Steps to Becoming a Champion Athlete

Dr. Harold Shinitzky

Table of Contents

Introduction

Dr. Harold Shinitzky

Introduction

A Champion's Mindset©:

15 Mental Conditioning Steps to Becoming a Champion Athlete

Heart pounding and muscles tightened as he stood over the 6-foot putt that he had made countless times before. Only this time it was for the US Open. As he drew the club back he thought, "This is for the championship". As he followed through, he watched the ball travel towards its eventual destination. Tasting victory but fearing failure he saw his ball caress the cup, spin around the hole and roll to a stop a foot away.

Have you ever felt your exceptional athletic skills vanish?

Have you ever experienced a change in your performance from practice to competition?

Have you ever wished you could quiet your thoughts and nerves during a game?

Imagine having freedom from stress when hitting your second serve, being laser focused when standing in the batter's box or relaxed during your pre-game routine.

Over the years, it has been a privilege to help Olympians compete at world-class levels, professionals become all-stars and high school teams win national championships. During the past three decades of working with athletes numerous patterns became clear to me.

This book will address 15 mental conditioning steps to becoming a champion athlete. These solutions have helped good athletes become elite, and elite athletes become great.

This book is written for athletes, coaches and parents of elite athletes. You will learn the secrets world-class athletes have mastered to become their best competitor. The earlier you learn these skills the better you will perform in your sport, and not your opponent.

And, if you are a fan of sports, you will love diving into the underlying psychology of a champion athlete.

As a Sport Psychologist with nearly thirty years of experience working with Olympians, professionals and nationally ranked junior athletes, I will:

- Share the steps of top elite athletes and the mental secrets that enable them to succeed when others fail.
- Provide personal accounts and stories illustrating each step.
- Discuss the reasons athletes struggle and the insights to overcome these challenges.
- Review the personality characteristics of successful, elite professional and Olympic athletes.

Now is the time to take your game to the next level. As you read through my book discover the secrets that create A Champion's Mindset©.

Step One: Master the Sport Psychology Triangle

Outline

1. A brief survey to prime you for your journey towards developing A Champion's Mindset©.
2. Athletic excellence is attained by successfully mastering the three components of the Sport Psychology Triangle (Behaviors, Thoughts, Feelings/Physical).
3. Review of the three components of the Sport Psychology Triangle.

The journey every elite athlete travels is an arduous one. Each athlete works with a coach on techniques and tactical skills, and another coach on strength and physical attributes, while some even work with a third on diet and nutrition.

The athletes I have directly coached as a sport psychologist have achieved the greatest success in their respective fields by honing their skills to be mentally tough as well. Each has applied the steps in my book that begin with mastering the **Sport Psychology Triangle** shown on p.11.

As you read this book you will find a range of skills, concepts and personal stories from some of the greatest athletes and coaches that will help you increase your chances of achieving your dreams on the competitive field as well as achieving personal success throughout your life.

In order to prime you for your journey towards developing A Champion's Mindset© take this brief survey.

To prepare to understand and use the **Sport Psychology Triangle**, consider the following questions:

1. (Behavior) Are you engaged in the following behaviors that require you to be your best on and off the competitive field?

a. Do you have tactical strategy coaching?

b. Are you involved in strength training?

c. Do you follow a healthy diet?

d. Have you established consistent daily routines?

e. Do you participate in competitive opportunities?

f. Are you living positively (avoid gambling, poor academic performance etc.)?

2. (Thoughts) What is your attitude about your performance on and off the competitive field?

a. Do you develop self-encouraging statements?

b. Do you dwell on the past?

c. Are you keeping sports in perspective?

d. Are you pessimistic about the future?

e. Are you unable to let go of negativity?

f. Can you stay in the moment?

g. Are you distracted by things outside your control?

3. (Feelings/Physical) How does your body react to perceived stress on and off the competitive field?

a. Have you been told you become too emotional?

b. Do your muscles tighten up before or during competition?

c. Does your breathing change during intense moments or when the game is on the line?

d. Do you fatigue at the end of a long tournament or intense game?

e. Do your mastered skills become inconsistent?

f. Do you worry about the upcoming competition?

Your answers to these questions will be vitally important as you read each of the following steps and consider the solutions.

Athletic excellence is attained by successfully mastering three components of the Sport Psychology Triangle (Behavior, Thoughts, and Feelings/Physical)

The Sport Psychology Triangle is comprised of three components that must be mastered to help an elite athlete reach his greatest potential. The three components of The Sport Psychology Triangle include: Behaviors, Thoughts, and Feelings/Physical.

The Sport Psychology Triangle

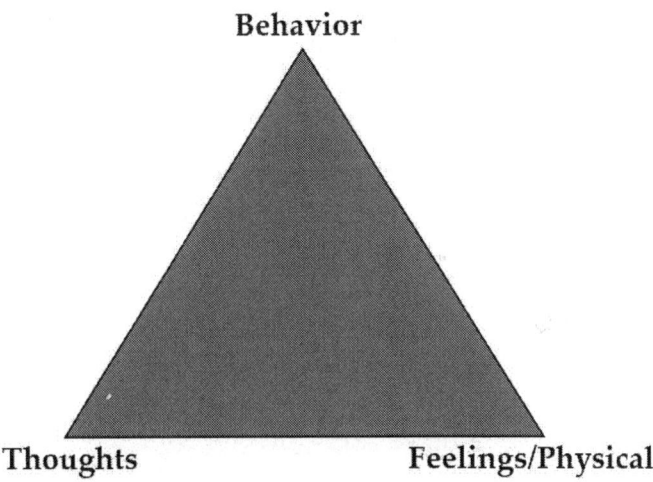

Behavior

Thoughts   Feelings/Physical

Consider this athlete's story: Joe, a top football prospect had a chance to reach his ultimate goal of playing in the NFL. He worked his entire life to make this dream a reality only to see it vanish because of his own actions. Joe was an exceptionally gifted athlete but was caught cheating on his college finals and was appropriately reprimanded by his institution. That should have been enough for him to change his behavior, but one night he consumed too much alcohol, became jealous of his girlfriend and in a moment of rage struck her. With domestic violence charges pending, NFL General Managers labeled him a bad investment, someone with a character flaw who would be a distraction to the team. In the blink of an eye his dream turned into a nightmare.

This story exemplifies the necessity to address the three key components of the Sport Psychology Triangle.

Behaviors

To be an elite athlete, working with a coach who addresses skill development, tactical strategies, and game planning for competition is a necessity. Additionally, a top athlete works with a Nutritionist to make sure his engine is properly fueled allowing him to perform at his highest levels from the start of the match until the finish of the game. Also, a top competitive athlete works with an Exercise Physiologist in weight training, speed work, and stretching.

The athlete also needs to determine if he is engaged in behaviors that might be distractions or negative factors in his life. These could include: gambling problems, substance abuse issues, extra marital affairs, poor business decisions, legal battles, negative peer relationships, and/or a lack of motivation to follow-through on confronting any one of the above.

In other words, *Behavior* means everything you are doing to reach and achieve your goals. These behaviors can include those things that are productive, effective, and beneficial, as well as behaviors which are destructive, unhealthy, and problematic.

If an athlete is not addressing his Behaviors, questions need to be asked…What are the reasons he is sabotaging his long-term potential? Why would he not do all that he could to increase his probability of success? If an athlete is struggling with an addiction, the probability of failure greatly increases with this monkey on his back. If an athlete is tens of thousands of dollars in debt because of a gambling problem, this albatross will interfere with his ability to concentrate and therefore increase the possibility of failure. Self-imposed distractions or external concerns invariably lead to less than optimal performance. Each athlete must ask, "Am I doing everything I can to be successful?"

Once the athlete has worked through these Behavioral barriers - unhealthy habits, poor decision-making skills, self-esteem issues – he can continue to progress towards developing the two other key factors for success as an elite athlete.

Thoughts

The lower left portion of the triangle focuses on *Thoughts* or as psychologists would say, *Cognitions* which include your personal, internal dialogues. Some athletes tend to ruminate on the past and emotionally beat themselves up due to the outcomes. Self-hate, self-loathing or catastrophic negative self-statements and thoughts are emotional toxins that will only poison the vessel that carries them. The past is the past. Learn from it!

Speaking to yourself with optimism, hope and motivation does not guarantee success, but this self-talk enables you to bring all your training, skills and experience to the moment. Having the right, positive statements in your mind is the beginning. All elite athletes have positive self-talk, and an underlying belief in themselves.

There are several aspects to your thoughts that are important. Being in the moment, thinking clearly, processing all the information and filtering out the distractions, allow you to manage competitive situations in which most mortals would crumble. To be a winner you must possess the correct mental foundation which enables you to maximize your physical, cognitive, and emotional aspects of the Sport Psychology Triangle.

I met with the center of an NCAA Division II basketball team after nearly toppling the top NCAA Division I team in the nation. Throughout the entire game, her opponent reminded her that she was not good enough to play for a D-I university. When crunch time arrived in the 4th Quarter she missed her last 4 shots and 4 free-throws. After this game, she couldn't let go of how poorly she played, how she let her teammates down, and how she wasn't as good as the D-I players.

Having the proper internal dialogue is the starting point for all that follows. Some movies give us excellent examples of a positive mental mindset, as in the movie, "The Last Star-Fighter." Prior to the hero realizing he will become the savior of mankind, he denies his potential and states, "I'm not a Star-Fighter. I'm just someone living in a trailer park." The alien recruiter re-states and confirms, "If that is all you believe you are, then that is all you are."

Many athletes have thoughts that focus on upcoming events. Considering worst case scenarios along with best case scenarios is essential for critical analysis in sports. "Managing" this thought process is what is key. When an athlete has thoughts, which are over-focused on worst-case scenarios he puts undue pressure on himself which often prevents him from performing up to his highest level and can lead to his worst fears of the future coming true.

The image below clarifies this point, Chances of Success (unknown author). In order to reach your goal, you must begin with the proper mindset.

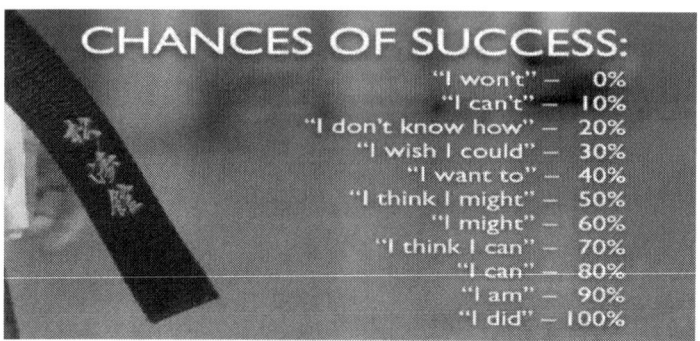

The probability of success starts with believing in the possibilities. To solve today's problems, an athlete cannot use the same logic that caused the problems. Each athlete must begin by challenging his own negative, obstructive thoughts. Many athletes close doors before they are open merely by not believing in their possibilities and by focusing on negatives. If only obstacles are what they see, the risk is they may lose sight of their goals. Words reflect internal thoughts and positive words always help to achieve goals!

As Henry Ford aptly said, "Whether you think you can or whether you think you can't, you're right". It all starts with your mindset.

Feelings/Physical

The lower right side of the Sport Psychology Triangle reflects the Feeling/Physical aspect of experiencing your life. Directly tied to your thoughts is the way your muscles, breath, and heart rate react to your perceptions of the world. When an athlete is in the "zone" he is relaxed, focused and allows his exceptional physical attributes to flourish.

Some athletes tighten up when they perceive a stressful situation. Their once magnificent athletic ability halts as they lock up their muscles. Many athletes physically tighten up from practice to competition and may allow themselves to be consumed with worry or dread. Their body reacts and their fluid movements, speed, and decision-making suddenly disappear. This demonstrates how a proper state of mind produces a proper physical state of being and an elite performance level.

When an athlete physically tightens up he expends more energy than usual. We have all heard an announcer declare that an athlete has "lost their legs" towards the end of a game. Though the athlete has played his sport for years and usually possesses the energy reserves to compete well beyond the final buzzer, they suddenly have heavy legs and fatigue.

Take away for Step One:

Addressing all three of the points of the Sport Psychology Triangle enables an athlete to reach his optimal abilities. When an athlete does everything he can, such as avoid engaging in distractions, carry

15

positive statements or thoughts, and remain relaxed and primed to release his best physical attributes, he is able to maximize his ability to perform, execute, and "shine under the brightest lights" and in the biggest moments.

Mohammed Ali insisted he was the "greatest" as though he was talking to both the world as well as himself. Positive self-statements and affirmations lead to an ultimate belief in self.

Step Two: Managing Stress

Outline

1. There is ACTUALLY no such thing as stress... Yet there is a Stress Reaction based on your perceptions
2. Normal reactions by the body and mind when you react to your thoughts and feelings
3. Three ways the body experiences arousal/anxiety
4. Three ways to assess your progress

The pressure of the moment weighed heavy. It was the AFC Championship and the Denver Broncos were 98 yards away from the end zone. As the clock ticked down, the camera focused on quarterback, John Elway. Yet, while the fans screamed, you could see a calmness in his eyes. The website of the Pro Football Hall of Fame quoted, *"the superb 98-yard drive...ranks as pro football's prototype performance in the clutch"* (*profootballhof.com*). As a unit, the team was unified in the positive belief that they were in the perfect position. As the team huddled for the start of this drive, Bronco's offensive guard, Keith Bishop said, *"We got 'em right where we want 'em!"* (*Sports Illustrated, Rick Reilly*).

With the score tied, 2.1 seconds left on the clock, and with the entire court needing to be traversed for the Duke Blue Devils chance to win the 1992 NCAA tournament against their vaunted enemy, the Wildcats of Kentucky, Coach Krzyzewski called a time out, and declared to his team, *"We're gonna win."* (*sports.espn.go.com*) Everyone and their grandmother knew that the ball was going to be inbounded to Christian Laettner. Grant Hill launched a heralded pass traversing three-quarters of the court to the top of the key and into the waiting arms of Christian Laettner. Back to the basket, from the free throw line, he faked to his right and then pivoted to his left. Just as Coach Krzyewski declared, *"We're gonna win"*, the ball went through the hoop, nothing but net. Where a lesser man would have been crushed by the sheer force and gravity of the moment, the confident (Laettner) ascends to great heights that few will ever reach.

There is ACTUALLY no such thing as stress… Yet there is a Stress Reaction based on your perceptions

The situation doesn't cause stress. What makes one person react doesn't mean everyone will react that same way. Your reaction is based on your perception.

Think about this for a moment. Your body doesn't react to reality but to your mind's perception of reality. If you don't think or perceive a situation as dangerous, your body will not react. You might have heard of the concept, Fight or Flight. It describes the way your body reacts when your mind perceives a threat. If there is a real threat but you didn't notice it or think of it as a problem, you won't react. In reality, the opposite is true. If you perceive there is a threat but none really exists, your body nevertheless will prepare to react. If you call the upcoming competition the biggest game of your life, you will lose it! Many youthful athletes who have skill "freak themselves out", freeze up or panic because of the way they perceive the opposition.

Additionally, what might be stressful to you might not be stressful to someone else. It all comes down to the way you perceive the situation. The reality is, situations are always neutral. In other words, there are no situations that are innately stressful. Words have been developed to explain our perception of our world. Words like nervous, anxious, and panic. What makes one person "nervous" might not make you "nervous." One person might feel that skydiving is exciting and is a way of having fun while another person might state, "Jump out of a perfectly good airplane, are you crazy!?" **The situation is not creating the anxiety, it's the person's perception of the situation.** Elite athletes look forward to the opportunity to perform at the highest level of ability. They have learned panicking does not benefit them, and keeping a level head is the best way to execute each powerful and graceful movement during their sport.

Bernie Madoff was clearly a dangerous individual. His Ponzi scheme robbed many individuals and organization of their financial savings. He behaved illegally, immorally, and without ethics, but people only saw what they wanted to see - his false claims without data of unbelievably consistent financial returns. His sociopathic ability to not feel guilt allowed him to manipulate, lie, and exploit other people to his advantage. His perception was that other people are suckers, ready and ripe for the picking. Most people would be consumed with angst and remorse knowing they were victimizing people. Again, everyone sees their situation through their "eyes or lenses." Every situation presents as neutral and therefore can be perceived as either positive or negative. It's your perception that creates the label.

Have you ever experienced a difference between practice and competition? What changed? Surely the Laws of Physics have not changed. In golf, it's always ball, club, and the Laws of Physics. It does not matter the name of an event, nor the prize money, nor the millions of people watching.

Successful athletes have discovered that if they focus on the task at-hand, they are able to perform the skill set without difficulty. Their muscle memory remains consistent. They don't focus on distractions. The millions of people don't affect them. The missed putt from the previous hole doesn't have any mechanical impact on their subsequent tee shot. The height and size of a basketball rim has not changed from the practice session to the actual game. The height and size of the rim did not change due to playing in the high school gymnasium versus competing for a major professional team. Top athletes realize that their reactions are based on what they choose to focus on. It is not the situation but rather their perception. What you choose to focus on occurs first, before your mind or body reacts.

To illustrate again the point that nothing is innately stressful, think about situations in which you just "wasted time." Lost time waiting in a line; lost time sitting on-hold on the telephone with Customer Service; lost time driving in rush hour traffic. These examples of "wasted time" would drive most people to total frustration. Now consider this example: a CEO of a company with 56 employees that required his constant supervision, or as he called it, "baby-sitting", and who is married with three children, a 9 year-old, 5 year-old and a newborn, when asked how he recharged his batteries or finds alone time, answered that driving home during rush hour traffic was his sanctuary. To him what is a major frustration to most people was his relaxing downtime. The reality is rush hour traffic is neither positive or negative. This situation is neutral. The key factor is your perception of the situation.

Here is a secret few know: You cannot tell your brain what NOT to focus on. If I tell you not to think of a big purple elephant, there it is. The very thing that I tell you NOT to think about is exactly what your brain focuses on. This has been scientifically proven. The key is to tell yourself exactly what to focus on.

An example to prove the point: The 13th Hole is a Par 4, 320-yard hole. 50 yards from the green there is a small creek. One man in a foursome said, "Oh, it's a water hole. I don't want to hit it into the water. But to be safe, I'm going to grab my water ball, the one with the crack in it." Guess who hit his tee shot right into the drink? Bingo! The guy who was telling his brain to focus on the water. He didn't tell his brain what to focus on, such as "I'll use my Driver and use proper form which will get my ball to travel 250 yards." In reality, if he focuses on what's important, the creek doesn't exist, the tens of thousands of people watching on TV don't exist, the prize money doesn't exist. And, if he focuses on the task at hand… hitting the ball at the correct angle, choosing the appropriate club, along with the laws of physics, the flight of the ball is predictable!

Your reality is based on the way you perceive and th
given situation. We all have our distinct reactions in life, but now ....
you manage and respond to situations is the key factor. I often use the
90-10 Rule: 10% of how well we succeed is based on what happens to us,
and 90% is how we respond.

Normal reactions by the body and mind when you react to your thoughts and feelings

It is important for you to understanding how your body and mind
naturally react to your perceptions of the world. When you perceive a
situation as "stressful" your body alerts, becomes aroused or primed and
ready for action.

The body naturally reacts to whatever you "perceive" as stressful.
I discussed in my book, Your Mind: An Owner's Manual for a Better Life
(Career Press, 2009) that emotions do not happen because of reality but
because of your perception of reality. What makes you nervous may not
make the person next to you nervous, and what makes that person
nervous may not make you nervous. It is your perception of any given
situation. Hence, your body reacts to what you define as "stressful."
Once your body reacts you can choose how you respond and regain
control. This natural reactive nature of our body is best described by the
Yerkes-Dodson Inverted U-Curve.

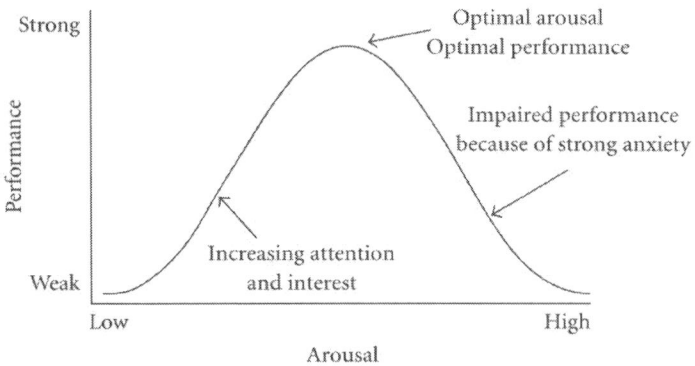

The following is an explanation of the above graph. The X-Axis is arousal or awakening of the body system. The Y-Axis is performance and functioning. If you don't care or are excessively overconfident, you wouldn't experience any arousal to the system. Your heart and breathing rate would remain unchanged. Your blood pressure and hormonal release of adrenalin would not change. However, as you begin to perceive demands, expectations, or "pressure", your system naturally awakens and your performance naturally increases. As an example: you're notified of an exam on Friday and it's Wednesday and you have not studied. Your mind perceives a threat of doing poorly on the exam, knowing you need a good grade. Your body reacts to this "perceived" stress or demand, so you grab your books and head to the library. This is reasonable and smart. However, if you react with panic and become overwhelmed, you might freeze up and forget the material or take no action because you feel like a failure and flunk the exam.

The apex of the above curve is the desired location an athlete reaches when he obtains his optimal level of arousal, which then leads to his optimal level of performance.

To help you understand this concept think about fertilizer at a golf course. If you have no fertilizer on the fairways, insects and bacteria can damage the course. So, you sprinkle some fertilizer on to keep the insects away and build healthy blades of grass that will withstand the traffic. There is an optimal level of fertilizer to sprinkle on the grass to make it lush and hearty. However, when you begin to dispense too much fertilizer, you begin to burn the grass. Pouring an excess amount of fertilizer will kill the desired beautiful, luxurious and green grass.

Yerkes-Dodson identified that there is an optimal level of arousal. Again, since your emotions are not based on reality but rather due to your perception of reality, you need to consider how you react to your perceptions, your definitions of the situations and how you respond to the reactions.

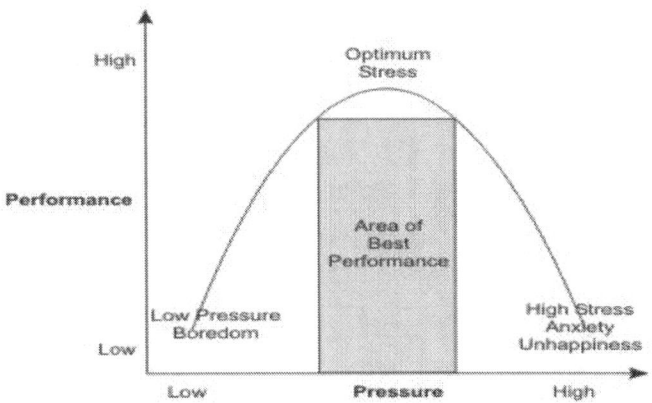

The Inverted-U relationship between pressure and performance

Often athletes will tell me they perform perfectly fine during practice, but once they enter competition, their performance drops. Other athletes will complain that during competition their performance is not consistent. The reality is that their focused, inner dialogue, and perception have changed from practice to competition. If left unchecked, the amount of arousal can become so overwhelming their muscles tighten up, fluid motion falls apart, and performance decreases.

Based on the above, the misguided goal would be to attempt to never react, rather than to respond as quickly as possible. Our bodies are built to have a natural reaction.

One of the soccer players I coached complained that he would "freak out" before a game. I asked what he meant by "freak out", and he said he would start thinking negative thoughts which led to anxious feelings. He became stuck in his head thinking, "I'm not good enough…My teammates will be disappointed by my performance…The coach will bench me." Reality demonstrated he was good enough to be recruited to the pro level, his teammates considered him a gifted physical athlete, and he was never benched due to his performance on the pitch. But he still retained negative thoughts which forced him to work even harder, fueling him to "over-achieve." He applied himself to prevent his greatest fears from coming true. In this case, he responded in a productive manner to his emotional reactions. Again, the misguided goal is to attempt to never react, the healthier goal is to respond as quickly as possible.

Three ways the body experiences arousal/anxiety

What I have been describing in the above examples is called anxiety which has three components: Physical Reactions, Thoughts, and Feelings. Most people are not aware what is referred to as anxiety can be experienced in three different ways. Knowing which one of the three you are experiencing is important for the solution to the anxiety. Each of the three components of "anxiety" can be separately addressed. You might only experience one of the three, or you might discover you have a combination of the three, or you may experience all three of the components of "anxiety" at once. Again, each of the three can be dealt with, addressed, and resolved.

Physical Reactions – An athlete who experiences physical anxiety usually is aware of changes to breathing, heart rate, muscle contractions, or other physical changes. Remember, it is normal to react to any perception, but the question is how well the athlete responds following that awareness. Whenever muscles tighten, skillful and fluid movements may begin to fail.

A common change that occurs when stressed is tightening of the abdomen which leads to short choppy breathing. Short choppy breathing decreases oxygen to the lungs at which point their heart must beat faster to get the limited amount of oxygen to the brain and body. When muscles tighten up and oxygen levels decrease, elite physical abilities begin to vanish.

Being in the "Zone" or the "Flow" presents an opposing, relaxed state where the brain and body act in unison, movements happen fluidly and without much thought.

Cognitive/Thoughts – The following stories illustrate the cognitive/thought aspect of anxiety: I coached a young woman who could not stop having negative internal dialogue, thinking she would hit her head on the diving board when preforming a back flip. Another woman I coached was competing in cheerleading as a Flyer and when her fellow cheerleaders launched her into the air, the base/catcher slipped, allowing gravity to step in. After landing on her hind quarter, she was taken to the hospital for a MRI. After that incident, she realized she could not always trust her base to execute responsibilities, which led her to avoid Flying. Even after the teammate responsible for the fall graduated that year, she still chose not to Fly because she felt there was the potential risk of an accident.

Thoughts create your reality and cause your body to react. Whether your thoughts are based on reality or your imagination your body with react.

Feelings/Worry - Many athletes I coach tend to worry about the future. Some worriers focus on the worst-case scenarios. One of my clients feared as a football coach, he would call the wrong play based on down and distance. As his panic grew he would focus more on what other people thought of him and if he was calling the best play, which would then lead to mixing up the proper blocking assignment for the called play. He clearly had the experience and knowledge but his fears led him to panic that his players would lose respect for him. In reality, the players respected his knowledge, valued his wisdom, and admired his professional experience. He worried incessantly the other position coaches would scoff at his incorrect play calling, but usually he did select a play which fit down and distance. The curious reality is even if he did call the "best" play, a player may not execute his responsibilities on the field. Likewise, he could call the "worst" play and the defense might be out of position which could lead to a broken play 60-yard score. It is important to realize there are never any guarantees, but only the opportunity to increase the probability of success. The coaches worrying did not resolve the problem but only led to dread and ruminating that intensified his panic.

Three ways to assess your progress

Progress can be determined in many ways. I coach clients to think about anxiety or arousal using three criteria: Frequency, Duration and Intensity. Once we structure an intervention, I ask each athlete to monitor and ask these questions:

1. How frequently do you experience the stress? How often do the symptoms occur? The goal is for it to be less frequent.

2. How long is the duration of the symptoms? How long did it last? The goal is a shorter duration.

3. When the symptoms occur, how intense are the symptoms? How extreme was the symptom when it occurred? The goal is less extreme.

I recently coached an athlete who struggled with catastrophic thinking. His thoughts traveled down a path of negative self-talk. To address this tendency, I coached him to use a two-step process called Cognitive-Restructuring. First, catch yourself as soon as possible when negative, intrusive thoughts begin. Two, replace the negative thoughts with positive, constructive, productive thoughts based on reality.

Negativity, if left unchecked, act as a predictable, irritating friend…well, a frenemy. Your frenemy is always there but brutal and negative. Most people are unaware of this negative voice until it is nearly shouting abuse. As we have discussed, the sooner to deal with an issue the better.

Many athletes are unsure what it means to self-state with a positive affirmation or thought based on their own reality. Determine this by asking yourself: Has a coach ever offered a compliment, praise, or observation about successful behavior? Has a peer given positive feedback regarding performance in a game? Have you ever noticed that when applying yourself, you are able to pick up the necessary skills? There are a host of personal, positive experiences, observations and feedback that can be verbalized or visualized to replace negative thinking. I coach all my athletes to drink them up, take them in, and use those moments to replace the negative pictures and thoughts.

Of course, learning to accept a compliment is necessary to this process. There are two parts to accepting a compliment. First, you need to actually say "Thank you." Not, "thanks," or "no biggy" or "anyone could have done that." Just say, "Thank you." Second, state why your accomplishment was important to you. This is not being a braggard, arrogant, or "blowing your own horn." It is recognizing the value of your accomplishment. To have a good sense of self and ego identity, you need to take in and accept compliments that have been based on your behavior.

An example of a compliment might be, "I am proud of you for earning the top honor this past season."

Accepting the Compliment – "Thank you. I worked hard to do my best, and I'm grateful to have been awarded this honor."

Only by taking in and accepting the positive feedback about your behavior will you develop a healthy and honest sense of self which will allow you to successfully complete the Cognitive-Restructuring intervention listed above.

Important Note: I also encourage an athlete to seek additional mental health services when needed. There are times when the struggles with anxiety or other mental health conditions can become debilitating. According to the Anxiety and Depression Association of America (ADAA), 40 million people over the age of 18 or approximately 18% of the national population suffer from anxiety. Numerous high-profile athletes have shared personal stories of their struggles with anxiety or other conditions (Kevin Love NBA, Dwayne "The Rock" Johnson, Olympic cyclist Chris Hoy, Mardy Fish ATP, DeMar DeRozan NBA, Olympic swimmer Michael Phelps, Brandon Marshall NFL, Bubba Watson PGA). Kevin Love offered an exquisitely detail recount of his personal experience (2018) while Mardy Fish shared his emotional challenges (2015) in articles published via The Players' Tribune.

Top athletes turn to coaches for skill development: strength coaches to physically prepare, nutritionists to fuel engines, and sport psychologists to maintain optimal mental conditioning.

Take away for Step Two:

If you maintain a healthy sense of control over arousal, respond quicker in a more positive manner to the natural reaction shown by your body, and accurately process positive feedback based upon your behavior, you then will be able to experience the world in a more positive, constructive and productive way.

Step Three: Mental Toughness

Outline

1. 10 Keys to Mental Toughness
2. Attributes of an Elite Athlete
3. 3 Barriers to Mental Toughness

An elite athlete realizes he possesses similar physical attributes to his opponent, has achieved the highest level of skill development, and performed his physical abilities in a consistent pattern and probability. He knows that developing the skill set and being consistent will provide him the greatest likelihood of performing at his highest level. While an NFL lineman probably weighs nearly the same as his foe across the line, and an NBA team has a limited array of plays which means the other team is aware of the plays, the elite athlete possesses the rare ability to execute. Heckling fans and poor officiating does not cause this athlete to lose focus and become distracted. Staying focused, disciplined and invested in the moment sets the stage for the elite athlete to become MENTALLY TOUGH.

10 Keys to Mental Toughness

Olympic and professional athletes possess a range of personality characteristics that help reach the apex of their athletic abilities and be the most mentally tough competitors. Athletes, parents of athletes, and coaches need to foster the development of these attributes. Consider these ten keys as vitally important if the goal is to possess A Champion's Mindset©.

I. Absolute Belief in Yourself -- You know the outcome of a game is partially out of your control, but choose the factors that give you a sense of personal belief and an internal sense of control. You know you have done all you can to achieve your highest level of preparation and performance and are fully committed to applying and preparing prior to an event. You take full responsibility for your performance during the event and do not blame your behavior on anyone else if the outcome is not what you had planned. You believe you can control the factors within in your purview and realize there will be positive experiences as well as unsuccessful outcomes, but you remain committed to doing your best. Doing your best is not an outcome, it is a process. This is not arrogance but self-confidence, and you know you are ready and prepared for the outcome.

2. Emotions Out-Information In -- You realize riding the highest highs means you could suffer the lowest lows. Your emotions are normal and you react. However, you learn from the past, and gather information and data from every opportunity whether it is positive or negative. After you experience your initial reaction to an event, stroke, shot, race, or tournament, you reflect by taking in the information which leads to a positive or negative outcome. Your goal is to assimilate the information, learn, and improve it. You learn quickly to release emotions out and process information in.

3. Focus-- You never lose sight of your goals, and remain focused before, during and after an event. Distractions are all around, but you filter anything and everything. Nothing exists that is relevant to your personal performance outside the lines of the field. You filter out irrelevant factors as white noise and learn how to manage changing situations. If it is warm, you hydrate. If it is windy, you adjust your stroke to compensate. Obstacles are what you see when you lose sight of your goals. By practicing focus, you will expand the amount of time you remain attentive, concentrated, and able to filter out externals.

4. Live and Learn from the Past-- You know dwelling on the past will only distract you from being in the moment. The past is history and you cannot change it. However, you can learn from the past by using both positives and negatives as private lessons from yourself to yourself so you don't repeat the mistake. Your commitment is to always improve.

5. Perseverance-- You stay the course. If at first you don't succeed, try, try again. Your goal is to improve, and every competitive moment presents an opportunity to practice reaching the apex of your abilities. You remember your aspirations are not a sprint, but a marathon, and you keep your eyes on the prize. It's always easy during the wins. Perseverance truly helps during the less successful times, injury rehab or across the long season.

6. Positive Self-Talk-- You remember your perception and state of mind create your reality. By practicing positive self-talk, you remain motivated during trying times. You have a choice how you react to any given situation, and you choose to listen to your positive self-talk.

7. Process Not Outcome-- You choose to focus on factors that move you in the direction of success. You don't worry about future events but remain in the moment. You have laser focus on the details, and trust your responsibilities which include the smallest to the largest. You minimize your errors and strive to maximize each moment to achieve your goals. As Confucius said, "Even the greatest journey begins with a single step." It is the commitment to the smallest details that make up the process which eventually leads to the outcome.

8. Reframe-- You don't get distracted by the name of a prestigious event, the number of people watching or the potential rewards that could come with victory. These distractions have nothing to do with your physical and mental performance. Let the fans, media, and other people become consumed with the glitz of the event. Remember the laws of physics don't change because of the event. Your job is to stay focused and do your best.

9. Resilience and Coping Skills-- You have the capacity to take a hit and get back up. As Confucius said, "Success is not in never falling but in rising every time you fall." You don't personalize negative comments and keep situations in perspective because you have learned not to let emotions rule you by responding rather than reacting. You now respond rather than react. You address areas of weakness to gain mastery of your life.

10. Time to Shine-- Your opportunity is today. You have put yourself in the best possible position to apply yourself during any given event. You hope your opponent performs at their best. Today you see the opportunity to rise to the top and you are filled with excitement at the possibilities that present themselves. Today is your time to shine.

I recently conducted a Needs Assessment of the players on a professional soccer team, 93% of the players self-reported that the topic which would be most helpful to learn more about: Mental Toughness.

Attributes of An Elite Athlete

The following graph reveals a wide range of attributes and beliefs embodied by successful, elite pros and Olympic athletes:

★ Name Attributes of Elite Athletes?

Driven - Motivated	Internal LOC, I control me Don't blame	Physically gifted	Postpone normal life	Committed
Advanced pain threshold	Disciplined	Competitive	Teamwork	Leadership
Absolute belief in self	Understand long-term goals (season, years)	Do my best is my best	Personal Accountability (Team vs. Ind)	Belief in Coaching - Mentoring
Passionate	No Guarantees, Increase probability	Never stop	Resilience – Steve Jobs – Something out of Nothing	Ego-Boundaries Don't personalize (Favorite fan)
Communication skills	Positive attitude	Emotion Management	Live and learn – short term memory	Realistic Expectations

Driven – Motivated

Sustained motivation exists as an underlying challenge for all athletes. Distractions consistently challenge attention span. An elite athlete does not have to be encouraged to apply himself because he already is holding himself accountable. No one has to remind him to review extra game film because he is continuously analyzing the opponent to better understand every detail, which could help the team reach its shared goal.

Internal Locus of Control

The athlete who believes outcomes are directly impacted by his personal behavior, invests his heart and soul into the sport. He perceives the direct link between the time in the gym or practicing his skills, and the eventual ability to compete at the highest levels. His conviction in working hard is based upon his belief that his behaviors will make a difference. This belief is referred to as Internal Locus of Control (LOC). This athlete is self-driven, loyal and committed.

Physically gifted

Clearly the elite athlete is more physically advanced than the general population. Yet he still needs to put forth the time to master the specific skill sets. A coach measures the physicality of his thoroughbreds, but they also look for the intangibles. Though his genetics have been passed along by their parents, it is what the elite athlete does with his body that allows him to rise beyond the others physical specimens.

Postpone normal life

When an elite athlete's friends are making plans to attend the school dance, he might need to skip it as he will be competing at an out-of-state event. Coaches appreciate when a young athlete is aware he will be missing out on normal activities and events in his life. His schedule will be more intense than his peers, with school followed by 4-6 hours of practice. With practice, travel, and tournaments he will be occupied, but he has made this choice and is willing to invest the time commitment. He does not harbor resentment, but rather makes the trade of a "normal life" in exchange for a chance to fulfill his dreams.

Committed

For an elite athlete to reach the highest levels of competition it requires a commitment to follow through on coaching recommendations, goal completion/follow through, and an abundance of personal pride to maintain unending drive until hitting the top.

Advanced pain threshold

Physical and psychological pain management is imperative when playing competitive sports. An elite athlete pushes his body to the limit in weight training, conditioning, and preparation. The football adage states, "The first day of football training camp is the first day an athlete plays injured." The elite push themselves through an injury, and maintains the mental fortitude to focus beyond the pain. The warrior mindset drives the strong competitor through practice, games, and towards his ultimate goal.

Disciplined

An athlete that is disciplined remains focused in light of external distractions. He stays the course and understands long-term goals have short-term steps that need to be mastered. No one needs to micromanage this athlete.

Competitive

Regardless of the sport, this player finds the challenge to make success his final outcome. Beyond mastering the skills, this athlete loves the opportunity to compete. He always applies himself at 100%. Dominating and being triumphant are concepts he lives by.

Teamwork

An elite athlete needs to work well with others and in unison with the team. He needs to take on responsibilities, and communicate clearly in order to identify concerns, address problems, and plan out strategies that will lead to the eventual team success. When an elite athlete is mixed with less experienced players he needs to help elevate his teammates play through good leadership, patience, and encouragement.

Leadership

When describing a leader in the sports world people often hear the comment, "He has that 'It' factor." This is the athlete that is selected as team captain by the coaches or by teammates. A leader helps make a teammate play better, leads by example and encourages everyone to apply themselves to the fullest extent. He is a natural motivator, great communicator, inspirational, and helps others reach for their personal best.

Absolute belief in self

For years I have encouraged athletes to develop the mindset, "If it's meant to be, it's up to me." An athlete that possesses an absolute belief in self knows he has applied himself fully, put in the preparation time, sought exceptional coaching, and acquired top flight competitive opportunities. His confidence is not dependent on the world around. This is not arrogance, but a sense being self-assured. He maintains mental toughness through the good and bad times and knows only he controls himself and believes he will always do his best.

Understand long-term goals

An athlete with a long-term career view stays the course. Every practice session, every game tournament, or competitive event provides an opportunity to work on new skills, plays, or techniques. Breaking down the long-term goal into short-term steps facilitates progress for both athlete and team. Meaningful growth flowers out of the awareness of little things done well.

Doing my best is my best

A top competitive athlete knows he only controls himself, and the only thing he can bring to the game is his best. This does not guarantee a victory. Doing his best increases the likelihood of reaching his greatest potential. The process of preparing, being ready, and putting forth his best effort is within his control. Doing his best is not an outcome measured by wins and losses. Maintaining a positive attitude, being in the moment, and applying the range of skills he has acquired into this competitive moment is doing his best.

Personal accountability

When an athlete is given specific responsibilities, he needs to realize teammates are counting on him to follow through. This athlete doesn't blame his behavior on anyone else. He doesn't make excuses. An elite athlete assumes personal responsibility and never relinquish this conviction. He puts in the time studying film of his opponent. He makes sure he is in the best possible physical conditioning, and has practiced with knowledgeable coaches, and embraces the opportunity to shine in competition.

Belief in coaching – mentoring

Exceptional coaches and teammates provide an elite athlete with a support network to help him achieve optimal performance. A top coach knows how to coach each personality on the team. Top athletes understand these same principles when encouraging their teammates. A good coach can communicate points with detail and clarity to assist the athlete in understanding the nuance of the play, technique or vision. The elite athlete believes in his coach's wisdom, knowledge and expertise.

Passionate

No one needs to encourage the passionate athlete. He will work harder than the other athletes. He will put forth his best effort during practice as well as during the games. His passion is not dependent on winning or losing. He applies himself to his fullest extent all the time. He knows the saying, "How you practice is how you play." Passion comes from deep within the athlete's core values and can be an inspiration to the team.

No guarantees - Increase probability of success

If the elite athlete learns this maxim as early as possible he will discover great success and magnificent possibilities. There are never any guarantees, yet he does have the ability to increase his probability of success. He can shoot his lowest round in golf, but not win the tournament. Higher ranked teams don't always win. However, there are a multitude of steps and activities for him to practice that will help him reach his potential. Hitting deeper ground strokes in tennis doesn't always win the point, but it will certainly increase the probability of success. Master the basics and work on increasing his consistency will put him in the best place to reach victory.

Never stop

Every Olympian has developed a "never say die" attitude. He has been working toward his dream and goals for years. His conviction is unwavering and commitment is unshakeable. Regardless of the length of the journey or the obstacles he confronts, this athlete never stops. This athlete has the mindset, "Today offers another opportunity to do my best against the best in the world." Through good or bad performance the elite athlete never stops.

Resilience

You might have heard about a team that, "Bends but doesn't break" or a football team that becomes impenetrable when the opponent reaches the Red Zone. This same concept applies to the individual athlete. His capacity to handle adversity and bounce back is remarkable. After a bad play, his focus is always to adjust and continue to compete at his highest level. If he is in a "slump", he maintains an attitude which allows him to continue applying himself through thick or thin. He doesn't personalize or generalize negatives. This athlete has the mindset to fight through any challenge presented.

Ego-boundaries

The top athlete knows himself well enough that external comments don't adversely impact him. He doesn't react to taunting or crumble when there is a negative headline. Ego-boundaries can be defined as knowing the difference between yourself and someone else. The top athlete knows who he is, and comments from others don't cause him to become overwhelmed, bothered or distracted. He knows how invested and committed he is to his sport. He knows his value system and always lives up to it. He doesn't personalize disrespectful comments because he knows who he is and isn't influenced by others. As a committed and passionate athlete, when a sport's announcer or fan makes a disparaging comment, he doesn't become devastated because he has good ego-boundaries.

Communication skills

An exceptional athlete understands exquisite detail of plays, techniques, and concepts. He wants as much detailed information as possible in order to improve and execute to the best of his ability. A good leader needs to be able to communicate with clarity and passion. He breaks lessons down into details, and thrives when quickly processing the information.

Positive attitude

An elite athlete will put in extremely long practice sessions, enduring physical pain and periodic frustration. However, throughout this experience the elite athlete remains steadfast with a positive attitude. The highs are easy to traverse and during the lows he doesn't give up. Though the frustrations can be challenging and the journey might be long, he remains positive for both himself and teammates.

Emotion management

Everyone has an emotional reaction to a situation regardless of triumph or loss. However, choosing to dwell in raw emotions does not provide him with any meaningful lessons to help learn from triumph or loss. Beating himself up with negative emotions will serve no benefit. An elite athlete uses every outcome in sport as a private lesson to himself. He learns from the past so as not to repeat it. He uses the Post-shot routine to ask three questions, 1) What was my plan? 2) What actually happened? 3) What did I learn so I won't repeat it? He also doesn't allow other players to "get under his skin." He controls his own emotional reactions and doesn't feed into the trash talking by his opponents.

Live and learn – Short-term memory

A top athlete realizes that he cannot change the past. If he focuses on the past, he is not focusing on the present. This makes a bad situation worse. By dwelling on a negative from the past, he loses focus on the one thing he can control, the present. Every outcome is a wonderful opportunity to learn something from the past. These lessons can occur in the moment (misreading the spin of a curve ball) or after the competition (what would I do differently the next time?). The best athlete has discovered ruminating on the past is a waste of energy, and moves forward from these lessons. He has learned the best solution after processing an outcome, is to live and learn from the past, so as not to repeat if the outcome is undesirable.

Realistic expectations

Every athlete works at improving his abilities. Yet, these goals need to be realistic. If he wants to progress he needs to make expectations attainable, realistic, measurable, and within a reasonable timeframe. Progress is incremental. The elite athlete bases expectations on current skill levels, and determines within a specific time period the exact details to increase the probability of success. These all lead to achieving his goals and expectations. Golfers strive to hit more greens in regulation. Tennis players work towards hitting fewer unforced errors. Baseball players set their expectations so not to expand the strike zone in their effort to increase their on-base percentage. There are no guarantees, but every elite athlete always increases his probability of success!

Three barriers to Mental Toughness

Equally important is the personality tendencies that could impede the ability to possess the mental toughness of a champion athlete. These three patterns of reacting to athletic life need to be monitored, addressed, and resolved in order to remove barriers to athletic success.

1. Being hyper-emotional or perfectionistic are probably the deadliest impediment to achieving mental toughness. The adage, "You live by the sword and you die by the sword" reflects a pattern of extremes. Hyper-critical athletes often begin from a natural belief in reaching the pinnacle. This can also be referred to as "Perfectionism" which drives elite athletes to achieve so much. It is also this "Perfectionism" that creates an unattainable belief hoping to never make any mistakes. Think about your favorite professional athlete. Do they always perform up to "Perfection"? Absolutely not. Think about a PGA golf tournament. Do any of the pros have bad rounds? Absolutely, yes. Do any of the top golfers miss the cut? You bet! Every single tournament many of the world's top professional golfers miss the cut. No

professional is perfect. As an amateur you must release yourself from this prison of perfection and strive for excellence. I coach my athletes to understand perfectionism should be a driving force to improve, but perfectionism should never be the criteria used to judge yourself.

2. Employing All-or-None reasoning is doomed to self-imposed barriers. If your tennis serve is on today, then you will dominate. If your tennis serve is off today, then you're going to lose. Each player must liberate himself from the irrational belief of All-or-None thinking. A single component of the sport should not be utilized as the criteria for self-implosion. A tennis player told me that when he arrived at the last tournament he was informed of the format for each competitive round. He claimed that because of the assigned format he was not able to find his rhythm. Yet the other players also had to deal with this format and amazingly they found their rhythm. In this case you can hear the tennis player blaming his performance. Since everyone had to deal with this factor, it is considered a constant like windy conditions of the British Open, excessive heat at the Australian Open or freezing temperatures at an NFL game in Green Bay. Rather than complaining or blaming his behavior on the format, he needed to figure out how he was going to adjust and adapt.

3. Focusing externally on everything outside of your control is fatal. There are players and parents who will complain about anything and everything. The umpires are terrible. The venue is not up to expectations. Focusing on external factors beyond your control removes you from the moment and unconsciously provides you a ready-made excuse for performing badly or losing.

Take away for Step Three:

Doing your best is only controlled by you. The motivational speaker Zig Ziglar said it best: "Success is the doing, not the getting; in the trying, not the triumph. Success is a personal standard, reaching for the highest that is in us, becoming all that we can be. If we do our best, we are a success." By developing these personality characteristics and these key attributes, you will increase your probability of success.

Step Four: Emotions Out/Information In

Outline

1. **How to Keep Calm, Cool and Collected**
   Emotions Out/Information In
2. **Overthinking: In Your Head, Not the Moment**
   Don't allow negative self-talk to cause emotional or physical paralysis
3. **The Slump: Making Bad – Worse**
   Allowing past frustration to interfere with current performance
4. **Brain Scan Scratch/10 Handicap**
   Show me a brain scan and I'll show you the difference between a scratch golfer and a 10-handicapper: Evidence-based fMRI Science
5. **Jawing: Trash talk**
   Understanding psychological gamesmanship
6. **Fan vs. Fanatic/Frenemies**
   Don't allow negative externals to determine your self-perception and emotional state

In high school, I was partnered with a classmate in doubles. We were taught, *"Rush and Crush…The team that controlled the net, controlled the match…Chip and Charge…Create angles…Move as if there was a rope connecting the two of you."* Interestingly, my partner and I would drive a deep ball against our opponent and charge the net. Our opponents would return the ball towards us. If a horizontal flying ball, strikes a flat plain object (the racquet) in which direction should the ball fly? Right, back towards the opponents on a horizontal path. Unfortunately, my partner's volley would end up at the bottom of the net. Horizontal flight, flat plain object, bottom of the net? My partner would then let everyone within a three--county area know just how frustrated he was. He would curse and strike the net with his racquet. Occasionally, he even attempted to propel his racquet into interstellar space. I would ask him, *"Did you teach the net a lesson? Next time, will it get out of your way?"* Unfortunately, rather than learning from the information right in front of him, he allowed his emotions to erupt and block his learning. In order for a ball to end up at the bottom of the net, my partner was swinging rather than punching at the ball.

How to Keep Calm, Cool and Collected

Emotions Out/Information In

Your emotional reactions reflect your assessment of your performance of the situation. When your performance is successful you feel positive. When the outcome is less than successful you feel frustrated or worse. The problem with either direction is you have not used the assessment and emotion to learn from and grow. Your emotions never offer helpful, detailed insights that allow you to replicate successful form or adapt and change techniques following negative outcomes. Your feelings don't provide wisdom, but rather momentary reactions. Jumping for joy and high fiving teammates when excited doesn't help you repeat the successful form. Verbally berating yourself after a bad outcome does not benefit your technique during future competitive opportunities. The earlier an athlete learns the concept, Emotions Out/Information In, will she be able to use every moment of competition as a learning tool to improve.

We have all experienced the moment when our emotions get the best of us. This is where the concept of Emotions Out/Information In begins. As with all athletes, once my tennis partner was able to learn from the past, so not to repeat it, he discovered a new level of consistency and success.

As my mentor Dr. Goldstein shared, "Emotions don't think and strong emotions obliterate thinking."

Over the years, many athletes implode by allowing a momentary event to emotionally overwhelm their ability to think. The best approach is: Live and Learn. Ask yourself, "What just happened I didn't want to happen, and what can I learn from this mishap?"

No one is perfect. Not even the best pro is able to attain perfection. Yet, everyday amateurs hold themselves up to this unattainable standard. Their expectation is perfection. Amateurs do not even possess the skills, nor have they mastered the nuances, and yet they expect to perform perfectly and consistently. If you could do this already, you wouldn't be an amateur, you would be a pro. The best pro.

When you emotionally react, it interferes with your ability to live and learn.

One of the greatest examples of just how devastating emotions can be is shown by one of the PGA golfers I coached. I observed when he was confident, he walked with his shoulders back, his chest pumped out and his chin up. When he was frustrated (emotional) he was slumped over. Think about this, "What is the physical distance the head of your golf club travels when you are confident and standing tall as compared to when you are frustrated and slumped over?" Sport is about repeating the same movement in precisely the same way. Any deviation from that exacting form leads to an increase in failure. When you allow your emotions to get the best of you, you allow yourself to alter your form. All of the teaching, coaching, and experience goes right out the window. What was once predictable now becomes erratic. Rather than focusing on the present, your raw emotions limit your growth. Rather than focusing on the here and now, you dwell on the past. Rather than learning from the past, so not to repeat it, you are venting, yelling, and decreasing your consistency.

The best starting point: understand your emotions are normal. You serve an ace in tennis and feel great. You sink a 3-pointer in basketball and feel you're in the groove. However, if you miss a 6-foot putt, grumble, fume, and kick yourself but never learn from your mistake, odds are that you are going to continue to make the same error. If a quarterback throws the perfect ball and you drop it, cursing like a sailor, thinking about how the fans want you traded, you will probably not learn from the past, so not to repeat it.

I always like to tell athletes, "Emotions out, Information in." Everything is a learning opportunity. Every play is a moment to learn, grow and improve by striving to be your best. As an amateur you are obviously attempting to decrease your errors, so you have a perfect opportunity to learn and grow. As a professional, you have a tactical coach to work on the details, practicing and striving to do your best and learn from the past. It's best to have short-term memory. Live and learn. Move forward. Emotions out, Information in.

In the movie *A League of Their Own*, Tom Hanks states, "There's no crying in baseball." He was encouraging his players to stay focused and not react emotionally. Like the Chicago Cubs fans, we all would experience the highs of winning the long-awaited championship, as well as feeling devastated when our Cubs fell short during the past 100 years. Post-game interviews often reveal heart felt sorrow, pain, and defeat as well as sharing the celebration of hoisting the championship trophy over their heads. The release of tears reflects the emotional investment committed by the individual to the event.

Notice, I referenced post-game. Allowing emotions to flow and consume you during competition is both the wrong time and the wrong place and you are no longer in the winning mindset. You don't think clearly or make good decisions. I share with athletes regardless of your intelligence (bright, average or below) if your emotions supersede your thoughts, you will always say or do something you later will regret. We react to a good or bad play but I am talking about degrees of reaction. A fist pump is one thing. Chucking golf clubs into the alligator infested pond after a shanked drive is excessive. When I receive a referral regarding an emotional player, it's usually anger management issues.

The athlete tends to wear their emotions on their sleeve, can't let something go, or becomes abusive to themselves to name a few.

All too often you impose inappropriate and excessive expectations on yourself which invariably leads to disappointment. Once an unrealistic goal is not achieved, an elite athlete is supposed to learn from the experience. Did the athlete fail because of lack of skill, inconsistent technique, or lost concentration? Remember, the goal was not achieved for a reason. Athletes need to learn what the reason was that contributed to the failure. Using the loss as a vehicle to learn is beneficial. However, that is not why I receive referrals. I get referrals because athletes become a raw, visceral, venting, caldarium of molten emotions that rage and spew forth in a toxic and destructive way. "I suck!" Cursing signals that the emotional flood gates are about to be released. Friends, fans and families downstream need to get out of the way.

I ask two simple questions that help an athlete to process any situation with more clarity.

1) On a scale of 1-10, how life threatening was this situation? (1 equaling no threat to life. 10 equaling terrible realistic threat to life)

2) On a scale of 1-10, how did you react? (1 equaling no reaction. 10 equaling an excessive reaction)

The goal of answering the questions is to realize that the reality of any given situation is not life threatening. As an athlete, you need to accurately determine where your emotional reaction falls on the scale. When you acknowledge that your reaction is above a 5 and closer to a 9 then you know you have overreacted and you need to keep your emotions in check and bring your emotional reaction down and in-line with the reality of the situation.

If you struggle with your emotions, you compound the negative event and allow it to snowball into other unrelated situations. You make a bad situation worse.

Working on developing short-term memory helps gather information from the situation and learn from the past so as not to repeat it. That is wisdom.

Overthinking: In Your Head, Not the Moment

When your emotions become overwhelming you might discover that you become "stuck in your head." You might begin questioning every nuance of your game. Your internal dialogue becomes a self-imposed obstacle. If you are stuck in your head, you might overthink what type of pitch the pitcher will throw and never get the bat off your shoulder. If your emotions keep repeating a negative self-assessment, you cannot focus on the moment at hand, or you might experience "paralysis through analysis" by overthinking. When you can learn to take a lesson from the previous experience, you will release yourself from your emotions and thoughts, and be in the moment.

One week I coached four golfers, a half-dozen baseball players, an elite competitive diver, a top ranked tennis player, as well as many military personal, and all of these elite individuals had one process in common, all were dwelling on an internal negative thought that kept repeating itself. I heard comments, "I suck!", "When is my slump going to end?", "I hate playing against this opponent!"

When one factor becomes all consuming, you become lost in your thoughts. Sadly, anything you think seems to make absolute sense. When you're feeling bad, sad, mad, or any negative feeling, your mind spins those thoughts in a downward cycle. Your words fit your perspective, and even if reality contradicts your perspective, your narrative only allows you to accept the thoughts that fit your momentary focus.

Do you over-think life situations? Certainly, you want to learn from the past, but over-thinking can be the ruination of many athletes. One of consequences of over-thinking is the loss of fluid, athletic movement.

The baseball player who said "I suck" played on an AAU championship team. He was their starting third baseman. In a few recent games, he went 1 for 4, 1 for 3 and 1 for 3. Was this worse than his usual performance? Yes. He usually exploits the opposing pitchers. But the more time he spent stuck in his head, the less time he was in the moment and was missing the beautiful cues provided by the pitcher. For years he had mastered reading the pitch, responding with cat-like quickness, and analyzing the situation to predict the upcoming pitch. Now, he was having an internal shouting match with himself saying, "I suck." Not only was the statement incorrect for his level of success, but it implied his recent decline was a measure of his overall success. We worked on getting him back to trusting his internal chatter and believing in his coach. Staying in the moment, he was able to trust his ability and "get out of his own way." Realize that hypercritical self-talk offers no positive value and is self-abuse. The healthier approach is to realize that failure is an event, not a person (Ziglar).

The Slump: Making Bad – Worse

Being in the moment is the only aspect in which you can control, focus and compete. If your emotions linger and become overwhelming you might become fixated on the previous negative outcome. Since you cannot change the past, your emotional focus on a previously missed opportunity will become a hindrance to focusing in the moment. By focusing on the past you contribute to not performing at your highest levels.

The slump usually occurs when an athlete does not take in the information but rather becomes overwhelmed by the emotions. As this occurs the emotions from the previous moment continue and interferes with the ability in the next moment. The athlete makes a bad situation worse. A slump is the incorrect externalizing of self-control onto an uncontrolled entity which you have no control over. This perspective stops you from learning and adapting. I had to help a golfer realize that golf was nothing more than one stroke at a time. When she was calm and quiet, she performed her best. It was her consistent form that provided her with the greatest chances to score low. It was her ability to be in the moment and not in her head that allowed her to be in the "flow." When she panicked she rushed her stroke, which changed technical skills and decreased her consistency. Her internal, negative dialogue interfered with realizing the flight of the ball was due to her swing. What was it about her swing that led the ball to eventually land in a location that she had not planned? Was she out of balance? Was the club face open? She returned to asking herself productive questions like, "What was my plan? What was the shot? What do I learn?" Rather than beating herself up and blaming her poor performance on the dreaded "Slump", she gave herself an opportunity to learn and grow.

In reality, there is no such as a "slump."

If you are stuck in your head, you create extreme, debilitating, obstructive thoughts which provide no beneficial impact. Terms like "slump" or "streak" don't explain what you are doing to be successful or what you need to change. One of the baseball players that I spoke with was told by his father that he was stuck in a "slump." Let me ask you, if you are facing the opposing team's starting pitcher in the first inning tied 0-0 at 6 pm, but then face a relief pitcher in the fourth inning at 7 pm with your team ahead 3-1, and later face another reliever at 9 pm are these the same situations? Clearly, they are not. Your muscle tone is different, the heat of the day has dissipated, the skills of the pitchers are different, and your strategies are different. If you are dwelling on the past and are filled with emotion you will not be in the moment. This is how consistency fails. If you choose to call each different at-bat a "slump", you probably aren't learning from the past and making the appropriate changes. The name slump doesn't help you learn from the past. Just like the word streak doesn't provide you with the wisdom needed to be triumphant over the long haul. Words don't offer insight. Negative words will be a weight that drags you down.

Being in the moment allows you to read the putt, see the ball, focus on your responsibilities, remain relaxed, stay centered, trust your experience, and take care of the process. Remember there are no guarantees. The only thing you can ever do is increase your probability of success. Take the lessons from your past and apply them in the moment. Emotions out/Information in.

Show me a brain scan and I'll show you the difference between a scratch golfer and a 10-handicapper: Evidence-based fMRI Science

Modern brain science now has the technology to show the brains of professional athletes behave different than regular athletes.

You might be asking yourself, "Is this title an exaggeration?" Is it possibly some type of false sensationalism? Actually, that's true.

A study by Ross JS et. al. focused on golfers of varying skill levels and handicaps. They utilized functional MRI images to assess the mental motor imagery of their swing. They found a correlation between the increased activation of neuronal regions and the golfers increased handicap. The opposite was also revealed in the findings which showed there was a decrease in brain activation in golfers with increased skills set in golf.

Amazing!

In a 2007 study by Milton et. al. (2007) using functional MRI (fMRI) during pre-shot routines pertaining to motor planning, they studied brain activity of golfers. The low handicap golfers had activation in the occipital area (visual cortex), dorsal lateral premotor area (determining the coordinated motor movements) and another other region. The novice golfers' fMRIs revealed activation in the amygdala-forebrain complex (emotional center), the posterior cingulate, and the basal ganglia. Laying these complex findings aside, the brains of professionals versus amateur golfers revealed a difference in brain activation. Show me a brain scan and I'll show you the difference between an expert and an amateur. The differences exist before the golfer swings the club. This suggests that the disparity between the skills performed by the novice and expert golfers lies at the level of the organization of neural networks during motor planning.

Yup, that's right. The scratch golfer has a deactivation of the brain while the higher handicapped golfers have an activation of the brain. The fMRI revealed the more skilled golfers trusted their read of the green, experience, motor coordination, and coaching in such a way their brains quieted. Unfortunately, as many of you have personally experienced, self-doubt, questioning all of the incoming information, apprehension of your motor planning and execution, your brain became the Peanut Gallery and started shouting negative comments and showering your internal dialogue with negativity. Your brain activated while Charlie the scratch golfer remained calm, cool and collected.

When you are in the moment, what is your brain doing? Internal chatter could increase the odds of poor performance. Suddenly your internal dialogue becomes your worst nightmare. Instead of quieting your internal thoughts, you are now shouting at yourself. Ross JS (2003) studied six golfers of various handicaps with functional MRI to evaluate mental motor imagery of their golf swing. The results revealed there was a correlation between an increased number of areas of activation and increased of the handicap of the golfers.

The results also supported the fact there was decreased brain activation in individuals with increased golf skill. These results are significant. Being able to trust your read and analysis of the information pertaining to your sport and skill is vital in knowing you have received the best coaching in order to manage any and all situations brings comfort. Lastly, appreciate and know you have practiced and competed across a variety of situations allowing you to feel comfortable during this event. All of this leads to a deactivation in the brain and a quieting of the brain. When the amateur begins to question his read of the green or the correct grip, club or distance, the activation of their brain leads to changes in his performance and a decrease in his consistency. Self-doubt becomes the reality. The Peanut Gallery comes alive and the brain activates.

Now we come to this statement, "Size doesn't matter." Let me correct you. In a study by Jancke L. et. al. using a different neuroimaging technique, they found the more skilled the golfer the larger their gray matter volume as compared to the less skilled golfer. This neuronal increase in volume is observed with the increased mastery of a skill set.

Guilo Bernardi et.al. assessed brain activity between Formula One race car drivers and a control group of volunteers. The Formula One race car drivers' fMRI results revealed that elite drivers displayed a deactivation in task-related cortical areas associated, and a greater volume of gray matter among task-related areas

Changes in the grey matter volume of elite judo athletes has been shown to help master their coordinated muscle dexterity (Jacini et al). Di Paola M. et al studied world class climbers and found larger brain volume in the cerebellum aids them in understanding the sensory consequences of their actions and making quick alterations.

You show me a fMRI and I'll show the difference between an elite athlete and a novice. The internal chatter of a professional athlete lessens as they approach and participate in a task. The rookie remains a rookie because he can't slam dunk a basketball during a pick-up game. Nor does the amateur judo student struggle during a competition just because he cannot flip an opponent. The novice remains off the PGA tour because he freezes up and can't sink a 6-foot putt after his buddy just bet them $10. What happens pre-shot and during the task is an activation in his brain. This internal negative self-talk, constant banter from the heckler in his head, causes him to tighten up, change his form, and predictably underperform during the fun-filled sporting event as an amateur.

The future is headed in the direction of post injury brain activation. Athletes will want to address their concerns and self-doubt when returning to competition. They will strive to quiet their internal chatter. Coaches and owners will want to know if their rehabbing injured athlete has progressed physically and mentally and is ready to return to competition. The fMRI will answer many questions regarding the player's readiness to return. Sport psychologist will be used to creating protocols to decrease brain activation for the returning athlete.

Science reveals a deactivation of the brain by more highly skilled athletes. As I am pointing out, emotions out/information in.

Jawing: Trash talk

Understanding psychological gamesmanship

Whether dishing out, or receiving trash talk, you need to control your emotions. If you're a trash talker and let emotions rule, you will focus too much on your opponent. If you are the recipient of trash talk and let emotions rule, you will lose focus on the task at hand.

The field of athletic combat breeds animosity, resentment, envy, anger, grandiosity, cockiness, and other negative emotions that can cause a player to react in the heat of the moment.

There are three different types of Trash Talk:

1) Random
2) Self-bragging
3) Opponent specific

Type 1) Random feels like a gnat is flying by your ear, annoying and distracting. This approach sounds like an odd group of belittling comments that really don't apply to the specific opponent. Type 2) Self-bragging is a strutting peacock who is his own marketing company. Type 3) Opponent specific is personal, cruel, exploitative, and feels vengeful, hurtful, and violates all acceptable levels of decency. In any other situation, opponent specific trash talk would sound assaultive and attacking someone's vulnerabilities.

The goal of Jawing or Trash Talk is to get an athlete to react. If an opponent on the offensive line in football is reacting to insults about his daughter, then he might not hear the Quarterback calling an audible, and he might be out of position when the ball is snapped.

Before you launch into insulting your opponent you need to be strategic and good at jawing. Sometimes insulting your opponent can backfire. Negative quotes in local newspapers may become bulletin board material or locker room targets that motivate your opponent. You never want to kick a sleeping dog.

Many examples of trash talk have become legendary:

• We all witnessed Lance Stephenson blowing in LeBron James' ear during the Game 5 of the NBA East Conference finals.

• Dennis Rodman and Rick Mahorn of the 1988 NBA Championship Detroit Pistons "Bad Boys" grabbed their opponent's butts during games to distract them from the game.

• The great tennis champion, John McEnroe would strategically have a temper tantrum during a match to disrupt play and express his frustration. Interestingly, he would respond to his own rant by refocusing with great intensity while his opponents would have become distracted.

- The NBA great Charles Barkley once made fun of the Chicago Bulls' General Manager Jerry Krause incompetence and why he remains in his position, "Jerry Krause must have pictures of his boss' wife having sex with a monkey."

- Arguably the greatest boxer of all-time, Mohammed Ali espoused on his own greatness, "I'm so fast that last night I turned off the light switch in my hotel room and was in bed before the room was dark." Additionally, "If you even dream of beating me you'd better wake up and apologize."

Also, I train my players to look for a player who has been emotionally reactive in any previous competition. Once he has assessed the opponent and identified their particular tendency to react (e.g.; receive a Red Card in soccer, be penalized 15 yards for a personal foul in football, be rejected from a baseball game for excessive arguing, or getting into a fight with a fan) we begin the process of determining what to say that would elicit the greatest emotional reaction from this player. Each one of these volcanic reactive individuals has triggers that will set them off. The specific statements (comments about their mother) or behaviors (holding a jersey) that are associated with creating the desired inappropriate reactive behavior are then developed, planned, and prepared (Intervene).

I also train athletes on the other side of Jawing - knowing where you end and someone else begins. Just because someone says something doesn't make it a fact. As a matter of fact, whatever that person says is a reflection of that person. You don't have to give power to someone else's words. Consider their agenda. Maybe the defensive back wants you to retaliate so he makes a comment about your mother. If you want to give his comment power, you choose to accept their insult as if it was real. Just because words come out of someone's mouth doesn't make the statement a fact. Knowing that his goal is to get a reaction, simply choose to ignore the made-up comment. Knowledge is power. Knowing he is saying this to get a reaction with no basis in reality, you then return back to the huddle and focus on the task at hand.

As the great W.C. Fields said, "It ain't what they call you, it's what you answer to."

Sometimes it's reasonable to fake strategy. Non-verbal can speak volumes. When your opponent is focusing on your game plan and how you position yourself in the field of play, you might want to use this strategy: walk over to your tennis partner and say, "Are they looking at us?" He confirms they are. "Ok, they think that we're strategizing but we aren't. But because they are focusing on us, they are not focusing on their game. Put your hand behind your back as if you're signaling me. All we want is for them to think we are sending signals." When you return to your net position, place your hand behind your back. Your partner audibly declares he understood your message and play on. The opponents are bound to be confused and spend so much energy focusing on us, that their performance suffers. The secret strategy is, there was no strategy. All you needed is for them to think you had a strategy.

Reverse psychology can also provide a fertile ground to cause your opponent to emotionally react. This approach would be referred to as, "Kill them with kindness." I was once playing against a tennis opponent who was struggling to get his serves in. The more he tried, the more frustrated he became. My coach recommended that when someone overreacts, I should underreact. So, I encouraged my opponent, "Don't worry about it. We're outside having a great time. Let's just enjoy being out here." This drove him nuts. The more I was enjoying the moment and encouraging him, the more frustrated he became and the worse he performed.

Cultural differences exist. In the United States, there has been a palpable change from the glory days of the Detroit Pistons Bad Boys.

There was a time if a player drove the middle of the lane he knew there was going to be a "hard" foul. As a culture, we accept loud and brash players. They are celebrated. There was a time when players believed they were bigger than the sport. Football player Brian Bozworth self-promoted an identity that was superior to all foes. His braggadocios persona and image were highly regarded. You either loved or hated this type of player, which led to higher television ratings and bigger contracts.

However, as time passed there has been a change which lovingly has been referred to as the "woosification of America." Now if you argue with an official in the NBA you will receive a quick Technical Foul. In US soccer, you could receive a Red Card for arguing with an official. Never in the history of soccer or futbol, has arguing with an official ever brought about a change in a call. Yet around the world players are able to react, vent, and loudly profess their disagreement with a call. Cultural factors need to be considered as the pendulum swings and shifts. In essence, there is a time and a place for everything and knowing the environment is vital. Strategically knowing how and when to jaw, challenging an official is more important than merely releasing your emotions. Some coaches or players might complain to an official with the goal of influencing future calls.

We review game films just to identify the opponent most likely to negatively react. We will identify reactive players and throughout the entire game, we have our athletes play within the rules but push the limits. Obviously, if we can get into the head of a player, we can influence him. We pull the strings to manipulate that athlete.

Ask yourself "who has received a red card in soccer?", "who has been thrown out of a baseball game for arguing with an official?", "Who has received a 15-yard personal foul for unsportsmanlike conduct in football?" Are there any athletes on the opposing team that Tweet, post on Instagram or rant on Facebook? We relish the reactive player who emotional vents on social media about the official, or the rival coach, or fans. This externally focused athlete tends to become easily distracted and blames his emotional tantrum on factors outside of his own control. We are pit bulls on a piece of beef when we come across one of these players. It doesn't take much fuel tossed on this pile of kindling to ignite into a full-blown inferno.

When John Salley of the Detroit Pistons read in the newspaper one of the players from the other team had stated, "If the Pistons want to be physical, we will be physical." Salley knew at that moment the Pistons had already won. His opponents were not going to be focused on their game but were already reacting on the physical combat ahead.

Are you guilty of any of these infractions? If you are, do not minimize the results. Because of your behavior or comments, you may have put your team at a disadvantage. It is the time for you to swallow your pride and take the first step. Instead of avoiding the truth, begin by admitting your behavior (regardless of how justified you think it is) and how you may have put your team or your match into a negative situation. Only by admitting these negative behaviors can you change your pattern.

I have worked with many young adults who believe they are the best at jawing. They find a sense of value and identity believing they can get under their opponent's skin. If you put your team or match into a negative position because you reacted, then you are an emotional, reactive individual. Eventually your behaviors or antics will cause you or your team to lose. Now is the best time to deal with this pattern and realize this is a problem. You need to be honest and willing to acknowledge this tendency.

If you plan on Trash Talking be wise, thoughtful, and strategic. Don't just bark your raw emotions, because they could turn out to be counterproductive. As with each subsection, monitor your emotions and be thoughtful, measured, and purposeful even with Jawing.

Fans vs. Fanatics/Frenemies

Your self-worth cannot be dependent on how other people judge you. Constructive feedback can offer helpful information that can be used to improve. When you receive praise, you will feel valued and affirmed. However, when you receive criticism you might find it disconcerting, agitating, and inappropriate. As an athlete you need to learn how to live up to your highest standards which will fuel your self-worth. Not allowing fanatics to adversely impact your emotions will always prove advantageous throughout your athletic career.

If you are in need of "atta-boys", you are also vulnerable to allowing your self-confidence to be determined by people outside of yourself. I always like to share with my athletes, "You are not as good as your favorite fan says and you're not as bad as your worst critic says." (Shinitzky)

How can you let total strangers drag you down? As Michael J. Fox says, "What other people think about me is none of my business."

Too many athletes allow social media to determine their state of mind. They Tweet or post something on Facebook, Instagram or Snapchat only to wait to see the responses from their followers. First off, your followers are not your friends. Ok, so on any social media site they either had to send a "Friend Request" or "Like" your page. Either way, they are not your friend. Your celebrity status draws attention to you. Just like other forms of power, wealth, beauty, etc. Celebrity status can be appealing to others. They feel that if they associate with you, it will increase their self-image, and want to connect in any way possible. They may want your autograph for their "cousin", or a picture with them, or to vicariously live through your social media posts.

One of my young athletes epitomizes this contemporary reaction to social media. His emotions were dependent upon other's reactions. Though 98 percent of the responses to his posts were positive, two percent of responses were negative. If you share your thoughts, feelings, or life events with the public, you open yourself up for every possible reaction. People will dissect every aspect of your life, regardless of your interest or purpose for sharing. "Monday morning Quarterbacks" have been in existence for longer than the internet has been around. This young athlete would become incredibly distraught when reading negative comments. If someone ripped into his character, he would spiral downhill. If someone made an inappropriate sexual comment about the woman he was dating, he would become offended. Even worse, when no one commented, this would invariably lead to a sleepless night. His identity was now directly tied to how social media reacted to his posts.

What he needed to learn is these people are "Haters." That's what they do, they hate. They hate on your post. They troll the internet for opportunities to spew their outrageous comments. They want to incite.

And Tweeting is another story! Once you hit send, there is no turning back. I recommend a 24-hour rule. Some people respect and understand the value of this buffer zone, while others unfortunately use a 24 second rule and post as quickly as possible. My generation never had to deal with the lingering effects of the internet and social media. A hard copy of a photo was the evidence de jour. However, now with cyberspace, the tweet, picture, video which gets posted is floating indefinitely in the cloud. Once you have unleashed your thought and press send, it's out there. This is a distraction and as an athlete, you should be focusing on your craft, vocation, and job.

The fan will defend you blindly and the critic will vilify you at every misstep.

Fan is short for "fanatic." Some fans obviously step over the line. When fans from one rival team fatally attack fans from the opposing team, they have crossed a line that clearly is flawed. A devout fan who follows you as though he was a soldier, and would never leave a comrade behind, is stepping over the line.

If you need attention as an athlete, you are vulnerable to "gold diggers" and stalkers. One of the baseball players I worked with came up the system very quickly. His celebrity status was overwhelming and he lost all anonymity. His picture was proudly displayed in all major sports publications, and 20-foot banners flapped with his likeness. After playing in Los Angeles, he came back with a story about meeting a young lady at the hotel who was very "into" him. She displayed an excellent knowledge of his sport, and the team standings as well as the current leaders in every position. He thought that he had died and gone to Sports Dating Heaven. Interestingly, he had noticed her in the stands during the day game, and the coincidence they would meet at the hotel was remarkable. It was then that we discussed his need for external validation and that he was vulnerable to praise and therefore easy to exploit. What I told him was that every out of town team is booked into the same hotel the night before every game. I had heard this same story to the exacting details of this young lady's appearance and comments from a previous baseball player. If you need "atta-boys" and external validation, you are at risk of being exploited.

In psychological terms, the way you see yourself is called your Ego. The more secure you are with the way you see yourself the more "Ego Strength" you have. Additionally, the feedback you receive from loved ones, and those that care about you is helpful to securing your sense of self. I like to tell the athletes I work with that if someone calls me a short, fat, hippopotamus, I don't have to give power to those words. At 6'2", 200 pounds and a homosapien, I wouldn't qualify to meet those descriptors. Just because words come out of someone's mouth does not make them facts.

Family members may exploit you as much as a stranger. Bizarre as this might seem, family members who have their own agenda might seek to make you feel bad in an attempt to prove them wrong. I worked with a baseball player whose uncle was running his financial affairs. When the athlete questioned some of his uncle's decisions, the uncle accused him of not trusting him and was appalled at the accusation. The uncle threatened to tell his mother and publicly embarrass him. The athlete backed off and passively allowed his uncle to resume his financial responsibilities. I met this athlete long after his uncle had invested poorly and paid himself excessively, leaving the athlete with almost no money. I recognized his uncle was a selfish, money hungry individual who took advantage of him. The uncle's aggressive comments were not truth. If I had worked with this young man earlier, he would have been able to differentiate his sense of self versus the distorted comments by his uncle.

Know your friends! Many of the elite athletes I have worked with reported they no longer can discern who their friends are. Just know, your friend would never put you in harm's way. Your Posse may see you as one thing, an ATM.

Be humble. Don't get a big head. "The day you think that you are "all that and a bag-o-chips" is the first day that you begin to lose because Number Two will be trying harder."(Shinitzky)

Take a hard look at your personal relationships. Remember you have chosen to voluntarily spend time with a person(s) (regardless of relationship status) and your relationship should be the best part of your day. If you have to make excuses for that person, then you are in the wrong relationship!

Take away for Step Four:

Managing your emotions is a vital ability elite athletes master. You will react, however the question is, how quickly will you respond? Control your emotions and learn from the past. Excessive emotions will cause you to tighten up. Learn to let go of the past in order to be in the present. Trusting your experience, skills, and coaching will help you quiet your internal chatter. If you trash talk, be strategic. Developing a good understanding of yourself will prevent you from being negatively impacted by the comments of others.

Step Five: Manage Your Thoughts and Emotions

Outline

1. "Pre-Shot Routine"
   Routines help remain calm, focused and primed to excel
2. Reaching the Zone and Mastering Flow
   3-Step Olympic Calm
3. Deep Breathing
   Increasing oxygen to the brain and body helps you be relaxed, think clearer and respond quicker
4. Muscle Relaxation
   Muscle tightness - enemy of top physical performance
5. Visualization
   Rehearsing physical activity (mentally or in reality), develops muscle memory
6. Home Court Advantage: Routines
   Structure and organization helps to focus on performance
7. ACT won, Scene won
   Quieting your mind and learning to be focused
8. "Post-Shot Routine"
   Three-step process to learn from performance

Pre-Shot Routine

Managing your thoughts and emotions begins with creating the right mindset before you compete. Being prepared, knowing you possess consistent skills, remaining relaxed, and maintaining positive self-talk, all help to keep your thoughts and emotions in check and increase the likelihood of competing at your highest levels.

Think back to when you felt the most focused and in the moment. Your mind was uncluttered and wasn't focused on externals. You didn't have distractions occupying your mind. You were relaxed. Everything felt as though it was flowing.

One way to increase this state of mind is to establish a healthy predictable pattern. This pattern is not a compulsion or a rigid pattern which you must adhere to, or else you will fall apart. In order to feel comfortable, establish a pattern that increases a positive state of mind. This is accomplished best by discovering what works for you, and will become your Pre-Shot Routine.

When the Baltimore Ravens played in the NFL Super Bowl in Tampa, the organization purchased all the billboards from the hotel to the stadium, and displayed images associated with either the Ravens team, or reflecting Baltimore culture. Imagine being in a different city and feeling at home. This was the beginning of their home court advantage.

I coached an athlete who traveled on her own to Europe for a competition. She didn't speak the language or know the easiest ways to travel from the hotel to the facility. Put yourself in this position. When she should have been focused on her sport, she had to focused on stress-inducing logistics. This was so distracting and distressing that she not only performed poorly, she seemed to internalize this negative experience as representing her identity. The lesson here is to have someone else organize the logistics, transportation, facility, and registration.

"Pre-Shot Routines" begin with knowing yourself. How much sleep do you require to achieve optimal performance? Which foods keep you fueled throughout your competition? Do you eat food that keeps you running in top gear? Do you pack bananas? Peanuts? Liquids to replenish fluids before you feel dehydrated? When do you automatically refuel? Regardless of the time of day, have you established a schedule to forestall the depletion of nutrients?

Remember, some aspects of your sport are within your control and some are not. The goal is to increase your control over those aspects you can address, while rehearsing as many different situations to feel skilled and more comfortable in arenas that are fluid and changing.

There are two types of pre-routine skills, closed and open. Closed-skills are specific control tactical patterns you can reproduce and repeat. These could include, free-throw shooting in basketball, target practice in archery, or toss during your tennis serve. These skills can be replicated and rehearsed to increase consistency and predictability. Open-skills situations are ever changing or outside of your control. These could include heading a soccer ball towards the goal based upon a centering kick from a teammate, the temperature at Lambeau Field in January, or the muddy conditions of the track at the Kentucky Derby. When it comes to open-skills beyond your control, the goal is to be exposed to many different possibilities or changing situation so you can manage unusual moments that come your way.

No one plans to fail but many fail to plan.

I've never known a golfer who wanted to hit from the deep rough, but at some point, all golfers are forced to save an errant shot in the tall grass. If you practice the skills required to recover, you will have the confidence to handle the unexpected circumstance.

No one wants to be down by five points with 52 seconds in a game, but if you practice time management and how to execute the plays called, you will have the confidence to know you can handle the challenging game circumstance.

One of the greatest golfers of all-time, Arnold Palmer, said he "goes to the movies before every shot." He would visualize the proper club selection for the distance and conditions, and see himself approach the ball. He would feel the breeze, see himself perform the stroke, and would see the flight of the ball and the landing. In essence, his pre-shot routine was to get into the proper mindset, both physically and mentally prepared by visualizing the entire shot before he executed the actual shot, and finally engage in the actual shot.

A new addition to the athletic arena is metrics, or data crunching. Since "Money ball" began, we now have a wealth of information that can be used to help you or your team improve its day-to-day routines in order to increase physiological and competitive performance. The new field is referred to as "Quantified Self" which analyzes data designed to increase strength, endurance and recovery. The U.S. Women's Olympic cycling team used this technological edge to win a Silver Medal in the 2012 World Championships. This field can track patterns between health and performance including sleep cycles, circadian rhythms, continuous blood sugar levels, blood biomarkers such as Vitamin D, and hormone levels. The data has also revealed the importance of establishing pre-competition routines including room temperature for sleeping, allowing for deeper sleep, releasing testosterone and human growth hormone.

Reaching the Zone and Mastering Flow: 3-Step Olympic Calm

The next three steps always go together. I practice these three skill sets with each athlete. These three physiological routines are the keys to the kingdom. The three keys are 1) Deep Breathing, 2) Muscle Relaxation training, and 3) Visualization. I coach athletes to practice these three steps when they are not in competition. They need to become proficient at these skills prior to implementing them during the competitive events. The premise behind this is very simple. You have to be excellent at your routine before you can successfully use it. Practice your routine before you need it, so when you do need it you've mastered the skills.

When practicing these three keys, begin by finding a quiet location with a minimal amount of distractions. Sit or lay down in a comfortable posture with your head supported by a chair or couch. Don't hold your head upright because that requires you to focus on keeping your head in balance. Once you're quiet, determine your resting respiratory rate. Take notice when your system changes due to some distraction, "stress", or "pressure".

The perfect state of mind for optimal competitive performance is called, "Flow." This term can best be defined as reaching the optimal state where a person's ability matches the challenge of complete absorption and focus on an activity (Csikszentmihalyi, M, 1990,).

To be in the zone during competition, you need to practice getting into the zone during non-athletic time. Getting into the zone is an active process, not merely magic. Remember, whatever you practice, you get better at. If you are a gamer I would bet that your skill level now is better than when you first learned how to use the controls. When you are still in the skill acquisition phase you are not at the point of competently applying that skill set.

To achieve the highest level of focus, concentration, and ability you must master the Three-Step Olympic Calming protocol. By achieving mastery over these three steps you are more likely to be mentally ready, be in the zone, and feel the flow.

Deep Breathing/Centering

In order to think clearly, respond quicker, and make better decisions, it's vitally important to maintain healthy oxygen levels to the brain during competition. To move effortlessly, skillfully, and achieve your greatest potential, you need to maintain oxygen levels to all of the muscles. Losing control of your emotions and thoughts lead to tightening of the muscles and decreasing oxygen levels throughout your body.

Let's begin with breathing or centering.

Assessing your resting heart and respiratory rates are critical abilities to be able to flow into the zone. Most young athletes need to learn how to focus on their body's muscle development, physical coordination, nutrition and recovery, and don't realize they perform best when in a relaxed state. The problem is if they don't know what their body is supposed to feel like in a resting state, they won't know when their body is in a stressed state, and won't know the steps required to re-gain control of their body. To reach the next level and gain absolute focus, first practice the Deep Breathing, Muscle Relaxation and Visualization routine.

Most athletes don't realize that when they become "stressed", think of a negative possibility, perceive some "pressured" situation, or worry about the competition, their body changes. Our central nervous system (CNS) reacts to "perceived" stress which causes our sympathetic nervous system to kick into the fight or flight reaction. The words, "stressed", "pressured", and "perceived" are in quotes because what makes one person stressed may not make someone else stressed.

As I discussed in my book, "Your Mind: An Owner's Manual for a Better Life", emotional reactions are not based upon reality but rather on the perception of reality. Breathing changes, blood flows more to the survival systems, and muscles tighten for the attack. One of the first muscle groups that tighten is the abdominal core or lower stomach area. The problem with abdominal muscles constricting is breathing capacity immediately decreases. You are no longer breathing normally. Less oxygen into the lungs with each breath, means less oxygen transferring into the blood stream, and less oxygen to the brain and body. You begin to take survival breaths, short, choppy breaths hoping to get the required amount of oxygen into your body. Because the abdominal core is tense and you are inhaling less oxygen, your heart must beat faster to circulate the limited oxygenated blood to your brain and body. The combination of increased respiratory rate and increased heart rate sends a message to the brain you are in a full-blown panic situation. DEFCON 1!

The reality is your body is built to handle "perceived" stress. There is a natural reaction you experience. What is important is not to develop the All-or-None belief system that says you are not to experience any stress. But far more realistically, how quickly can you respond to your body's reaction? Your response is completely in your control.

Since, your body reacts to "perceived" stress, you choose how to respond. Realizing you have tightened up and your breathing pattern has now dramatically changed, you need to implement the new breathing technique.

The first key to the trilogy, deep breathing or centering requires expanding the abdominal cavity. This forces the diaphragm down and draws in maximum lung capacity. Though a moment earlier your body reacted to "perceived" stress, you are now regaining control by addressing the first component of adaptive responding. I encourage athletes to take a deep breath in and hold it for one count longer than they normally would and then gently breathing out. Many people find breathing out of their mouth aids in this process. Don't force your breath when you exhale.

Repeating this process, you will discover by increasing the amount of oxygen, the lungs gather with each deep breath, the longer and slower your breathing rate becomes. Many people find that by merely doing this first step they begin to feel tired, relaxed and clear headed.

As you increase your lung capacity, you increase the transfer of oxygen to your blood stream. The more oxygen to your blood stream, the more oxygen to your brain and body. Your heart no longer has to beat faster in order to get the plentiful oxygenated blood to your brain and body. The curious reality is now that your breathing and heart rate slows, you immediately send a message to your brain you are relaxed. The more oxygen your brain gets, the clearer you think, the more relaxed you stay, the quicker your physical movements become. This is perfect state of mind!

Regardless of what is going on around you, you control the response and state of mind. As I often say, "When a dramatic event occurs, in a panic many options are overlooked, but the person who keeps a level head is able to think clearer and make better decisions." We all react. We react to what we perceive, think, or feel. The question is how quickly do we respond. Regaining control of breath and oxygen levels throughout the body is the first step.

Muscle Relaxation

World-class athletes have learned to keep themselves as relaxed and primed as possible to compete at the highest levels. When individuals become stressed their muscles tighten. In addition to controlling thoughts and emotions, learning to control your body offers an invaluable solution to perceived stress. When performing at peak levels, elite athletes coordinate muscles in a symphony of motion.

The second key of the trilogy is Muscle Relaxation Training. This intervention has the longest name of any therapeutic approach I employ. It is associated with the "Jacobson Progressive Muscle Relaxation Training" approach.

Many athletes point out that when "stressed" they tighten up, muscles lock up and are no longer able to relax. This involuntary contraction of muscle groups is a normal process to a "perception of a stressor." The reality is we have a process of reversing the experience from involuntary to voluntary, from feeling out of control, to feeling in control. Ironically, the process of gaining voluntary muscle control begins by contracting the muscles. As you voluntarily contract the muscle group, it purposefully burns out (Hydrogen ions build up), takes control of the involuntary contractions and regains personal control.

I have developed a process that reverses the above protocol. Because I have found the mind and head to be the most vital parts of the body in the relaxation process, I begin at the head and work down, from head to toe. I coach all of my athletes to get into a comfortable position with their heads supported. Again, try to practice this in a quiet location. If you sense any distractions (ie; car, hallway door, phone) merely acknowledge the distraction. To deny the reality that you heard a sound increases stress to your system. However, by merely acknowledging the distraction, and comfortably allowing yourself to return to the relaxation rehearsal, you will eventually become skilled at filtering out distractions.

After the athlete has progressed through the Diaphragmatic Breathing, I have him focus on furrowing only his forehead/Frontalis muscle. Voluntarily holding this muscle group for five counts, leads to it voluntarily burning out and naturally relaxing. He repeats for a second voluntary contraction of the Frontalis muscle, allowing gravity to take control upon relaxing. He then combines the Frontalis with the Eyes/Cheek muscles, holding for five counts and by voluntarily contracting these muscles, he voluntarily burns out these muscles, leading to relaxation. The muscles elongate as he releases them.

The third in this combination is contracting the Frontalis, Eyes/Cheeks, and jaw muscle or Mandible. He contracts for five counts, burns them out as they naturally release. Unfurrow the brow, release eyes/cheek muscles, and release the Mandible. (As an aside, he can't fall asleep with Frontalis and Mandible clinched. Watching someone falling asleep and the Frontalis and Mandible muscles unwind and relax). The final muscles to include in the first group are the shoulders. He voluntarily tightens the Frontalis, Eyes/Cheeks, Mandible and Shoulders, becoming aware of the dissolving tension after the contraction. He holds for five counts and releases. He observes the sensation of calming, unwinding and how the muscle elongates as gravity takes control. He does each combination twice.

Now he moves down to the next group. Making a fist, curling his hands, bending at the elbows as though he is curling a barbell towards his shoulders. He is now activating his biceps, triceps, hands and fingers. Again, hold for a five count voluntarily allowing Hydrogen Ions to build up and burn out the muscle groups. After he releases these four muscles, he repeats contracting all four in his arms. Noting the distinction between the stress and strain from contracting the muscles to the sensation of calm, relaxed and peaceful from releasing and sensing the flow of blood out to the extremities of his fingers. Many people report they feel their own heart beat somewhere in their body.

Moving to his abdominal core and contracting this area mirrors the same experience as what naturally happens to his body when he perceives a stressor. When he locks up his abdominal cavity, he starts taking short, choppy breaths. Obviously, that decreases the oxygen to his lungs, blood stream and his brain. Hold the abdominal core for a five count, burn it out and then release. He notices the contraction of muscles, when he inhaled, and he stopped breathing. When he relaxed, he exhaled and followed up with a deep breath. He repeats a second time.

Lastly, he shifts down to his quads, calf, feet and toes. He tightens up these muscles and curl his toes underneath, feeling the stress and strain. He holds for five counts, then releases and notes the changes in his body between voluntarily contracting, and achieving voluntary relaxation.

Remember, he takes a deep breath in, then tightens each muscle group, holding for five counts, then gently breathes out, and releases the muscle group.

As mentioned earlier, I find this sequence vital to achieving a peaceful state. It is best to experience the benefits by first focusing on his head and face followed by the cumulative benefits from relaxing successive muscle groups down throughout the body.

As I noted above, The Jacobson Progressive Muscle Relaxation technique starts from the feet and moves up to the head. The procedure has the athlete voluntarily contract each major muscle group for five counts, then relaxing and contracting the same muscle group again for five counts, and then relax.

He contracts toes downward. Feel the stress and the strain, holding for five counts, then slowly releasing, feeling the blood flow to the extremities. He takes a breath in and release and repeats the process for a second time. He curls his toes under and feel the tension and pressure and holds for five counts and slowly release the muscles.

Moving up to his calf muscles, he is to focus down to the singular muscle group, and contracts calf muscles and holds for five counts. Again, he feels the tension he has created by contracting the muscles and becomes aware of the state of distress when muscles contract. After a five count, he releases and elongates the calf muscle, and repeats noting the difference between contraction and relaxation, involuntary contraction, and voluntary control.

He repeats this process with the Quadriceps. When he voluntarily contracts these major muscles, he notices how he rises in the chair or on the couch and notes the tension exerted on these muscles because the fast twitch muscles in his Quads are powerful. He holds for five counts and then releases, again noticing the difference between tense and relaxed. He notices through voluntarily contracting the muscle group, he can burn it out and then regain control of the muscle.

He repeats the process with his Gluteus Maximus and Minimus, better known as his bottom, (your Ba-Dunk-A-Dunk) and squeezes and tense up his behind, holding for five counts. He feels the tension he has created by locking up the muscle group.

He does this again with the Abdominal muscles. Tightens them, feeling the strain and the tension, and notices when he physiologically reacts to perceived stress he locks up in his abdominal cavity. This is nature's way of coping with stress. Fight or Flight kicks into gear, and the athlete locks up his abdominal core, and shifts to survival breathing, taking short, choppy breaths. By locking up the abdominal core, he decreases his lung capacity. Less oxygen into his lungs leads to less oxygen transferring to the bloodstream and less to the brain and body. This process naturally causes more stress to the system. He repeats this voluntary contraction to his abdominal group for five counts and then releases.

The Jacobson protocol finishes by moving to shoulders, arms and face, finishing with the forehead.

When one muscle group is contracting, he might feel other muscle groups contract at the same time. Also, he locks many muscles when breathing in, and releases muscle groups when breathing out.

When stress is perceived the body naturally tightens the abdominal core. When he locks up the tummy area he does not take deep breaths but shallow ones. Shallow breathing decreases oxygen in the brain and body and the heart begins to race to compensate and distribute lower oxygen levels. This physical state is referred to as panic.

The solution is to combine deep breathing and with the muscle relaxation techniques.

I have adapted this protocol to a shorter procedure. I suggest to breathe in, hold one count, breathe out, relax forehead muscles/Frontalis. Interestingly, individuals can't fall asleep with a tense Frontalis muscle or a tense Mandible. He breathes in, holds one count, breathes out, relax muscles around his eyes and cheek bones. He breathes in, holds one count, breathes out, relaxes jaw muscle/Mandible.

These two preliminary steps make the third key component more effective when preceded by deep breathing and muscle relaxation exercises (Short, S. E., et. al, 2001).

Visualization

A key component of mental conditioning is the ability to imagine the exact steps, form, technique, and situation. Visualization, or mental imagery provide the final component to reach the "zone." The more you create a mental map and visualize the activity, the more muscle memory is developed. Muscle memory occurs by doing the behavior, and is solidified by visually or imagining the skill and action. The more you practice visualizing every skill and situation, the more control you have over thoughts and feelings.

What your mind's eye "sees" becomes your reality. You have to "see" it before you can believe it. The internal belief that you deserve to be an elite athlete is a first step towards success. When you get to the big event, it will not be a BIG event because you have already "seen" it and been there. Zig Ziglar said, "You've got to 'be' before you can 'do', and you've got to 'do' before you can 'have'.

The three steps: Diaphragmatic Breathing, Muscle Relaxation, and Visualization are deliberately placed in this order and sequence. Deep breathing increases oxygen to the brain and body and begins the calming process. Muscle relaxation creates a peaceful state which prepares for the controlled explosion of coordinated muscles during competition. And lastly, visualization or mental imagery, establishes the neuro-circuitry that increases muscle memory and fosters a positive internal mindset, leading to performing your best.

Many people use the visualization terms Visual Imagery and Guided Imagery interchangeably. That's fine but I will separate them into two categories. Visual Imagery is non-specific while Guided Imagery is specifically directed.

In a 2011 publication, Mousavi and Meshkini studied the impact of visual imagery on the reduction of a tennis players' anxiety during his sport. They found that visual imagery reduced the tennis players' anxiety and improved his performance. The use of mental imagery or visualization modulates arousal, decreases maladaptive behaviors, increases positive self-talk, and increases concentration/focus. This was enhanced when other strategies were implemented, including self-talk, relaxation training, and goal-setting. (Mousavi, SH. and Meshkini, A. 2011).

Munroe, et. al., (2000) the four W's of imagery: Where, When, What and Why.

1. Where does the athlete use visual imagery? The most common location was the training facility or competitive environment.

2. When does an athlete use visualization? The most common time frame is just prior to, or following the training session.

3. What does athlete imagine when he visualizes? The content an athlete most visualizes is a vivid depiction of his accurate, coordinated movements. He implements as many sensory systems as possible (sight, sound, touch, taste, and smell).

4. Why does an athlete utilize the technique of visualization? The reasons most often fall into two categories: Cognitive - enhancing the learning of new or advanced skills and prepping for game strategies; and Motivation - psyching up, modulating arousal, and improving self-confidence/self-talk.

I am often asked, "When should an athlete use visualization?" I reply, at every stage of the sport; during skill acquisition through performance expectation, and during learning the new plays, all the way to recovery from injury. Hall (Hall, C,. 2001) published his research that revealed the benefits of visualization. Visualization facilitated skill development, and partially takes the place/contributes to the physical practice for improving performance.

To refine the techniques, I often coach an athlete to practice the "Bird's eye view." In golf, I like to use the Bird's Eye View to teach an athlete to focus on the individual stroke. I suggest he imagine a golf course and start slowly deep breathing. He imagines looking down on the entire course and sees the green grass of the fairways, the holes, the sand traps, the trees, and the water. He only sees the course. The outside of the course is black, as though nothing exists beyond the boundaries of the golf course. Now, he lowers himself down to one of the holes. As he descends, all of the other holes disappear. The only hole he sees is this one hole. He sees the tee box, the fairway, and the green. Nothing exists beyond this one hole. He brings himself onto the tee box, and takes deep breaths in, and holds for one count longer than he normally would. He then breathes out, feeling relaxed and calm. Depending upon the length of the hole, he confidently decides the club for the distance and the condition. The only thing his mind's eye can see, is from the tee box forward. Darkness lies behind him and outside of the fairway. He tells himself exactly what he plans to do with this club in this situation. He begins his pre-shot routine, comfortable, relaxed, and confident. As he addresses the ball, he takes a deep breath in, holds for one count longer than he normally would, and as he breaths out, remaining relaxed, using perfect form, staying balance, coiling the club around his body, head still, he releases the torque to allow destiny to be achieved. He allows himself to feel confident with his plan.

Our motivational mentor Zig Ziglar would say, "If you want to reach a goal, you must 'see the reaching' in your mind before you actually arrive at your goal."

Now I ask the athlete to imagine himself from his point of view. This is referred to as 1st Person perspective.

Start with 1) practice, 2) warm-up, then 3) visualize competition.

Step 1. When he visualizes, he always imagines proper form. He imagines the skills flowing, to executing each skill to the optimal form. He sees himself following the instructions of his coaches and integrating all of the experience he has participated in over the years as coming together.

Step 2. Whenever possible he utilizes as many of the five senses as possible. The more senses he utilizes during the visualization the more real it becomes to his neuro-circuitry. As he sees the vibrant colors, images, motion, and relevant imagery, the more real the experience becomes for his brain. Within his scene he listens for the sounds, hears the noises of his sport whether it is a team or an individual. He rehearses the dynamic auditory sounds from the image.

Now you imagine this…Feel the temperature of the heat of the Australian Open penetrating on your arms, the driving water as it passes your fingertips while you surf the Bonzai Pipeline, or the frigid cold of the Green Bay Packer's stadium on your face. Sense the breeze as it blows through your hair. Feel the strain on your legs as you pass mile marker 18 during your visualized marathon. Taste the salt in the air while imagining the treacherous waterfront holes of St. Andrews, or the chlorine from the pool during your meet. Smell the aroma of sweat in the gymnasium during your tournament. The more you can integrate your five senses the more real and impactful the skill of imagery becomes for solidifying the link of neuro-circuitry and muscle memory.

Step 3. After he visualizes the situation and integrates his five senses, he imagines the same scene, but from a fan's point of view. He places himself in the crowd and looks back at himself. He observes himself executing proper form, exuding confidence, shoulders back, chest out, chin up, and radiating pride. Again, he imagines the positive techniques, the five senses, but now he observes the way he carries himself when he is in command of his skills, form, tactics, strategies, and execution. This is referred to as 3rd Person perspective.

I recommend to all my athletes that they practice these three steps at least three times per day. Remember, whatever they practice, the better they get at doing it.

Some athletes scoff at the idea of visualizing. They avoid anything that might be "touchy-feely." Interestingly, research has shown the benefits of visualizing in all sports. One study focused on the benefits of visualization on weight training revealed that people who carried out virtual weight training workouts increased their muscle strength by 13.5%. By creating a mentally positive focus and thinking about weight lifting, they achieved nearly half of the gains seen by the group that lifted weights (they saw a 30% increase in muscle strength) (Ranganathan V.K., 2004). Amazingly, doing both the actual physical task and mental practice is more effective than either alone.

Athletes have been researched to assess the benefits of visualization in order to manage arousal. Whether it is "psych up" or "calm down" visualization, scripts are created for the specific sport which can help athletes reach their optimal level of functioning (Jones, et. al., 2002).

Scanning an individual's brain when receiving feedback from an external source (parent, coach or friend), the tone and word usage of the external source, reveals a tendency to become defensive. If the terminology doesn't fit the individual, his brain does not naturally take in the information. However, if he converts the external information into words he would normally, use and then record himself saying these same phrases, the individual's brain scan reveals he is more likely to assimilate the information. Consider recording yourself offering positive self-statements about your abilities, and then add the reworded comments you have received from others that are true and accurate. Then replay the recording back and let the beauty and dramatic impact of these comments wash over you and add to your positive state of mind.

Additionally, consider taking any areas of struggle, and reword them into future positive observations. If you are struggling with maintaining a healthy and constructive attitude during competition, consider rewording this internal observation into a future positive self-statement (eg; I am proud of myself for reaching this state of positive thought. It's comforting to have mastered the ability to remain in the moment). Again, record these future positive self-statements and listen to them many times. The more you engage in this type of mindset, the more you remain in this chosen state of mind

One of the leaders in this field, Dr. Wolpe of Temple University, uses the combination of Progressive Relaxation and Systematic Desensitization. Once having practiced and mastered deep breathing, muscle relaxation techniques, and visual imagery, consider the issue that causes you the most stress. Generate a list from the least stress inducing activity/person/place to the most stress inducing activity/person/place.

As an example, I had a young patient who was terrified of flying. We created a list of 10 progressive steps from comfortable and calm (1) to fear-inducing and dread (10). Her list began at 1 with her relaxing in my office. The second step was merely having a discussion about flight. Her third step was discussing her flight. What was her most stressful activity/person/place? Flying!!! So, this would represent tenth place on her anxiety continuum. Just short of this would be going to the airport. The goal is to rehearse anxiety reducing strategies while at the lowest number. As you move systematically up the hierarchy, continue to employ the relaxing techniques in order to quiet your body and mind. Never force the movement. When you reach an activity/person/place on the list that is too overwhelming, revert to the previous step on the continuum until you are calm, quiet, and relaxed.

Another example - one of my patients was afraid of dogs. She was dating a MMA fighter who owned a mutt that he saved from a local shelter. Because of that, she wanted to desperately resolve this lifelong struggle. When she saw a dog being walked down the street, she panicked and crossed the street. This provided only temporary relief until another dog crossed her path. Her continuum progressed from (1) sitting in my office, (2) sitting in the office discussing dogs, (3) sitting in my office discussing being in the same room as her boyfriend's dog. As she systematically progressed up the list and employed the visualization techniques and relaxation skills, she eventually started to feel comfortable with his dog. Now she totally enjoys spending time over at his condo. Using the combination of relaxation techniques and systematic approach allowed her to have a more loving and close relationship with her boyfriend. Recently, she even offered to clean his place even while he was not at home. She survived the potential frightening solo experience, and found that his little "doggie" was incredibly friendly.

In another case, I was working with a hockey defenseman who was terrified of skating across the blue line and entering the territory of skilled athletes on the offense. He was always bigger than his competitors and played the role of team "enforcer" on the ice. If you messed with his teammates, he was given the authority to go "biblical" on adversaries. In light of his assaultive abilities, he never felt as skilled as his smaller, faster, frontline teammates. The consequences of this perception created tension as he skated from blue line to blue line. When his team went on the offense, it was his responsibility to keep the puck within the blue line or everyone on his team would be off-sides. Needless to say, when he started to panic moving forward, he would state some rather disparaging self-appraisals and tighten up his muscles. This combination turned into a self-fulfilling prophecy. His fears led to a decrease in his talents, abilities, and performance.

After practicing positive self-talk and relaxation training together we created a continuum from the least stressing inducing place to the most stress inducing experience, skating across the blue line on offense in an ice hockey game. He was diligent and motivated, practicing the relaxing techniques at least three times a day. He became exquisitely skilled at reducing his respiratory and heart rates, his blood pressure chilled, muscle tone remained calm, and his thoughts repeated the reality that he does possess exceptional skating skills. Once he implemented this on the ice and discovered he moved fluidly, he was able to track down the flight of the bouncing puck and keep his team in scoring position. Again, the combination of relaxation techniques, visual imagery, and successfully progressing through your own hierarchy of stress can make the cowardly lion a first-string all-star.

When you put these skills together, they create a powerful ability to focus on the moment. No one, not even the pros are focused 100% of the time. No one can focus perfectly an entire competitive event. Remember to stride for excellence, not perfection. Each athlete needs to practice three aspects of focusing. The first is entering a focused state. The second is lengthening the time you are able to remain in a focused state. The third is the recovery back to a focused state. If you lose focus, practice this four-step process to refocus.

Four-Step Focus Protocol

1 – Breath deep. Increase oxygen to your brain and body which facilitates focus and relaxation.

2 – Relax Muscles. Calm your muscles to allow their fluid, consistent movement.

3 – Visualize. See the maneuver that you are about to engage. Muscle memory initiates.

4 – Use a verbal prompt. Find a word that refocuses you into the moment.

This four-step focus protocol will help re-orient the moment for you.

Home Court Advantage: Routines

A wonderful aid that influences thoughts and feelings, is establishing routines to increase a sense of control, helping to focus on the competitive task at hand.

These are not compulsions, but routines. These are not rituals, but a set of behaviors allowing to focus and remain relaxed. These are not superstitions, but a pattern of behavior that brings about a sense of comfort, regardless of playing at home or on the road. These routines include bedtime, food, and drink rituals.

One of the NFL players I work with had a game in London, England. This international game was a fun opportunity to spread the sport of football to other regions around the world. The problem for most teams traveling east is adjusting for the earlier time differential due to time zones. But I instructed my athlete to put himself on the time of the destination as soon as he gets on the flight. He switched his watch from 9pm to five hours ahead, which was 2am. Though the flight departed at 9pm EST, it was actually 2am London time and he immediately decided to zone out and go to sleep. When he arrived, he was refreshed and ready to charge forward. The idea is to, whenever possible, create a *Home Court Advantage.*

The tennis players I coach fuel themselves throughout their match regardless of other possible distractions. They have created their *Home Court Advantage.* And working with a nutritionist helps other athletes determine when and what to eat/drink in order to compete at their highest levels throughout a competitive event.

Some coaches have players at away games who are sitting on the bench, wearing ear buds playing their fight song. In the locker room of the away games, assistant coaches have been known to pin up pictures and posters of their home stadium. Even major professional teams now secure, along the route from the hotel to the stadium for their away games, signage and advertising.

Farrukh Quraishi former GM for the Tampa Bay Rowdies told me their first game of the season was against the San Antonio Scorpions who had won the NASL the previous year. We knew the Champions Ring ceremony was scheduled during the fifteen minutes before the game. I suggested after the warm up to take the players back to the locker and provide a pep talk and relaxation period to help them focus. The Rowdies ruined the Scorpion home opener and ring ceremony by defeating the champions.

ACT won, Scene won

Rather than fighting thoughts, accepting the state of mind you experience helps to find comfort, and facilitates controlling thoughts and feelings. The Acceptance theory (ACT) is another technique to keep athletes in the moment by going with the flow.

Imagine this scene: You are up to bat in the bottom of 9th inning of a baseball game. Your team is losing by two runs, the bases are loaded, and there is one out. What are some of the thoughts you imagine having in this scenario? Perhaps you have helpful and confident thoughts such as, "I got this" or "there is nobody better to win this game than me." Other thoughts might be less helpful such as, "The fate of the game rests on me," "If I don't connect, I'll be the laughing stock of the team", or "My father is going to freak out if I don't make contact." You have probably experienced these or similar thoughts during your lifetime. If you get too caught up in these thoughts while stepping up to the plate, there is a good chance you'll swing and miss...or never swing at all.

When faced with these distracting and uncomfortable thoughts, most athletes attempt to eliminate, alter, or avoid using various methods. In Cognitive-Restructuring, athletes replace negative thoughts with positive ones. Remember that you CANNOT tell your brain what, "Not to focus on." If this works for you, Keep it up! However, for many, the unwanted and unhelpful thoughts eventually come back, and at times, they come back even louder and more distracting than before.

So, if fighting with unwanted thoughts can lead to having more of those thoughts, what is an alternative? There is an up-and-coming branch of psychology encouraging those who struggle with disruptive thoughts to stop fighting against them, and instead, change the relationship they have with these thoughts. One of the more popular models is Acceptance and Commitment Therapy or ACT (Hayes, S.C. et. al. 1999). This model is based on the theme of learning how to commit to what truly matters to you, while learning how to effectively cope with, or accept unwanted thoughts and experiences that inevitably occur along the way. Acceptance, makes room for thoughts without attempting to avoid, change, or minimize them by gaining a different perspective in your mind.

One of the foundational exercises ACT therapists teach to help with this type of acceptance is called mindfulness. Russ Harris, a well-known author in the ACT community, defines mindfulness as consciously bringing awareness to the here-and-now experience with openness, interest, and receptiveness (Harris, R, 2009). This means intentionally focusing your attention on this moment regardless if the experience is pleasant or painful, and to be curious about what thoughts, feelings, or sensations arise in this moment.

For example, take a moment to notice what you are doing at this moment as you read this book. Start your sentence by saying to yourself, "I notice I am [fill in the blank]." The most obvious response is, "I notice I am reading." But after a moment, you might come up with other responses too, such as "I notice I am sitting/lying down," "I notice I am breathing," or "I notice I am listening to music." Being aware of these actions is what mindfulness is all about. To take it one step further, mindfulness asks you to bring a sense of curiosity and openness to the actions you become aware of.

The principles and exercises in ACT, including acceptance and mindfulness, have been shown to be highly effective for many different types of struggles. Among these struggles are anxiety, depression, panic attacks, trauma, chronic pain, and problems with focus, concentration, and attention (A-Tjak, J. G , et. al., 2015). There have also been several studies showing how athletes benefit from acceptance and mindfulness strategies, and they suggest athletes who practice these exercises show better performance (Hayes, S.C, et. al, 2015), enjoy the sport more (Moore, Z. E. 2009) (Bernier, M. et. al., 2009), and are less likely to give up the sport due to frustration and fatigue (Gustafsson, H., 2015). This might be helpful for athletes because the focus shifts from attempting to control unwanted thoughts and feelings, to focusing on each game moment as it occurs without attempting to rid or avoid these thoughts and feelings.

Now ask, "What are some ways an athlete might practice some of these exercises?" One way to begin mindfulness practice is in your daily routine. The next time you complete one of your morning activities, see if you can bring your awareness to the sensations. If you are doing the dishes, for example, notice feelings of frustration, irritation, and hesitation, along with thoughts such as, "I don't feel like it", or "I just want to rest." Keep in mind, this is not an attempt to make washing the dishes more pleasurable, but instead being more aware and conscious of the experience as it is happening in real time. At first (and many more times after), your mind will become bored and drift back to some thought or fantasy. This is normal and natural, and it happens to everyone. As soon as you notice your mind wandering, take note of whatever it was that distracted you (thoughts about work, sports, tests, family, etc.), and bring yourself right back to noticing the experience of washing dishes.

In addition to informal exercises of mindful daily routines, practice more formal mindfulness exercises, such as sitting in a comfortable position with your eyes closed and allowing a mindfulness instructor to guide you through an exercise. Most of these exercises involve noticing your breath, the same way you noticed the sensation of brushing your teeth, or washing the dishes; with openness and curiosity to whatever thoughts, feelings, and sensations arise in the moment. You can find guided mindfulness exercises from one of the seminal teachers, Jon Kabat-Zin (2012), or from a variety of ACT practitioners and teachers.

The more you practice mindfulness, the more you create a space for all kinds of thoughts, feelings, and sensations without attempting to change, avoid, or eliminate them (Acceptance). Cultivating a regular mindfulness practice opens the door to working on acceptance exercises. To begin acceptance, intentionally engage in an activity you find slightly annoying or irritating. Once you have chosen an activity, see if you can be mindful of the experience while allowing all thoughts, feelings, and sensations to be there without attempting to change them from negative to positive, or without trying to get through the activity as quickly as possible. The idea is to try turning into, instead of away from, these unpleasant experiences in order to be less bothered when they arise.

Eventually, with enough regular practice, many people soon notice a difference in the way they interact with everyday experiences. Let us look back at the imaginary baseball scenario. You are up to bat in the last inning of a big baseball game. Your team is losing by one run, the bases are loaded, and there are two outs left. The fate of the game rests with you. Instead of spending time battling with unhelpful thoughts, use your acceptance/mindfulness skills to hone in on the sensation of the bat in your hand, the position of your body near the plate, and the way the pitcher and other players are lined up. As I have shared there are no guarantees, but you may now be in the proper state to increase your probability of success. Now, acceptance and mindfulness can help increase the likelihood your swing will be executed with awareness and focus without interruption by unhelpful thoughts.

"Post-Shot Routine"

Emotional reactions don't provide helpful input to improve. Your emotional reactions can impede your progress. Mastering the lessons learned from the three-question process of the Post-shot Routine will help improve your skills and become more consistent. Most of the greatest lessons in competition come from events that are not positive, nor victorious. We must learn and grow from defeat. The most embarrassing defeat could offer the greatest lesson.

There is a three-question process of the Post-Shot Routine:

1. What was the plan?
2. What actually happened?
3. What did you learn from the outcome, both positive and negative?

After every competitive moment you have a plan, an action, and an outcome. Use this reflective process to analyze your ability. The great

NFL Dallas Cowboy's Coach Tom Landry suggested, "I always learn something from a loss." Failure is not a loss if you learn from it.

You become your best coach. First, review your plan. Second, shift from raw emotion to beneficial cognition. Outline what occurred. Third, interpret how and why the action occurred the way it did. There is no blaming, no externalizing, no pointing of the finger to someone else. You now take full responsibility.

A golfer would ask,

1) What was the plan? Drive the ball 250 yards with a slight draw.
2) What happened? My ball ended up in the right rough.
3) What did I learn from the outcome? "Why did the ball slice off to the right and into the deep rough? Somehow, I created the angle of the club face to generate direction and spin in that direction. How did I do that? It certainly wasn't part of the initial plan. I somehow changed my technique and form, and it led to inconsistency, and to taking a stroll into the deeper greenery. I lifted my head which opened my stance, causing the club face to open slightly, which created the left to right side spin on the ball."

A soccer player would ask,

1) What was the plan? Head the ball into the right upper corner of the net.
2) What happened? I headed the ball over the goal.

3) What do I learn from the outcome? "Why did my header sail above the cross bar of the goal? If I blame my opponent, then there is nothing for me to improve upon. If I don't take personal responsibility I will never learn from the past. I took my eye off the ball, which altered my timing, and caused the ball to move upward rather than straight."

Another example of the Post-shot routine was shared by a gymnast. She asked herself,

1) What was the plan? Have a positive attitude and successfully compete in the state championships by consistently performing the routine that I have practiced all season.

2) What happened? My internal self-talk was negative and I struggled with my maneuvers on the floor routine and balance beam, and scored lower than anticipated.

3) What did I learn from the outcome? "When I met the competitors, I felt inferior to their accomplishments. During the competition, I felt I needed to increase my height on all my skills. But once I changed my technique, my form began to break down and I struggled. My way of handling the struggle was push harder, which led to more sub-par performance. I realize that when I compare myself to other competitors at the higher levels, I tend to speak to myself with doubt and become insecure. When I become insecure, I try to push myself by slightly altering my form and technique. This change leads to inconsistencies and sup-par performance. I need to become more secure with my skills and abilities regardless of the competition. If I focus on my already proven abilities I will be consistent. I need to return to positive self-talk. I need to recall my competitors never touch me during my performance. There are never any guarantees, but I realized it was my perspective and negative self-talk that caused me to perform worse. It will be my positive self-talk and confidence in

my practice, coaching, and experience which will bring me closer to my dreams."

Another example of the Post-shot routine was an AVP men's volleyball player. He asked himself,

1) What was the plan? Return from my elbow injury and compete at the highest levels.
2) What happened? I was inconsistent and re-injured my elbow.
3) What did I learn from the outcome? "I probably came back too quickly from my rehab. While I was not competing, I felt like a slacker and thought others would see me as "weak." The pain meds and spray masked most of the pain. I adjusted my form to protect my injured elbow and my performance decreased. I re-injured my elbow during a match. I lost a few matches to lower rank opponents. Because of my injury I was not able to play at the highest level. My consistency decreased because my form had changed. My form had changed to protect my elbow from re-injury. I might have returned to competition too quickly, leading to poor performance. I will need to take the next couple of weeks off to recover and return at full strength. Once I return fully recovered I'll be consistent."

Here are a few positive examples of using the Post-shot Routine. A pairs figure skater asked herself,

1) What was the plan? To stick every jump throughout my two programs.
2) What happened? I landed every jump.
3) What did I learn from the outcome? "I realize that when I prepare I can compete against the best in the world. My coaches have helped me reach the top of my sport. My partner really cares and puts in the time with me to practice. I did my pre-competition routine and stayed focus throughout the performance. I didn't get

ahead of myself. I took each jump one at a time. I realize I do my best when I stay focused and in the moment."

A baseball player asked himself the three questions from the Post-shot Routine.

1) What was the plan? To have situational awareness and do what's best for my team.
2) What happened? I advanced my teammate to a better scoring position by going with the pitch to the opposite field. The pitch was low and outside. I extended my arms, made contact, and drove the ball to the opposite field.
3) What did I learn the outcome? "In this situation, I have the ability to help my team. I successfully completed the task. I stayed with the pitch and made solid contact to the opposite field. I want to learn that I can be successful, and that I need to continue taking what the pitcher gives, and exploiting it for my team. I don't have to hit home runs to be a good teammate. I can always be totally in the moment and understand how best to help my team."

An elite diver used the three questions from the Post-Dive Routine by asking,

1) What was the plan? To complete a reverse dive and not get stuck in my head with negative thoughts.
2) What happened? I successfully completed the gainer by staying calm and coming up with many positive comments from the past.
3) What did I learn from the outcome? "When I relax before a dive I do really well. When I challenge negative thoughts with positive statements (Cognitive Restructuring) I'm able to do my best. I practiced changing negative thoughts; Instead of saying I'm afraid of hitting my head I change this to positive statements that were based on reality. I've never hit my head on the board, and My momentum carries me away from the board, Over the years I have

mastered each dive without a problem and when combining these two steps I was able to get out of my head and into the moment."

When things don't go the way you planned, the first step in making any change is admitting that there is something that needs to change, and then not blaming the outcome on external factors.

Take Away for Step Five:

Develop pre- and post-shot routines. Most world-class athletes have mastered a pre-competition routine which often includes the 3-Step Olympic Calming techniques of deep breathing, muscle relaxation, and visualization. Additionally, the best athletes learn from the past. Practice the post-shot routine by using the three-question process. Mastering these pre- and post-routines will help you stay in the moment, remaining calm, cool, and collected and to compete at the highest level.

Step Six: Strive for Excellence Not Perfection

Outline

1. Happiness and success is not reaching perfection, but how to handle imperfection
2. To err is human, to forgive divine
    Excellence is a process not an outcome

Happiness and success is not reaching perfection, but how to handle imperfection

Self-worth, happiness and sense of personal success is based upon your awareness that you have done your best and lived up to your highest standard. Life rarely turns out exactly the way you plan. Being the best is a remarkable and rare achievement. Not achieving the absolute top position is not a statement of failure. Being honest with yourself that you have given your best is your best. Seeking excellence over perfection will lead to personal improvement and personal satisfaction.

In the road of life there will always be potholes. Invariably, you will drive your car right into one of these potholes. Unfortunately, you will have to stop whatever your goal and address this problem. You will need to contact the towing company, take the time to rent a car and wait for the repair shop to contact you when the repairs are completed. After spending time and money to get this accomplished, what will you do the next time you're driving down the same road and come to that pothole? Will you drive right back into it? Will you get into a different lane? Will you contact the county DOT and ask them to fill in the pothole? All but one are good possibilities. Which one do you think you would choose?

If your happiness and success is based upon perfection you are probably setting yourself up for disappointment.

If you live by an All-or-None perspective, then you will always beat yourself up for anything but the singular outcome. This style is oftentimes taught to us by our family during our childhood. Critically demanding parents can inadvertently create this type of perspective. Your effort, diligence, steadfastness and willingness to keep applying yourself are not valued. Only the outcome is the basis for determining your sense of accomplishment. Remember, long-term goals have short-term steps, increasing your probability of success. This is not merely a one-shot deal. You don't become a professional basketball player because you played one season in high school. It is the process, not the outcome. Goals have steps while dreams vanish upon the light of day. If you want to do your best, then strive to be your best. I have a funny feeling that if you were the best player on your high school basketball team, you would be willing to accept the role of being the Sixth Man on a NBA Championship team. You might not be the best athlete or player in the league or even of your team, but being an integral part of the championship team would be something you could feel proud of achieving.

The fictitious character of Ricky Bobby in *Talladega Nights* had the All-or-None way of looking at racing, "If you're not first, you're last!" The truth was he learned this from his father who had abandoned him at an early age. Many perfectionistic athletes wrongly think, "Second Place is First Loser." This mentality drives them forward to attain greatness, but it also sets them up for disappointment and negativity.

An ancient proverb, "If you are not a better person tomorrow than you are today, what need have you for a tomorrow?" "The purpose of human life is to improve one's character traits by working on oneself every day. That's why God gives us today – and tomorrow." Sara Yoheved Rigler

To err is human, to forgive divine

No professional athlete has a perfect career or remains number one in their sport for their entire career. The best athletes in the world occasionally fall short of expectations. Understanding that doing your best is a process not an outcome is vital to pursue excellence not perfection.

"Life is not about perfection but rather how you handle imperfection" (Shinitzky, H.) Recalling the difference between Amateurs and Professionals, Pros get paid. Amateurs don't. If you are not being paid and therefore an amateur, you make too many errors. If you are celebrating your successes but not learning from your losses, you will remain an amateur as you will not address the inconsistencies in your performance that prevent you from reaching the summit of your sport. In reality, even professionals aren't perfect. Few teams go undefeated for a season. Even those rare undefeated teams probably did not perform ideally in every situation and every moment of their season.

When discussing sports or business or social life we should consider swapping out the term perfection and insert the word, excellence. Strive for excellence that is definable and attainable. Perfection and impossible in terms of human behavior are identical words in performance. The use of excellence provides a softer, reasonable and accurate objective. Does Derek Jeter reflect excellence in sports? Is HE perfect? Some would say yes to both. You know, like that, Yankee thing. Ridiculous, ill-advised choice descriptor (ie; Cub fan speaking). Since perfection is an impossible goal the best anyone can hope for is doing your best and striving for excellence.

The main emphasis in this is to keep sports/life in perspective. Don't let perfect be the enemy of good (Voltaire)

We are human. We lack the ability to maintain the vigilance and focus required to perform eye-hand coordination with exact repetition over a period of time. Robotics has inserted itself into our lives for repetitive tasks. Humans fatigue. Humans become distracted. Humans react with emotions. As in the movie, *The Andromeda Strain*, the scientist loses his focus on the electron microscope for just a moment and hence misses the life-threatening particle.

Too many athletes struggle not with their abilities but with their perspective. They self-impose a belief that they must be perfect. Curiously, most of such individuals are amateurs. Get where I'm going with this? The Miller's Analogies Test would ask the comparative question, Amateur is to Errors as Government Bureaucracy is to Gridlock.

Think about your favorite athlete. This could be someone you looked up to during your childhood or someone you follow on your fantasy sports league. None are perfect. Not one of them. They might have a short period of time in which they string consistency together but even those experiences are short when compared to the entire season or their career. No one attains absolute perfection.

Yet, there are those athletes who hold themselves accountable to an unattainable, unrealistic, irrational expectation followed by the requisite verbal berating and negative judgement reserved for the lowest form of species on the planet. Their tirade doesn't even appear to offer lessons to learn from but rather emotional meltdowns creating an abusive dynamic between the athlete and their own mind. As we had previously discussed there are no guarantees. There never was and never will be. Ok, death and taxes. Interesting if a pro is not perfect how silly is it that an amateur would hold themselves up to this standard. Again, that's why you are an amateur. Errors.

As the title of this step reflects, To err is human, to forgive divine (Pope, A.). As Zig Ziglar famously is quoted, "If you learn from defeat, you haven't really lost." What you do with this information is more important. Keeping this information in perspective is vitally important. Why did I do what I did? What do I need to change, learn, improve, address, etc? You plan, practice, study, apply yourself, execute and the results are rarely perfect. We are human. We err. The aspect of this quote from Pope emphasizes the rule that we as humans make mistakes, struggle to maintain consistency, and fall short of perfect. The capacity to forgive is the key. Forgiveness is the solution to the problem. You could offer forgiveness to those that you have expended too much energy focusing on as the cause of some negative event. You might need to offer forgiveness to yourself.

Lack of perfection is human. It is normal. "Perfection should be used as a driving force to improve as we all have room for improvement but perfection should never be used as criteria to judge yourself." (Shinitzky, H). Strive for excellence not perfection in life and sport. Excellence is definable and attainable. Perfection is impossible.

Take Away for Step Six:

Self-worth, happiness and a sense of personal success is based on the awareness that you have done your best and lived up to your highest standard. What leads to personal satisfaction and improvement is striving for excellence not perfection. If you live by an All-or-None perspective anything less than a perfect outcome makes you feel incomplete and a failure. No professional athlete has a perfect career. The best occasionally fall short of expectations but they pursue excellence not perfection. Remember that humans lack the ability to maintain vigilance and focus to remain perfect over a period of time. Strive for excellence not perfection.

Step Seven: Increase Your Probability of Success

Outline

1. There are no guarantees in life: All You Can Do is Increase the Probability of Success
2. It's all Practice: The Laws of Physics Don't Change
3. This is the biggest tournament of my life and other children's fairy tales
4. Five steps of SMART goal-setting
5. The opportunity of a lifetime is only as good as the lifetime of the opportunity

There are no guarantees in life

You can do everything right and still not win. Remembering there are other competitors vying for the same goal which impacts and determines the final outcome. Since there are factors outside of your control you need to take care of your responsibilities. As you execute your step-by-step techniques, tactics and performance you invariably increase your probability of success.

You can spend your life preparing for THE event and something derails your plans, ie: the Olympics could be boycotted, the number one running back for your fantasy football league gets injured and is out for the year, shot your lowest round in golf and still not win. The only action you can do is apply yourself, do your best, and put yourself in the best possible situation.

As an example: A jockey can prepare for the race, become one with the thoroughbred, practice the distance and replicate the conditions. The steed can receive the best care from the trainer. But on the day of the Triple Crown, the gate position might be further out than you had hoped, the horse might fall too far behind the lead pack, or he might get pinned against the rail without a clear escape. Remember, "There are no guarantees in life: The only thing you can do is increase your probability of success."

This concept applies to life beyond sport. You could attend class and do your homework you still don't guarantee an "A" in the class. You can leave for work as usual but due to an accident be delayed. In life, the only strategy that you truly ever employ is to increase your probability of success since there are no guarantees.

The great coach, Lou Holtz once opined, "Life is ten percent what happens, and ninety percent how you react to it."

You might unwittingly increase your probability of failure by participating in activities that have the potential for becoming a distraction such as gambling. I have worked with extraordinarily wealthy professionals who view gambling as a simple hobby which doesn't impact their financial life. Yet, I have also worked with athletes who gamble to such a level that they fell millions of dollars behind the eight-ball. Imagine that every tournament you have to give your winnings away to someone who could break your knee caps for non-payment. Hmm, like that would be a distraction?!

As Albert Einstein said, "Insanity is doing the same thing over again and expecting a different result." Repeating unhealthy behaviors and decisions unfortunately make the problem worse.

In life, there are never any guarantees. You make decisions everyday of your life. You could increase your probability of success by removing negative choices. You could also increase your probability of failure by including poor choices as acceptable options. You might choose some fun activity because it sounds interesting. Yet you might end up experiencing some unintended consequences which not only impact you but also your team. Even worse, your choices might have terrible consequences for you and your supporters.

A powerful example of increasing your probability of failure is revealed by research study from the University of Michigan, Monitoring the Futures (Schulenberg, et al. MTF 2016). It reported the average college student often consumes five or more drinks in one night. A cascade of tragic outcomes was identified. In many sexual assaults that occur, alcohol was reported as involved (Abbey, 2002). Many physical assaults are attributed to the consumption of alcohol (Wechsler, H. et. al, 1994, Powell, LM, 2002). Poor class attendance is oftentimes associated with alcohol (Ansari, WE, et, al. 2013). This is presumably due to the hangover and not due to drinking in class. Alcohol also has a rather adverse effect on the developing brain. Documented evidence supports potential effects on short-term memory, sleep cycles (NIAAA) as well as attention and concentration. Let's not forget DUI and the consequences/distractions associated with this legal situation.

As noted, alcohol is frequently identified as a contributing factor for sexual assaults or domestic violence. Flatly, sexual assaults or domestic violence are never acceptable. Period!

There are no guarantees. Doing your best is the process, it is not an outcome. I had a student who had struggled in college to maintain the minimal grades needed to be active and play her sport. She studied hard for her math exams but just couldn't understand how Sine and Cosine were a number, a curve and an angle. As feared, she could only muster a "D" which dropped her grades below the minimal standards. She was suspended the next semester and was not eligible to play with the team. Though she worked hard and applied herself there was no guarantee she would earn a high enough grade to play. She put forth the effort which was her attempt to increase her probability of success yet still fell short.

Many examples exist in which a coach called a good play for the circumstance but the defense stepped it up and blew up the play. As an example, the Seattle Seahawks had marched down the field as the game clock was running out and were in position to win Super Bowl XLIX. They had reached the one-yard line with 26 seconds remaining. Many Seahawk fans felt Coach Carroll should have given the ball to "The Beast", Marshawn Lynch. He chose to throw the ball. Of note, during the NFL season of all the times in which a team was on their opponent's one-yard line, the offensive team chose to throw the ball 66 times. Of those 66 passes they either scored a touchdown or had an incompletion, zero interceptions. By the numbers, the Seahawks called a good play for the circumstance. They had a "pick" or "rub" pass play called but in this moment, rookie Malcolm Butler made a game-saving interception which "iced" the game and the Patriots won the Super Bowl. There are never any guarantees and in this case, they made a decision which left most Seahawks fans crying.

Of course, no matter how an athlete tries, there are times they do not reach their goals. Dan Jensen, the renowned US Olympic Speed Skater had practiced, prepared and won world championships and was the favorite to win every race he was in. However, in 1988 he fell during his events and in 1992 he did not reach his goal. There are no guarantees but by putting yourself in the best possible position increases your probability of success. Dan Jensen's story does have a happy ending when he set a world record in the 1,000-meter event winning the elusive Gold Medal at the 1994 Winter Olympics.

It's all Practice: The Laws of Physics Don't Change

The name of an event doesn't change the laws of physics. Every opportunity you have to compete is an opportunity to improve. Regardless of the fact you are practicing or the game clock has started, each is an opportunity to work on your game, improve your skills and address some specific lesson you learned from previous opportunities. Since the laws of physics (e.g.; gravity, magnetism, etc.) have not changed and improving is a lifelong pursuit, every opportunity (practice or play) is an opportunity to practice and get better.

"Even if there are failures, it brings experience. Experience is what you get when you didn't get what you wanted. And experience is often the most valuable thing you have to offer." (Dr. Randy Pausch, 2008).

Focusing on the basics, staying consistent, remaining in the moment, using the skills acquired from years of practice, are the factors that make professional athletes.

As an example, Ted Williams -- arguably baseball's best hitter -- failed six out of 10 times. Consider the math: Williams failed *more than half the time!* Williams' ability still serves as an example of excellence in baseball. Regardless of the episodic highs and lows, remaining in the moment took care of the fundamentals: A ball thrown by the opposing pitcher has a fairly predictable path. He processed the pitch's release point, integrated the pitcher's tendencies, and reacted by putting the movement of the bat in the rotational path of the ball. His coaching and skills along with his experience allowed him to hit .406 in 1941. He entered the Baseball Hall of Fame with a lifetime .344 batting average. This took years of practice, to stay in the moment and not get stuck in his head

There is a humorous story attributed to Michael Jordan which states, *"I've missed more than 9,000 shots in my career. I've lost almost 300 games. Twenty-six times I've been trusted to take the game winning shot and missed. I've failed over and over and over again in my life...That is why I succeed."* Michael possessed the skill set which allowed him to focus on the task, the moment and the goal. He did not become consumed with the pressure of the moment or the significance of the goal or the magnitude of the task. What he had done was practice the form over years, mastered the technique to be consistent and visualized the moment hundreds of times. As he practiced with his teammates, they created game-like conditions, rehearsed specific plays on scouted defenses, and amassed the experience, coaching and abilities to remain focused on repeating his form. He was aware that the form in practice was the form in competition. Newton and Einstein's theories did not falter because he was playing in the NBA Championship. The Laws of Physics did not change. His form, technique and skill didn't change because of the name of the event (practice versus NBA Championship), the number of people watching, or the potential financial windfall of endorsements.

Coaches have long been aware practice, consistency and mental focus are the basic components to a winning program. You've probably heard a coach interviewed before, during and after competition, "We just have to continue doing what brought us here." The coach is right. By keeping the situation in perspective, we realize that it is all practice. What brought the team/player to this point is exactly what the team/player needs to continue doing, play the game. If you change up the skill set, form and techniques you will likely display inconsistency and probably underperform. If you bring your best A-game and lose, then you have lost to a better opponent on this day. A better way of looking at this outcome is you didn't lose, rather they won. You didn't give away the game because of poor performance, they performed better on this day. You shoot your lowest round in golf does not guarantee victory as another competitor doing their best could shoot lower. You execute the proper play in soccer but it doesn't mean you win every game. Once you realize if you use what brought you to an elite level of skill is practicing proper form, technique and skill and not becoming distracted by the name of the event, the prize money nor the number of people watching. All of competition is, in essence, practice.

Professionals practice to warm up, maintain their skills and improve technique. Everyone practices to be their best, and regardless of the competition, games, tournaments, rivalries, matches, the opportunity is there to do your best. You begin your sport learning and developing new skills to advance to a higher level. Every opportunity to play your sport is an opportunity to improve, become more skilled and consistent.

Why do the pros practice? Why do the pros have coaches? Why do the pros watch videos of opponents? Why do the pros workout? Stretch? Eat well? Simple, because everyone has room for improvement.

Let me repeat, everyone has room for improvement!

The only thing you can ever do, is be your best. That is not an outcome that is a process. There are no tournaments. There is just another opportunity to practice your craft and improve.

How do you win a tennis match? You have to win the most sets. How do you win the sets? You have to win the games. How do you win the games? You simply have to win the points. Last question, how do you win the points? You get it! You have to win this stroke. The singular stroke is your victory. This moment in time must be executed to the best of your ability. If you don't take care of the basics, you will never get to the promised land. Victory comes from mastering the process. By stringing a series of singular processes together you eventually reach an outcome. There are no guarantees, there is only increasing your probability of success. There is no competition, there is only another opportunity to practice your craft, improve your skills, do your best and become more consistent.

I heard one golfer during an interview say, "I looked at the Leaderboard and saw that I was two back, so I decided to bring my A-Game." All I kept thinking was, "Now you're going to bring your A-Game. What were you bringing before realizing you were two back? Maybe you wouldn't be two back if you had been bringing your A-Game all along."

Practicing game like situations helps to translate to competition. Yet competition is no different than practice if you are always bringing your A-Game. Perfect practice makes perfect. Since we are human perfect might be a goal but it is not your destination. Doing your best is all you can ever do. Put yourself into the best possible situation. Strive for excellence rather than perfection.

Remember that the difference between a Pro and Amateur is the pro hits winners and the amateur makes errors. Of course, we are talking about consistency and predictability in your performance. At this point in your career, you need to focus on decreasing your errors. It's not about perfection, it's about skill development and realizing you are using every opportunity to improve your performance. That would mean in the big picture, it's all practice. Practice increasing your focus. Practice developing the basic and then advanced skill sets. If you have not achieved the top position in your sport, then you have the opportunity to improve. Every opportunity to improve is an opportunity to get better whether it is during practice or game time.

Imagine that you are preparing for an upcoming tournament. You practice during the week and feel you are improving. However, when you arrive at the tournament, you tend to get nervous. Your form breaks down and your consistency disappears. Now imagine that you are preparing for an upcoming tournament and when you attend the tournament you focus not on the event but rather on the skills you have been practicing. If you look at the tournament as another opportunity to improve and practice then you are not distracted by the label of the event (tournament, meet, competition, US Open, Championship, etc.).

When you work on your form in practice the goal is to master the details and nuance of biomechanics, timing, consistency, visual-perceptual processing, and positive mental focus. Everyone is striving for that holy grail with respect to transferring their form from practice to competition. In essence, can you repeat that form to the best of your ability? Can I toss the ball in my tennis serve in the same place each time so that each service form becomes rote and predictable? Am I able to swing my 7-iron in a repetitive manner such when I strike the ball it will loft into the heavens in a reasonably predictable way and the ball will land in approximately the same area? Have my pairs figure skating partner and I spent enough time practicing with my coach to develop the muscle memory, allowing us to appear graceful while completing a triple throw loop that has the requisite elevation, proper rotation, and correct vertical posture so my partner will land on one skate making it look effortless?

Here is an example that shows how developing a new routine in practice can translate to world-class competition. One of the Olympic sailors I worked with had previously been diagnosed with Attention Deficit/Hyperactivity Disorder. He had been prescribed Ritalin which helped him to focus. When he earned a position on the US Olympic Team he was informed that he could no longer take his medication because it was considered a banned substance. Initially he panicked. Once we began to address this reality, he was highly motivated to come up with a plan to increase his probability of success. Fact, though he could not focus on anything for a long period of time, he was able to focus on everything for a short period of time. Between his coaches, his understanding of his strengths and our techniques for mental focus, we developed a five-step protocol that facilitated his masterful skills as a sailor. While racing he focused on five key points which help him be successful. The five-step sequence of tasks included: Wind direction, sail aloft, current, tiller, and opponent. Again, he could not focus on any one task for a long period of time, but he could focus on each one of these tasks for a short period of time. These strategic tactics were based on reality and the laws of physics to remain competitive at an elite level. He would rotate sequentially from each tactical skill. He would determine the direction of the wind which was his source of power. He would visually assess if his sail was a full deployment or optimal trim. He knew never to sail with an approach of less than within 45 degrees as his sails would luff or flap. In sailing terms, he would be "in irons." He would take into consideration the direction of the current and adjust accordingly with his tiller. Finally, he would be aware of his opponent and ready to tack in order to give "dirty air" to his competitors. His routine helped him to regain his Olympic skill set and compete on a world-class level.

What's amazing is in most sports you are not being asked to do something new. The goal in practice is to expose yourself to every plausible situation and circumstance. You want to rehearse and master the tactics, skills and abilities during practice in such a way that you will feel comfortable and confident during competition.

As a matter of fact, some sports have you doing exactly what you have been practicing, performing and competing over the months. Biathletes will cross-country ski and then shoot a rifle as they did in practice. A gymnast will do the exact floor, bar, beam and side horse routine they have been working on in previous practice sessions and competitions. Swimmers, distance runners, cheerleaders repeat exactly what they have put months of effort into and if they are able to focus on only their routine they display consistency which puts them in the best position during competition.

I was working with a basketball player who could drain free throws during practice but would struggle during games. What was the one thing that changed from the time he practiced to the time he was competing? Did the bucket get raised to 10'2"? Did the ball become inflated to a size that could no longer fit into the bucket? Did the free throw line get moved back? The reality was that none of these took place. The singular thing that changed from practice to competition was the way he thought about the circumstances. His thoughts or perceptions led him to make unconscious or even conscious changes to his form. Negative thoughts might have begun or he might have started to fear bad outcomes. His breathing changed, his muscle tone changed, his motion changed, his thinking changed. The Laws of Physics did not change, gravity remained intact. The process of trajectory and force maintained the predictable impact on the flight of the ball. When he stopped focusing on competition or the game he began to focus on his skills. Yes, the very skills he had been working on and mastering during practice. The reality is that it's all practice!

While a faculty member at the Johns Hopkins University School of Medicine, I was fortunate to consult with the DeMatha Stags high school football and basketball programs. Their great basketball coach, Morgan Wootten had requested outside assistance with some of his players. His philosophy was to practice like you played. It didn't matter if they were playing against Lew Alcindor (known now as Kareem Abdul-Jabbar), they always practiced with the mindset that they all could improve. Typical comments were, "We practice just to make us a better team...Hopefully I learned from every single game I was involved in...Sometimes you learn more from a loss than a win" (Wootten, 1994). Coach Wootten understood how practicing game-like conditions translated to in-game success.

Adrian Dantley rates as one fo the greatest free throw shooters in NBA history. Danley's practice routine was described in a wonderful exposé describing how Dantley walked onto the court, "His face is a study of concentration. He does not smile on the court and rarely says much to the other players. Instead, Dantley concentrates on his shooting. He is thinking . . .Backspin. Over the rim. Follow through." (http://articles.latimes.com/1986-01-06/sports/sp-13578_1_adrian-dantley). He reminded himself of the basics every time he approached the free throw line. Dantley realized that regardless of the name of the event (eg; NBA game, collegiate game at Notre Dame, or high school game at DeMatha) it was all practice. The same form, predictable and consistent.

Whenever you experience the change in your ability between practice and competition, you are focusing on the competition and not skills. Remember you have earned the right to be competing in this event. You have spent countless hours practicing. You have invested time and money into receiving the best coaching to master the physical and mental aspects of your game. Your practice is in fact your ability. If you allow yourself to break down the entirety of competition you realize the whole is made up of the parts. Stay in the moment and focus on the part. Focus on what you have done, mastered and developed consistency with your practice. It's all practice!

"This is the biggest tournament of my life" and other children's fairy tales

Labeling an event doesn't change your muscles, your coordinated skills or the fact that you have qualified to compete in this event. By labeling an event you personally change the way you judge it and therefore create a false narrative. By focusing on the details of each maneuver within your control, you increase the probability of success.

I received a call from one of the nationally ranked female high school golfers. She was frantic. She was heading to the state tournament that weekend. Her voice was more animated than usual. She quickly stated, "Doc, I'm freaking out 'cause this is the biggest tournament of life." As we talked she identified her fears of not achieving her long-term goals, disappointing her parents, and failing to score low in this tournament.

She had created a monster in her head, a monster as scary as Beowulf or some villain in a Grimm fairy tale. Imagination can cause many sleepless nights. As Mark Twain once wrote, "The greatest fears in my life never happened." As President Roosevelt stated, "The only thing to fear, is fear itself." The Boogie Man, the state tournament, the Toe Monster under your bed or the US Open are nothing other than what you make of them.

Perception and Perspective

This concept has existed for centuries. The Taoist stories of perspective and perception run long and deep. For more detailed lessons you might want to check out the following web-site, http://www.katinkahesselink.net/tibet/zen.html).

114

There are many ways to waste your limited supply of energy and decrease your probability of success. You can choose to invest your energy in activities which offer exceptional return on investment (ROI), or you can choose to invest your energy in counterproductive behaviors, feelings and thoughts. Three of the ways to waste energy are referred to as the 3 W's: Wishing, Worrying and Whining from 'Your Mind: An Owner's Manual for a Better Life' (Shinitzky, H. et. al., Career Press, 2009).

Wishing. You invest energy in the past. You cannot change the past. If you dwell on the past, "beat" yourself up because of the past, ruminate on the missteps of the past, you run the risk of not living in the here and now. If you miss a short putt and become frustrated you might hold onto that frustration. You make the past interfere with the present. You are making bad – worse.

Worrying. You fear the future. You think of the worst-case scenarios in your thoughts regarding the future and not focus on the present. Coaches direct athletes not to focus on the outcome but rather on the process. As Mark Twain surmised, "Most of the biggest worries in my life never happened."

Whining. You complain about incidents outside of your control. A football player complaining the weather will be cold in Green Bay during the month of January. Well it's not just cold for that one player. Mother Nature is not plotting against this one athlete. It's going to be cold for everyone. A golfer complains the winds will be howling at the British Open. Again, Mother Nature isn't creating these winds just to interfere with this one player's success. The winds are infamous at the British Open. It will be windy for everyone. These events are referred to as constants. As if there is a mathematical constant. Whenever you are presented with a constant that is outside of your control, consider how you will adapt to that factor.

Examples:

- I was amazed a few years ago when one of the MLB players came in after he was traded away to the other team in the same city. He went from the National league to the American league. He wasn't bothered by the trade. He wasn't bothered by the new team identity. He was however bothered by the change in the strike zone called by the umpires when he was batting. Now that he entered the National League, the strike zone was bigger. Balls down by his knees were now being called strikes. What do all of these facts reflect? He was complaining about a constant for that specific league. We discussed two options, 1) Start a grassroots movement and file a formal complaint to the commissioner or 2) He could stop whining about something outside of his control use his energy to adjust and adapt.

- Several of my Olympic Figure Skating hopefuls expressed their concerns above the integrity or bias of the judges at the upcoming Olympics. The background that led to this discussion was the Olympic judges form Russia and France a few years ago colluded and agreed to score their teams mutually high regardless of the actual performance. The Russian Pairs Figure Skaters fell during the landing of a jump which usually receives a major deduction. Not in this case. The Russian team won the Bronze with much controversy. Afterwards, the International Olympic Committee investigated and discovered the nefarious agreement. The Russian team was stripped of their Bronze medal which then was awarded correctly to the Canadian team. The figure skaters and I discussed the fact the judges have no effect on performance. Focusing on externals distracts from performance. Remember, if the external is a constant that effects all competitors equally, such as temperature or wind, consider how to adapt and adjust. If you choose to focus, whine and complain about things outside of your control you create your own fairy tale.

- Research supports these observations. Cheng & Hardy (Cheng, W.N. & Hardy, L. 2016), studied 485 national and international dancers performing at the university level. The goal was to rate the dancers' perfectionism and establish a correlation to their levels of self-perceived anxiety (How they handle their stress?) versus cognitive/psychological anxiety (What are you feeling and thinking?) and to determine which aspect of performing creates the most significant stress. This evaluation consisted of two aspects: perfectionistic strivings (focusing on personal standards) and perfectionistic concerns (doubts about action). The studies found that perfectionism was most correlated with regulatory anxiety (How they handle their stress) more than cognitive anxiety (How they think or feel). In accordance to that finding, personal standards proved to be the strongest predictor of regulatory anxiety (How they handle their stress). These results confirm the pressure of failing during performance is self-imposed anxiety. They created their own story in their head rather than focusing on the task at hand.

- Another study identifying the adverse impact of your negative thoughts, revealed by Hodge & Smith, 2014. When it comes to athletic performance it's not only your expectations but also your external focus on the expectations of others. In a study focusing on the fear of public disappointment, Hodge & Smith, 2014 conducted research over the years of 2004-2011 on the All Blacks, New Zealand's national rugby team, players and coaches. The interviews focused on four facets: public expectation, pressure, choking and coping. When winning becomes an engrained belief by you and the fans, the perceived pressure can mount. The All Blacks achieved a 75 percent winning percentage at the time of this study and public expectation massively rested on the team's shoulders.

- The interview results validated just how impactful the pressure of the public's expectation is for players and coaches. All Blacks player Anton Oliver expressed the pressure on the team from outside supporters was "emotionally draining" (Hodge & Smith, 2014, p. 379) and although the team's legacy was continually treasured, it only heightened the trepidation of failing. Interestingly, if the public's expectations were not enough, Assistant Coach Wayne Smith admitted he continuously reminded his players of his expectations during the Rugby World Cup (RWC). The All Blacks' legacy of success was in fact shattered in 2007 when they, according to Team Captain Richie McCaw, froze under pressure. Due to stress stimulated by expectations of the outcome, the team lost clarity and choked.

These findings highlight the effect of expectation on performance. The expectations of supporters and the fear of disappointing them is an external stressor that all athlete dwell on, instead of focusing internally or on routine execution, and performing their absolute best.

The only thing you control is yourself. Focusing externally removes you from what you have personal control over, you. If you become consumed with the expectations of others, the name of the event, the number of people watching, the prize money or trophy or your negative self-talk, you will lose sight of focusing on the process and doing your best.

As demonstrated by the choking of The All Blacks team, an athlete's perception and concentration in high-pressure situations affects performance. Further research conducted by Oudejans, Kooijman, Kuijpers & Bakker focused on how the athletes attempted to ease the pressure and prevent the failure. The responses were categorized in five attributes: 1) movement execution, 2) worries, 3) external task-relevant factors (concerning equipment or opponents), 4) external task-irrelevant factors (concerning the audience) and 5) positive monitoring (constructive self-talk). The following responses were the most common reported by the athletes.

-        57.8% of the responses focused on positive monitoring

-        25.9% of the responses were concerned with worries

-        4.1% focused on movement execution

Lastly, research (Oudejans, 2011) was done involving the same participants by concentrating on the self-talk of the athletes. Interestingly, high-pressure situations do not prompt skill-focused attention. On the contrary, distracting worries occur more commonly and correlate with choking. During practice, where the perceived degree of pressure is small athletes concentrate solely on skill execution, however the study proved the outlook changes immensely as the perceived pressure rises. Remember, "pressure" is based on perception. If fixated on the magnitude of the event, (Olympics, Super Bowl or Pee-Wee League Double Elimination Championships) self-impose stress will alter performance.

Five steps of SMART goal-setting

Breaking long-term goals into short-term steps helps you reach your goals. Hoping is not a plan. Having a roadmap guides you down a path toward your goal. Remember there are no guarantees but by goal-setting you increase your probability of success.

The following mnemonic helps generate a game plan to facilitate achieving goals. The SMART goal-setting mnemonic (SMART) helps organize your long-term goals and short-term steps.

S=Specific

M=Measurable

A=Attainable

R=Realistic

T=Timely

Make sure each goal is <u>specific (S)</u>…"I want to work on hitting more ground strokes deep on each point during my tennis matches" is a specific goal. Set up each goal so that you will be able to <u>measure (M)</u> your progress. Determine your present level regarding your goal and identify the method to evaluate both your progress and the eventual goal. If you currently hit 60 percent of your ground strokes deep in the opponent's court, strive to reach 65 percent. This is a measurable goal. "Hitting 10 percent more deep ground strokes is a goal that I can attain this season" is a specific <u>attainable (A)</u> goal within a certain amount of time. Too many athletes set unrealistic goals which can lead to failure and burnout. Be <u>realistic (R)</u> about your goals. "I want to hit 100% of my ground strokes deep to my opponent on every play in every match" is clearly an unrealistic goal that no professional tennis player could achieve. Lastly, set the goals to be time specific. Consider setting up your goal for a short period of <u>time (T)</u> based on realistic and attainable steps…"By the end of this season I want to increase my deep ground stroke percentage by 5% and use the specific tactical skills provided by my coach." Using the SMART goal-setting template will help achieve your goals.

Following is a story that shows SMART in action.

I received a referral from a Big Ten golf coach regarding an athlete suffering with anxiety. The athlete was worrying about becoming a PGA golf professional. The athlete chose to invest his energy on the future. The athlete needed to refocus on factors that he controlled (ie; physical and tactical skills).

S – Specific goal(s)	Increase hitting the greens in regulation by 5 percent and decrease the number of recovery strokes by two strokes per round by the end of this season.

M – Measurable	Monitor his percentages of both greens and recovery strokes per round.
A – Attainable	These goals do not require a new skill set. Therefore, these goals would be considered attainable.
R – Realistic	A five (5) percent improvement on hitting greens as well as a two-stroke improvement in recovery strokes per round are both realistic.
T – Time	Striving for both goals, increase greens by 5% and decreasing recovery strokes by 2 by the end of the season are both reasonable for practice, coaching and timeframe.

People often state competitions, tournaments, or matches exasperate their nerves beyond the daily practice of their sport. It is important for each athlete to determine if he is performing the same routine in competition as in practice and, in turn, practicing how they compete. However, if the only difference is self-thoughts then he needs to re-write his mythical fantasy story he created in his own head. Fear can make even the simple task become overwhelming. The most common fears include disappointing coaches, parents, and occasionally the public. Self-imposed stressors also include the fear of making a mistake or the fear of a missed opportunity.

The opportunity of a lifetime is only as good as the lifetime of the opportunity

Missed opportunities are also a common fear many elite athletes confront. Qualifying for the Olympic Games, for example, is a privilege given to athletes once every four years and could be the only chance to achieve the greatest title of their sporting career. To be considered an Olympian is a substantial feat in itself. Arnold & Sarkar (2015) examined the significant stressors of the Olympic Games. They asked 15 sport psychologists who worked first-hand with athletes in Olympic competition to offer their knowledge. Surprisingly, they acknowledged the heaviest degree of pressure rested in the qualification process, even more than competing in the Olympics. These study results emphasize the belief pressure can be derived from opportunity. Qualifying for Olympic competition is one opportunity, but throughout a competitive season there are endless opportunities for an athlete to perfect their skills. As I say, "The opportunity of a lifetime is only as good as the lifetime of the opportunity."

Here is another example to show how fear can debilitate competitive athletes. Two of my internationally renowned athletes, gymnast and a principal male soloist in ballet were both competing in the elite international programs. They both possessed the skills required for the program directors and coaches to recruit and offer them scholarships. They had won every major award and were consistently receiving accolades by respected authorities. However, both athletes found once they had reached this level, they began to fixate their identity and self-worth on the singular factor of the subjective decision of the coach or director. This singular external focus led to fear and dread, which led to all-or-none thinking and self-doubt. This pattern is displayed by individuals judging themselves negatively if they are not the absolute best. They began comparing themselves to other exceptional athletes, "Did you see the quadriceps muscles on that guy?" They were investing their finite daily energy into aspects outside of their control and not focusing on the one thing within their control, their performance.

Still another example: one of the NCAA Division I High Jumpers had the ability to challenge the laws of gravity by transferring lateral energy into vertical energy and utilizing the Fosbury Flop clear 6' 10." He could throw his entire body over a bar that stood 6'10" in height. However, when he was participating in a tournament against another top national competitor, he would begin saying negative thoughts and comments, "I'll never beat him. He clears 7'2"." When he began this hostile internal verbal barrage, he would never consistently clear 6'6." Again, his choice to invest his finite amount of energy into an external factor and "whine" about the opponent, became shackles around his ankles.

An exceptional perspective comes from golf teaching pro, Michael Hebron (Youth Golf, powerpoint online live, 2017), he reminds people to consider, "We learn best when it is ugly. Good learners are ok with the ugly. Bad learners resist it. Great learners seek it out."

Take Away for Step Seven:

There are no guarantees, therefore your goal is to increase your probability of success. Stay in the moment and don't get stuck in your head by focusing on externals. If you stay in the now, focus on doing one step at a time, pride will come in knowing you did your best. The words you use to describe an event cause you to emotionally react. The Laws of Physics don't change because of the event. Focus on your abilities. Maintaining a healthy perspective and set realistic goals which will help you continuously improve while remaining positive.

Step Eight: Develop an Optimistic Attitude

Outline

1. **Winners find solutions, losers look for excuses**
   If it's meant to be, it's up to me.
2. **Fears**
   You have to get past your fear of falling in order to learn your next jump.
3. **The Five A's of Success and Winning**
   Acknowledge, Approach, Address, Adapt and Adjust
4. **Change**
   I would never damn your future because of your past

Winners find Solutions, Losers look for Excuses

If it's meant to be, it's up to me.

Elite athletes see themselves as winners. They are optimistic, see every situation as an opportunity and a challenge, and reach for the highest standards.

These stories prove just that…

- As one of the greatest middle linebackers in the NFL, Michael Singletary was quoted, "Do you know what my favorite part of the game is? The opportunity to play." He sought out the opportunity to display his skills and never blamed an outcome on someone else.

- The flamboyant world champion boxer Muhammad Ali declared, "I done wrestle with an alligator, I done tussled with a whale, handcuffed lightning, thrown thunder in jail only last week, I murdered a rock, injured a stone, hospitalized a brick; I'm so mean I make medicine sick." Just feel his confidence, regardless of what obstacle is put in front of him in the boxing ring or in life, Muhammad Ali was determined to overcome and be victorious.

- Zig Ziglar is one of the top business consultants and motivational speakers and often encourages clients to understand that, "It is your attitude, not your aptitude that determines your altitude."

Each champion looks forward to the battle. This is key to A Champion's Mindset©. I always ask the athlete, "Where would you rather be, the Bottom of the Top, or the Top of the Bottom? If you take 100 and divide it into two halves, then the Bottom of the Top would be 51 and the Top of the Bottom would be 49. However, if you divide 100 into 10 segments that changes the question. Now, where would you rather be? The answer says a lot about your self-worth, goals, dreams and beliefs. Your answer speaks volumes about the standards you hold yourself up to. The Bottom of the Top would be 90, while the Top of the Bottom would be 10. The champion athlete strives to reach for the top tier.

If you focus on external factors, you begin to develop excuses for your potential loss. An example of this was displayed when one of the nationally ranked junior golfers declared he was concerned about the weather for the upcoming tournament. Interestingly enough, he mentioned he was paired with an obnoxious player who "drives me nuts." When I asked him if he planned on losing, he replied with a perplexed look and stated, "No, why would you say that?" I followed up with winners look for solutions, losers look for excuses. He was already planning an array of reasons for his eventual loss.

I have always encouraged athletes to live up to their highest standards. On the next page is a representation of the levels athletes currently have attained along with the potential of future growth as they advance to the next level. The lowest level is the range of athleticism in high school athletes. The most gifted high school athletes are clearly developing physically and mentally. These elite athletes will be recruited for college scholarships. The middle level is the range of athleticism possessed by college or nationally ranked athletes at top training programs, IMG, Florida Southwest Skating Club. These athletes are still maturing physically and developing their athletic acumen. To compete at this level is impressive. Yet there is a higher range of athleticism achieved by professional or top nationally ranked athletes.

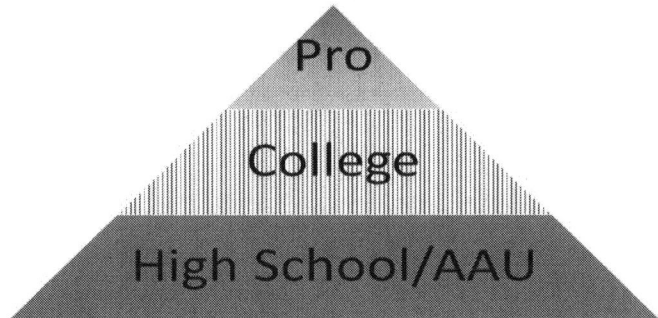

By looking at this chart, young athletes in the lowest level can appreciate the tremendous amount of improvement that awaits them. They can see they have not reached the pinnacle of athleticism. However, once they move up to the next level there are fantastic aspects ability, physical growth, mental maturity and competitive experiences that remain untapped.

As this next story shows, living up to your highest standards is key to being a professional/elite athlete. Nicholas, a high achieving soccer goalie, for years held aspirations to attend college on a sports scholarship and eventually go to the pros. He was first-team goalie playing for a championship club team. He submitted video resumes and applications to several colleges. One particular Saturday coach relegated him to the second team and when discovering this news, Nicholas blew a gaskett. He had no idea why coach made such a pathetic decision and was offended since he was clearly the superior goalie. Also, the second team goalie who was also the coach's son. Nicholas was so upset that he could barely focus. When the second team began their game, the opposing team advanced the ball and dominated the game. He was so upset with the sub-standard play of his teammates, he was cruel to them. There were numerous shots on goal and he fumed as the opposing team scored against the second team.

The next week he received a letter from one of the colleges that he had applied. The coach wrote a personal letter to him. The letter was brief. It stated,

Dear Nicholas,

Thank you for applying to our college. I am sorry to inform you we will not be offering you a scholarship to attend our college and play for our soccer team. I had informed your coach that I would be coming to your area last weekend to watch your game. I had asked him to move you to the second team because I wanted to assess your character and leadership skills. I specifically asked your coach not to tell you the reason for this decision. Your behavior on the pitch was not to the standard we are looking for in a student-athlete. We had hoped your leadership would show you helped your teammates rise to the occasion, coordinate the defense in a well-orchestrated manner, and defend your goal against more shots on goal than is typical on the first team. What I observed was none of these characteristics.

Again, thank you for considering our program. Best of luck with your future.

Sincerely, Coach

When I met Nicholas, you can imagine how depressed he was after receiving this letter. We discussed how the opportunity had passed and how he needed to learn to manage an emotional response teetering on self-destruction. We decided to use the painful emotions as a catalyst to help him take personal responsibility and become the best player and person he could. His new mantra was, "If it's meant to be, it's up to me."

As the season progressed Nicholas was voted by his teammates as their captain because of his level of motivation, commitment, leadership and support. As Nicholas reoriented his focus on doing his best and helping his teammates shine, he received another letter. This time it was from one of the Italian Football Clubs. They had sent their assistant coach to scout him as he had displayed all of the winning qualities of a champion. The letter was worlds apart from the previous letter. They complimented him on displaying elite characteristics and offered him a contract to be back-up goalkeeper. In a matter of six months, Nicholas had experienced the fullest range of emotions, from the depth of depression to the ecstasy of achieving his dream. The trajectory of his life changed because he had accepted personal responsibility, accountability, applied himself to the highest standards.

Being optimistic and having a positive attitude shows you are a winner. This story proves this point.

A women's Field Hockey player was initially referred to me because her coach saw a pattern that needed to be addressed. She could best be described as an Eeyore from the childhood cartoon Winnie-the-Pooh. Whenever there was a "big game", she acted like a pessimist. Her body language reflected discouragement, and her focus on obstacles became barriers to success. She admitted to this tendency and justified her perspective, "Well of course, our opponent is ranked number two in the conference." She would do the math in her head. Her team was ranked second to last in the conference. She sounded like a curmudgeon complaining about life. If she could have bet on this game, she would have given the points and taken the higher ranked opposing team. The curious reality is anyone on any day has the potential to win. Unknown to her was the opposing coach sat out two of their top players for a week before the post-season was to begin which clearly made the two teams comparable. That's right. Once she saw the lineup was minus the two "superstars" she filled with confidence. Over the years of working together, she realized personal self-control and positive internal self-talk was always within her control and not dependent on who she was playing against.

It has been said, the best teams make it to the playoffs, but the hottest team wins the championship. Often the underdog maintains a positive attitude and triumphs over certain defeat. But obviously, the best doesn't always win. Mike Tyson lost his heavyweight fight to underdog, Buster Douglas. The prohibited favorites, the New England Patriots lost to the New York Giants on two separate occasions in the Super Bowl. The University of Houston Phi-Slamma-Jamma lost to the Wolfpack of NC State. Developing and maintaining a positive attitude doesn't always guarantee the outcome, but that mindset allows you to be ready, invested, committed throughout the competition.

Also consider that an athlete/team could have an off-day in competition. Sure, the odds are in the favor of the favorite, but there are too many variables to simply assume that to the higher ranked team/player goes the victory. That's why we play the game. Anyone can win on any given day. We would never have to actually play any sport if the outcomes were victory to the favored. Choose to have a positive attitude. Don't always think the victory will always go to the higher ranked team. Remember, winners/optimists seek solutions, focus on what they control, and accept personal responsibility while losers seek excuses.

Fears: You have to get past your fear of falling in order to learn your next jump.

"I've missed more than 9,000 shots in my career. I've lost almost 300 games. Twenty-six times I've been trusted to take the game winning shot and missed. I've failed over and over and over again in my life. And that is why I succeed." Michael Jordan

Confucius eloquently addresses this reality, "Success is not in never falling but in rising every time you fall." The reality is we all "fall", literally and metaphorically. To expect you will never "fall" is a sure-fire way to set yourself up for failure. Whether you are Michael Jordan or

Confucius realizing it's not about being perfect, but rather how you respond when things don't go your way, and you "fall."

News Flash. In baseball if you don't get a hit seven out of 10 times, you go to the Baseball Hall of Fame. Think hard about this fact. If you fail six out of 10 times, you go down in history as one of the greatest Baseball players ever.

All Olympic figure skaters start somewhere. Learning how to shift their weight from the inside edge to the outside edge of their skate is vital. Eventually, they attempt a jump. Olympian Dick Button was the trend setter in 1948 when he landed the first double axel jump in competition and when in 1952, he landed the first triple jump of any kind. Most skaters must work up to achieve the coordination and timing to accomplish these feats. So, what happens along the way to greatness? Lots of falling on your behind! What I'm focusing on? Falling. Guess what I'm not focusing on? The proper skating techniques. To advance, you have to get past your fear of falling. Falling is a part of achieving.

What is *"falling"*? Messing up? Not winning? Becoming injured? Everyone has a different definition of falling, but *falling* is most definitely not failing. Every moment serves as an opportunity to learn grow and adapt. It is through analyzing the mishaps the details are identified and improvements revealed. Learning from your past makes you a better competitor.

I can remember my high football coach encouraging all the receivers to sacrifice our bodies in order to catch the football. He used to say, "If you can touch it, you can catch it." He helped us understand "falling" was a part of catching the ball. Catch the ball and then worry about your body. All we needed to do was lay out our bodies, make the catch that was in the best interest of the team. The fear of getting hurt or injured diminished because the team goal of victory superseded the individual concern of bodily harm. I took this same philosophy to tennis. If I could touch the tennis ball on the top of the outstretched racquet I would make full contact with the ball when I just laid myself out. Hit the ball and then worry about my body. The momentary physical pain served the pursuit of winning the point.

Falling is not choking. Falling offers great wisdom, lessons in life and opportunities if you are open and willing to accept that falling is only part of rising to greatness. It is not a loss if you learn from it.

The opportunity to excel is the elite athlete's mindset. They want the responsibility and opportunity. They are prepared and do not shy away from the elite level of performance. Yet for the majority of athletes, moving up the levels of competition requires years of addressing flaws, weaknesses, technique, strategy and so much more. "Falling" is the willingness to seek out advice, and put in the time and effort of applying yourself.

"Falling" is stepping out of your comfort zone. You have not made it to the most elite levels because of your great shots, or wonderful plays, but rather by overcoming inconsistency and erratic performance, while recognizing the need to master your form. The perspective that I encourage is, "Become excited about stepping into your discomfort zone." As Andre Gide said, "Man cannot discover new oceans unless he has the courage to lose sight of the shore." Regardless of gender, in order to break from your predictable routine of falling short, challenge yourself. Become excited about sailing away from your familiar shores, and the potential discoveries that await you beyond your comfort zone.

"Falling" is not the problem. Quitting, giving up, negativity, pessimism are the toxins that curtail growth. To become an elite athlete, rise every time you "fall."

Many fans of competitive sporting events state, "How does she do that? If I was on the ice in front of millions of viewers, I would just freak out."

In figure skating, all athletes must get past their fear of falling in order to learn the new jump. Fear leads to avoidance. But

132

acknowledging the challenge leads you to anticipate the development of the new more advanced maneuver in a positive perspective.

You choose your perspective. Avoidance is what the general population does. The elite athlete realizes he yearns for the challenge. He seeks to do his best and absorb the lessons shared by his coaches.

He doesn't hold himself up to perfection. Remember, success is not based upon perfection but how you handle imperfection.

When the going gets tough, the tough grabs the challenge by the throat and jumps on top of it. As the mantra states, "It ain't over 'til the fat lady sings." In tennis, it ain't over until the ball is rolling. In football, it ain't over until the whistle is blown. His willingness to apply himself more than anyone else brings him to the top of the mountain.

I always share, "Obstacles are what you see when you lose sight of your goals." If you are keeping your eyes on the prize you will adapt and adjust your direction to attain your goal. If all you do is focus on the obstacles, then that focus will dwindle your energy. Consider the steps you need to move past and beyond any obstacles.

As the late Dr. Randy Pausch said, "Brick walls are not there to keep us out, the brick walls are there to give us a chance to show how badly we want something." (Pausch, 2008) "Remember brick walls let us show our dedication. They are there to separate us from the people who don't really want to achieve their childhood dreams." "We cannot change the cards we are dealt, just how we play the hand."

The Five A's of Success and Winning

Acknowledge, Approach, Address, Adapt and Adjust

Acknowledge a challenge. Feel the fear, don't avoid it. By yearning for the challenge, you will anticipate the skill development in a positive light and acknowledge the need to change your technique.

Approach the negative behavior. Avoidance never resolves issues. It only provides a short-term delay. By approaching negative behavior, you are open to developing healthy strategies, skills or answers to the problems.

Address your shortcomings. Addressing shortcomings, limitations or weakness will be the key to seeking feedback and coaching to improve and grow.

Adapt to improve your talents. Change behaviors and perceptions of your life. Learn from the past in order not to repeat destructive patterns in the future.

Adjust perspectives, strategies and techniques. By adjusting you show insight, and acknowledged the need to change and improve. Without insight, there is no change.

The Five A's of Winning and Success will help you stay in the game. In order to invest the time and energy in improving your game, you must Acknowledge you have room for improvement. The first step is to Acknowledge. Admitting there is an issue you must Approach the negative behavior. Avoidance never resolves the issue, it only provides a short-term delay. By approaching the behavior, you are open to developing healthy strategies, skills or answers to your problems. This occurs via Addressing your short-comings, limitations, or weaknesses. Getting feedback, coaching, reviewing film all help you Adapt in such a way so you can improve your talents. Lastly, adjusting your perspective, strategies and techniques can lead to previously unattained levels of success. In doing so, you have displayed insight and Acknowledged the need to change, improve or make a difference. Without insight, there is no change. When the athlete is willing to acknowledge that there is an issue that needs to be stopped or changed, he opens the door to better understanding the reasons he does what he does and what he can do differently in the future.

A female basketball player acknowledged she had issues that were out of control. She had significant gambling debts causing her ongoing anxiety, and distracted her from being on top of her game. Also, she had cheated on her husband, not because she didn't love him, but because she needed constant approval from other men.   This behavior led to the end of previous relationships, and she feared it would end her marriage.

Once she <u>acknowledged</u> the problem, she then <u>approached</u> her issues by focusing on the patterns that had previously landed her in trouble. For years she had harbored unhealthy coping skills, but now she was willing to talk about them to a professional. She <u>acknowledged and approached</u> the underlying issues, and identified the reasons she acted out in unhealthy ways.

By <u>addressing</u> the problems, she began to develop healthier coping skills and a more positive identity. She realized her acting out behavior was how she dealt with her dysfunctional family dynamics, and she now chose to make different, healthier choices. Her need for male validation was <u>addressed </u>in therapy, and as a result, her self-worth and self-esteem blossomed. She <u>adapted</u> by realizing that encouraging men to "hit" on her was a non-productive way to fulfill her unresolved needs. She <u>adjusted</u> her life by making a concerted effort to invest her energies in her marriage, realizing a deeper love for her husband. She also resolved her financial problems and gambling debts.

Change: I would never damn your future because of your past

The father of a young golfer said, "That's just the way she is. Whenever she has to answer, she freezes up." I followed that statement up with my usual comeback, "Please excuse my indelicate language but I would never damn your future because of your past." Telling lies throughout the majority of your life, doesn't damn you to a future of telling falsehoods and lies. Just because you stole things in your past, doesn't damn you to a future of stealing. If you want to change you can, but change is not easy. Changing behavior follows a five-stage process. Research identifies five stages of change which include; Pre-Contemplative, Contemplative, Preparation, Action and Maintenance (Prochaska & DiClemente, 1982). You can only move through one stage at a time, and at times you may slip backwards.

1. The first stage reflects unawareness or hyper-resistance. A person doesn't even know his behavior needs or could change. He perpetuates the behavior without any awareness of the negative impact and could be defiant, resistant to input or advice. He is highly invested in not changing. (Pre-Contemplative)

2. The second stage reflects the point he is willing to think about changing. He is open to considering the possibilities, and begins to weigh the pros and cons. He begins to analyze the costs and benefits of action or inaction. He still is not changing, but is considering the possibilities. At the conclusion of this stage, he has decided to make a change. (Contemplative)

3. The third stage begins when he has decided to either stop a negative or start a positive. He is aware altering his behavior is a good idea but is still not changing. He has to get his ducks in a row, construct a plan of action and find a tactical coach, identify a stop date, organize resources, or recruit a friend to go through the process for support. (Preparation)

4. The fourth stage, he decides to change. Think about New Year's resolutions. Just because he is in the process of changing does not mean he has changed. People start out with the best intentions but often fall short of keeping the change up for the long haul. (Action)

5. The fifth stage, he has engaged in this changed behavior for more than six months. The changed behavior has become a part of his lifestyle. Reinforcing the changed behavior increases the likelihood it will continue. (Maintenance)

People change at different speeds. Some see a problem and immediately tackle it. Others are aware of a problem, take years before they attempt to change and possibly even longer to resolve the unhealthy behavior. As a colleague said, "People don't change unless the cost of not changing is more than the cost of changing."

Self-concept plays a role in changing and refers to how you see yourself in a specific situation. If you perform well at singing, you feel confident in a singing situation and have a good self-concept. If you avoid singing situations because when you sing dogs coming running, your self-concept might be rather negative.

Self-concept is not static: When first introduced to the mathematical equation of long division, you probably were confused and struggled to understand the steps. Your teacher slowly covered the material, went over examples, and had you practice long-division for homework. Over time you began to understand basics, and you progressed to more complex long-division problems. By the end of the year you could quickly run through long-division without any struggle. So, at one point in time, you were green and confused. Your self-concept regarding math was poor. However, with practice in-class and with homework, tutoring from your parents and teacher, your self-concept regarding long-division became accomplished and solid.

Whatever you repeat you get better at it. Previously struggling with mastering a skill, situation or ability does not mean you are forever doomed. Unless of course you choose to force the past into your future. This falls in the category of insanity when you do the same negative behavior and expect a different positive outcome. Again, whatever you repeat you get better at it.

The following athletes demonstrated their ability to develop improved self-concept abilities:

- A golfer struggled executing a purposeful slice but with one-on-one training with a swing coach he developed his tactical skill and now utilizes consistent technique command of dog-leg holes.

- An elite figure skater struggled to cut deep edges allowing judges to hear grinding but with the tutelage of exceptional precision coaching, now glides effortlessly across the frozen surface like a champion.

Both above athletes would have initially doubted their ability (poor self-concept) but they addressed their deficit and did not "damn their futures because of their past" liberating them to practice and learn the skills required to develop solid confidence in their ability (positive self-concept).

- A tennis player was coached to, "Live by the sword. Die by the sword." He had consistent form and could blast his ground strokes like missiles. Unfortunately, when confronted by competitors with equal skills he would attempt to up the ante and generate more power, but hit balls long. His internal self-talk was, "I just can't seem to beat these guys", feeling as if they somehow had his number. When his coaches challenged his belief system and directed him away from being the most powerful competitor, he realized he could outlast his opponents by playing smarter, not harder. His positive self-concept went from "I can't beat these guys" to "bring it on, I'm ready."

- A baseball pitcher could release a thunderbolt from the mound pushing nearly triple digits. Unfortunately, his belief that he was "The Man" left him watching his pitches launched by his opponent's bats sail well over the outfield fences. When he moved from college to the minor leagues the competition had caught up to his pitching speed. His self-concept went from "The

Man" to "I'm never going to make it to the bigs." His self-concept shifted from strong to fallible. Fortunately, with good pitching coaches and practice he kept his opponents guessing. His self-concept went from fallible to strength.

When an athlete believes his past identity can't be changed, he sabotages his future performance. His internal negative self-talk limits his ability to be open to future possibilities. He creates self-imposed barriers and damns his futures because of his past.

Take Away for Step Eight:

Your past discretions do not automatically need to be repeated through your life. Acknowledging behaviors that need to change open you up to seeking solutions. Realizing change is never easy but with personal conviction, excellent coaching and developing productive behaviors, you can become a champion.

Step Nine: Establish Realistic Goals

Outline

1. **The Difference Between Pro and Amateur?**
        Skill Acquisition vs. Performance Expectation
2. **The Medical Model**
        See One, Do One, Teach One
3. **The 7 Steps to Successful Goal-Setting**
        Your Personal Game Plan

I ask my athletes, "What is the difference between a professional athlete and an amateur?" Is it the length of time they have been playing? No. There are many athletes who have played their sport for decades and just enjoy the fun, semi-competitive play within a local league. Is it skill? No. There are a significant number of amateur athletes who possess the same level of skill as the pros but have never made it to the big leagues.

The difference between a pro and an amateur is four-fold:

1) Pros make money playing their sport while amateurs do not.
        Ask yourself: Am I making money for playing my sport? If you are not then you are an amateur.
2) Pros are consistent, amateurs are inconsistent.
        Ask yourself: Do I perform my skills, at a level that I predictably, consistently achieve my goal of doing my best? As a figure skater, do I land a triple throw? As a golfer, do I chip close to the hole? As a tennis player, do I serve at a high percentage? If you are not predictably consistent, you are an amateur.
3) Pros hit winners while amateurs make unforced errors.
        The reason most elite amateurs haven't made it to the pro ranks is they make too many errors. If I am an amateur and focus predominantly on my winners, I am focusing on the wrong part of

my game. Ask yourself: What are my most common errors and what can I do to decrease this pattern?

4) Pros set realistic goals while amateurs set unrealistic, unattainable goals.

Progress is incremental. Pros understand focusing on the step-wise improvement of the process while amateurs frequently set goals that don't focus on acquiring the specific, basic skills to increase the probability of success. Ask yourself: Are my goals within my ability? Am I setting realistic goals?

Realistic with goal-setting is vital every step of the way. However, if you have not acquired the skills you should not expect to attain certain levels of performance.

A Big 12 university golfer was referred to me by his coach due to concerns about not achieving his goal, "To get down in one." Certainly, an admirable goal. Optimistic. But when he didn't one-putt he got upset and berated himself and his muscles tightened. I suggested he find out which PGA golfer had the lowest putts per hole average and what the number was. If you are a math major you will love this section. When you land on the green and it takes you one putt to sink the ball on each hole, then your average putts per hole is one (1). When you land on the green and if it takes you two putts to sink the ball on each hole, then your average putts per hole is two (2). He discovered the lowest PGA tour pro shot a 1.67. He realized he was holding himself accountable to an unrealistic, unachievable goal not even the best PGA professional attained. His goals needed to be realistic, quantifiable, measurable, and attainable. He became upset for not achieving perfection which led to a poor performance. Armed with this new insight, he focused more on the process and less on the outcome. His goal was to trust his experience and quiet his mind which led to a shooting a course record 63.

Again, if you are not being paid money for playing your sport, you are an amateur. Hence, every second of every moment is practice. It's all practice to improve for the eventual long-term goal of college,

Olympic or professional competition. Your goal is to decrease errors rather than be victorious. You can find specifics aspects of your skill set you can improve. Every step you take can be assessed and evaluated in such a way you learn from the experience. As an amateur if you were successful, analyze the form, timing, technique that facilitated the positive outcome. On the other hand, if you determine the outcome was not what you had planned, use this opportunity to learn from the past so not to repeat it. Utilize the post-shot routine.

As an amateur you are still in the Skill Acquisition mode. That's right, if you are not making money at your sport, you are still in the Skill Acquisition phase. Your goal is to increase your probability of success, decrease your errors and be realistic.

All too often an amateur athlete struggles due to the demands imposed by his coach or parent…The parents of a Lacrosse player were frustrated he occasionally performed exceptionally well while at other times he underperformed. His parents loved their child and only wanted the best for him. His parents' expectations for consistent top-level performance was unrealistic. Because of the discrepancy between performance expectations and skill acquisition the father blew a gasket, fried his motherboard, became emotionally volcanic. The obvious consequence of dad's fanatical reaction induced fear, apprehension and dread in his son. Rather than focusing on his own performance, the young man was filled with anxiety, dread and fear as to his father's reactions. When his father was not in attendance at his game, his performance excelled. There were two major issues with this family: 1) The young athlete's personal skill level. Even though he possessed numerous physical attributes which propelled him to success, he was still developing more consistency. 2) His father's belief and haste to have his son possess consistency before he was ready. Hence, skill acquisition vs. performance expectations. Improvement is incremental.

By the way, why do the pros continue to practice? Why do the pros have coaches? Aren't they done learning? Never. Pros always want to be prepared, fresh, and there is always something to improve. Former New York Yankee star Derek Jeter stated, "There may be people that have more talent than you, but there's no excuse for anyone to work harder than you do." Practicing is always a part of being your best.

To better understand the top level of athleticism, ESPN's Sports Science hosted by John Brentkus reveals the magnificent unity of human potential displayed by only the most skilled professionals. The show highlights the rarified air of the professional or Olympian as a beautiful synthesis of visual-motor, eye-hand, brain and body coordination combined into a symphony of movement. This ballet of grace and power often appears effortless to people sitting in the stands or watching on television. The show focuses on every major sport from, the scientifically determined speed advantage in baseball of running through a base rather than diving to the base, to the physiological advantages and techniques leading to quicker speed and footwork by the most lauded soccer players. This program shows us the very best of the best. Amateur athletes now have a visual analysis to appreciate the difference between their skill level and the top level in their sport and therefore set more realistic goals.

The Medical Model

Now let me introduce you to the three-step process of the Medical Model that was taught to me during my training at Johns Hopkins University School of Medicine. It is an excellent model to use as you incrementally grow from an amateur to a professional. The Medical Model is comprised of, See One, Do One, Teach One.

Step One – See One: If you have never been exposed to a specific procedure (skill, technique), there is no reason to assume you should be aware it. Once taught, the amateur starts the journey to mastery. No one would presume that he possesses the artistic skills of Rembrandt after drawing a picture of Bambi. I doubt he would feel comfortable entrusting his life to a medical student who has begun reading about cardiothoracic surgery.

Step Two – Do One: After years of practice, supervision, feedback, opportunities and more practice, the amateur develops the skills and consistency of techniques.

Step Three – Teach One: Eventually, the amateur learns to appreciate the details, subtleties and fine points and now has the capacity to share his wisdom with others. This is the transformation from amateur to professional.

To become a professional the amateur starts with the basics, advances through the appropriate steps, and only then does he reach the ultimate goal, professional status.

Often people impose unrealistic expectations on others (or themselves) while still in the skill acquisition phase. This clearly leads to disappointment, frustration and occasionally hyper-critical judgments. It is not until an athlete has attained the mastery of the skill before imposing exceptional performance expectations. A competitive figure skater was frustrated she was not easily mastering her new choreography combined with the accompanied music. She was not comfortable with the more advanced skill maneuvers. But once she mastered the skills, she could alter the pace to match the music.

The concept of skill acquisition versus performance expectations is helped by another concept, effective before efficient. In other words, I do not rush a behavior before the skill has been mastered. If you attempt to rush or be efficient before mastery you are likely to suffer failures, errors and problems and therefore not be effective.

Skill acquisition versus performance expectations is explained by the following example. When setting goals, start with realistic goals. Using metrics can help to better understand the skills displayed by the best athletes. Golf offers an example: PGA's Shot Tracker reveals tour players on average make, 99% of putts from 3 feet and in, 60% of 6-foot putts, 54% of 8-foot putts, and 31% of putts between 10 and 15 feet. But, remember if you are an amateur you need to focus on developing your basic skills and minimize your errors. In golf, that would be three-putting. Start by counting how many three-putts you have per round and then work to decrease this frequency, not trying to match touring pros.

The 7 Steps to Successful Goal-Setting: Your Personal Game Plan

"Today is the tomorrow that you dreamt about yesterday." Dr. Shinitzky

Goal-setting is a vital aspect to become an elite athlete in sport as well as in life. As mentioned earlier, hope is not a plan.

Goal-setting requires vision, planning and implementation. Prominent motivational speaker, Zig Ziglar stated, "You've got to 'be' before you can 'do', and you've got to 'do' before you can 'have'." Goal-setting is not merely passively dreaming. There is a difference between a dream and a goal. The dream vanishes upon the light of day. While a goal has steps that must be accomplished to increase the probability of success.

7 Principles of SUCCESS: Your Personal Game Plan

7 Principles of SUCCESS
Dr. Harold Shinitzky, Project Champions, 1993

- S – Set your goals
- U – Understand your passions
- C – Critically plan your steps
- C – Challenge yourself through adversity
- E – Evaluate your progress
- S – Stay focused
- S – Savor your accomplishments

This 7 Step Formula helps athletes increase their probability of success and move from amateur status to pro status.

No one plans to fail but many people fail to plan. Using the 7 Step Formula of SUCCESS, I encourage athletes to consider Setting Your Goals (Set your goals), any and all of them, great and small.

But, athletes don't have unlimited amounts of time, energy or resources, so they have to narrow it down to their top one or two goals (Understand your passions). Once they identify their passions and what they are willing to focus their energies on, they have to critically establish the steps that will increase their probability of success (Critically plan your steps). Realistically, the reason they haven't already reached their goal is that it is difficult to achieve. They need to determine how to challenge themselves through adversity (Challenge yourself through adversity) and are always moving forward and in the right direction, so they evaluate their progress (Evaluate your progress).

Every once in a while they may need to remind themselves of the reasons that they are pursuing this difficult goal, so they need to stay focused (Stay focused) and identify the reasons they are passionate about this goal. Behavioral research teaches if a behavior is reinforced it is more likely to continue. Savor your accomplishments and reward yourself along the journey and when you achieve your goal (Savor your accomplishments).

If you are currently a professional athlete, you constantly compete for a spot on the team, for your career, for your personal pride. Success doesn't come by blind luck. Effort, commitment, perseverance, possessing a high pain threshold, and many more characteristics are mandatory to maintain the highest level of performance. In reality, you never make it to the top. You are aware of the need to continually strive to improve, to refine your technique, to stay competitive. Just because you won the greatest event in your sport, now requires you now to readjust your goals. You are always applying the Principles of Success!

One figure skater I coached had a problem though he had just won the national title. His dream had always been to win the national title. His dream was now the problem. He had worked diligently ever since he was a youngster. He had finally ascended his Mount Everest. The journey was fraught with obstacles which he directly confronted and triumphed. However, that was his previous goal. Now he found himself stuck, not preparing for the world championships. What we needed to do was readjust his vision, goal and plan. We needed to take the 7 Principles to Success and reconfigure his plan of attack so he could re-energize himself to put forth the time and effort required to compete on the world's stage. To do this he had to:

Set his goals – Compete in the Worlds

Understand his passions – Compete in the Worlds (same short-term goal)

Critically set up the steps – Rededicate practice time on the ice, meet with coach daily, stop eating unhealthy foods, stretch/rehab daily, commit to partner on mutual goal, create a countdown calendar, recruit a support network

Challenge himself through adversity - Catch himself and stop negative self-talk and insert positive self-talk, have support network available, visualize attending Worlds, remind self that Worlds is the new personal goal

Evaluate his progress – Daily feedback from his coach and partner, honest self-appraisal

Stay focused – Remind him that he earned the privilege to represent the United States at Worlds, remind self that he has a long history of success when applying himself

Savor accomplishment – Tap into his personal level of pride for doing his best, after competition celebrate the opportunity to compete against the world's best pairs figure skating teams, rekindle friendships with his international competitors.

Every day in every situation we have to choose our destiny. Do you take a left or a right? Do you keep your eyes on the prize or do you take a break and make a different choice?. Our choices impact our lives. Every decision you make (or not) or action you take (or not) leads to an outcome.

Competitive sports require the athlete to understand and appreciate the journey that awaits them. Rome was not built in a day. God did not create the earth in one day. It takes more than one lick to get to the chewy Tootsie Roll center of a Tootsie Pop.

Long-term goals with short-term steps must be coordinated over a protracted period of time. As Confucius stated, "Even the greatest journeys begin with a single step." Put in the hard work, don't expect guarantees. Receive fantastic coaching from a seasoned professional with no guarantees. Be the off-spring of genetically loaded parents. Always remember that there are no guarantees in life, except death and taxes. Again, I tell my athletes the only thing you can ever do is "increase your probability of success."

The **SUCCESS** Formula does not offer a guarantee. What it does do is increase your probability of success.

1. **S** - As you begin this process, first determine and <u>set your goals</u>. What would they be if you requested the whole Enchilada, any and all. Be fun-loving and crazy and start with a simple goal then consider the most extreme.

2. <u>U</u> - Now take a step back. Since you don't have unlimited funds or time, and you don't have unlimited energy to invest, <u>understand</u> which goal(s) are you most passionate about. Based on the reality of time, money and resources, what do you want to expend your energy on? This one goal is vital to your dreams and aspirations.

3. <u>C</u> - There are no guarantees. Consider the <u>critical</u> steps that will increase your probability of success. You may not engage in each one but each one leads toward your passionate goal. On a daily, weekly basis, participate in as many of these short-term steps as possible.

4. <u>C</u> - Let's be real, since you have not already achieved certain goals, it probably means you have tried but failed. You had the best intentions but fell short. In light of this reality, consider how you will <u>challenge</u> yourself through life's future adversities. You might find distractions or other priorities and when they present themselves, how will you go about managing them differently?

5. <u>E</u> - Though you are moving forward you might not be moving towards your goal. <u>Evaluate</u> your progress. Reassess the decisions, choices, and behaviors you are participating.

6. <u>S</u> - Sometimes you lose sight of the reasons behind your goal selection. Remind yourself of the rationale, the reasons, the purpose for this goal. Rekindle the fire that burns within you to <u>stay focused</u> and motivated towards achieving this goal.

7. <u>S</u> – A goal that is <u>savored</u> and rewarded is more likely to continue. Determine what you value and offer yourself an incentive and motivator towards your efforts and conviction. It can be tangible, emotional, something you provide to yourself, or request from someone you respect. Behavior that changes should be rewarded and savored, and are more likely to be repeated.

Following is an example of an athlete using the seven steps of the SUCCESS Formula.

1. A soccer player wanted to be the best and get recruited by a major league team (Step 1 <u>S</u>uccess). Though his range of goals included futbol, girlfriend, wealth, sports car, and villa on the Riviera, he decided to set his focus on a more realistic short-term goal that would move him in the direction of his goals.

2. He determined a reasonable short-term goal would be to gain more agility with ball control and foot speed (Step 2 s<u>U</u>ccess). <u>U</u>nderstanding his passions, by narrowing the many goals down to one or two helped him achieve his goals. He was specific and realistic with his behavioral goal.

3. He began the process of determining what steps he would need to increase his probability of success. He contacted one of the top exercise physiologist and trainers in the area. He became a student of this skill set, practiced coordination, drilled, and watched videos of the best futbol players online. He would work privately on foot speed and ball control and agreed to meet with one of the more mature players on the team to learn from a master (Step 3 su<u>C</u>cess). Step 3 required him to <u>C</u>ritically set up the steps that increased his probability to succeed. He consistently reminded himself that he knew the steps, realizing there are no guarantees.

4. He was aware he had tried this in the past but failed to follow through to completion. He needed to learn from the past so as not to repeat it. He frequently expressed a quote from Zig Ziglar, "Failure is a detour, not a dead-end street". Once he determined what factors, reasons, excuses or distractions occurred previously to throw him off his goal, he created a list of methods, internal encouraging comments, and gathered peer support (Step 4 suc<u>C</u>ess). He <u>C</u>hallenge himself through adversity. He realized in the past when in an intense match, he would often think negatively and beat himself up. His internal negative dialogue would contribute to a fatalistic mindset and he considered not continuing to put forth the effort required to compete at the

highest level. He needed to challenge his catastrophic tendencies and reminded himself not to make permanent decisions to temporary problems. He remembered that, "The difference between success and failure might be trying one more time." And he often thought about the remarkable and inspiring Dr. Randy Pausch (Pausch, 2008), while suffering through his battle with a terminal disease, shared a part of his now famous Last Lecture,

> *"The brick walls are there for a reason. The brick walls are not there to keep us out. The brick walls are there to give us a chance to show how badly we want something. Because the brick walls are there to stop the people who don't want it badly enough. They're there to stop the other people. You need to plan for obstacles and how you will manage them. You need to consider the potholes that you previously ran into and discover how to operate your vehicle safely while pursuing your goals. You need to figure out how to keep yourself focus, motivated and committed to your goal."*

5. Because you are moving forward does not mean you are near the finish line. Step 5 (succEss) required him to evaluate his progress. His direction might in fact be off target and reminded himself the light at the end of his tunnel might be a train barreling down on him. Having regained his focus and reoriented himself to personal commitment and to focusing on the process while striving to be his best, he rekindled his physical attributes that he gained on the all-star team.

6. Once he readjusted his goal (Step 6 succeSs) he reviewed the reason he chose this goal over all others. He reminded himself why he pursued this goal and what were the important reasons he started this goal. He determined the underlying driving factors and motivators that emotionally sparked his interest to change his behavior, improve and grow. He created a vision board picturing the important and motivating factors in his life. It had a picture of

his parents who encouraged his soccer skills, participation and love of family. He had a picture of the FIFA World Cup and a few pictures of top soccer players. He pictured his younger siblings because they provided him with unconditional love and he had pictures of himself as a child to remind himself how far he had grown.

7. His ability to attain his dream and make it a reality needed to be reinforced (Step 7 succes**S**). He reminded himself that he worked hard to traverse his path and he had the fortitude to set, work and achieve his goals. He had created a plan that helped him find the promised land. As Step 7 states, **S**avor your accomplishment. When he finally achieved his ultimate goal by scoring a goal in the winning match, he took a much-needed break to savor his accomplishments. He rejoiced in victory and took the time to drink up the joy and thrill of making his dreams a reality. He spent the next several weeks with his family and shared the joy with his parents and siblings.

Take Away for Step Nine:

Winners display consistency with elite level behaviors while amateurs are inconsistent and make more errors. As an amateur your goal is to develop the skills and decrease your errors in order to compete at the highest levels. Find a coach who can share, mentor and monitor your development of the basic skills as you follow the three steps of the Medical Model, See One, Do One, Teach One. Finally, the best way to increase your probability of success and achieve your long-term goal is to establish a plan of action of short-term steps using the SUCCESS formula.

Step Ten: Finish Strong

Outline

1. Champions remain focused from start to finish
   Remarkable Comebacks
   Celebrating too early - Run Through the Finish Line
2. Do you believe in miracles?
   Never give up
   Sometimes David beats Goliath

Sports history is filled with front-running athletes and/or teams that dominated opponents and crumbled in the finale. Fans, historians and media love a great underdog story. But the once-dominant athlete or team is left to wonder how or why they collapsed.

Remarkable Comebacks

One of the greatest comebacks in all of sports, comes from the 2013 America's Cup by Oracle Team USA. They were trailing the New Zealand team 8-races-to-1. All the Kiwis needed to do was win one final race but Oracle stunned the yachting world by winning the next eight races to win the America's Cup.

For all the non-Yankee fans, the 2003 Boston Red Sox were on the verge of elimination in the ALCS as the New York Yankees were up 3-0 in the best of seven series. All they had to do was finish them off and move on to the World Series. However, no one told the Red Sox this and the Yankees snatched defeat from the jaws of victory.

The long awaiting 2016 Chicago Cubs left the Cleveland Indians with drooping jaws as they became the World Series champs after overcoming a 3-games-to-1 deficit.

Celebrating Too Early

All too often athletes begin their celebration while running to the finish line instead of through it.

During the fourth quarter of Super Bowl XXVII, the Dallas Cowboys' Leon Lett scooped up a fumble and ran for the end zone. Leon began his ESPN highlight reel celebration at the 10-yard line. Unknown to Leon, Don Beebe of the Buffalo Bills had not given up on the play. At the last moment, just prior to crossing the end zone line for a touchdown, Beebe knocked the ball out of Leon Lett's celebratory hand.

In the 2014 NCAA Women's College World Series, victorious Baylor Bears were down 7-0 to Kentucky in an elimination game. However, it ain't over till the fat lady sings and Baylor rallied to a stunning victory.

In the 2006 Torino Winter Olympics, American snowboarder Lindsey Jacobellis had established a commanding lead and was priming for victory. On the last straight away she performed an entertaining kick maneuver which left her on her back only to watch her competitor race by for the victory.

When competing on the world stage or at a local tournament, finish the race, run through the finish line, not to the finish line. Save the celebration for after being triumphant.

If you google https://youtu.be/BqhK55JVEd8 spend the next five minutes fully appreciating the consequences of celebrating too early.

Do you believe in miracles?

Everyone is aware of dramatic and unexpected upsets in sports, either by an individual or team. Every year there is a Cinderella team in the NCAA March Madness tournament. Clearly a lower ranked team has defeated a higher ranked opponent. Happily, this encourages every player or team to realize anyone, on any day, can beat their opponent and create a miracle.

Here are a few examples of "miracles":

1. 1983 NCAA Division I Men's Basketball Championship between the Houston Cougars vs. North Carolina State Wolfpack. Houston's powerful, mature roster earned the nickname, Phi Slama Jama. The roster included: future NBA player and Hall of Famer Clyde "The Glide" Drexler, future NBA player Hakeem Olajuwon, future NBA player Michael Young, future NBA player Rob Williams and future NBA player Larry Micheaux. Fans, media and some opponents concluded Phi Slama Jama would dispatch with the lower-ranked Wolfpack. However, as the basketball gods would play this one out, Dereck Whittenburg shot a 30-footer with microseconds remaining on the game clock. The shot fell short, but was miraculously dunked on the rebound by Lorenzo Charles with the unexpected and spectacular results. This moment in time epitomizes the slogan that "It ain't over till the fat lady sings." Never give up.

2. The vaunted Russian national hockey team was the dominating force in international ice hockey competitions for years. They were the favorite to win the 1980 Winter Olympics in hockey. But to the surprise of all fans, the underdog United States team triumphed with a 4-3 victory. The now famous colorful commentary and emotionally call by Al Michaels transcends time as he declared, "Do you believe in miracles? Yes!"

3. The odds were on favorite New England Patriots against the New York Giants in the NFL Super Bowl. The Patriots had dismantled most of their competitors throughout the year and had amassed the greatest scoring offense in NFL history, and were undefeated going into the Super Bowl. Winning the Super Bowl would leave them as the only other undefeated team in NFL history (Miami Dolphins 1972), and the greatest offensive powerhouse the NFL had ever witnessed. However, nobody told the New Your Giants they were supposed to just lay down and lose. Vegas bookies lost

the financial house when the Giants were crowned the Super Bowl champions.

4. In 1991 the ninth alternate, John Daly, was invited to compete in the PGA Championship. Though the field was loaded with former champions and familiar names in the golfing world, the opportunity presented itself and John took the bull by the horns. He displayed uncanny driving ability, soft irons and fantastic putting. After the four rounds, Daly stood atop the leaderboard as the unexpected, underdog for the championship.

5. Many of you might not be familiar with the Nic Vujicic. He was born without arms or legs and could have easily given up and declared the world as unfair and cruel. Instead Nic has climbed to the top of the speakers' profession and is an author and motivator. He participates in surfing, swimming, boating and fishing all because he focuses on what he has rather than focusing on what he doesn't have. Nic always encourages the attendees to look inward and discover the reality that it's not how you start but how you finish. "Are you going to finish strong?"

6. In the history of all sports the greatest odds listed against a team to win the championship was the Leicester City Football Club. In 2015, they narrowly avoided relegation to a lower league. No one could blame bookmakers for slapping 5,000-1 odds to win the English Premier League title in 2016. Such odds did not deter the players from always competing to their best. The entire soccer world cheered as the underdog Foxes finished the 2016 Premier League season 10 points ahead of some of the richest, most-famous and star-studded teams in the world including Arsenal, Tottenham, Manchester City, Chelsea and Manchester United. Previously unknown players such as James Vardy, Danny Drinkwater and Riyad Mahrez earned call-ups to their national teams for international matches. Regardless of the hand or circumstances you are dealt in your life, drawing strength from

the reality and making the best out of the situation is within your control. Though there are no guarantees, you can choose to be your best.

Consider the lessons from history; David versus Goliath, Jack and the Giant, St. George and the Dragon, Rudolph The Red Nosed Reindeer, and The Little Train That Could. All were the underdog and could have given up. Yet, they persevered, overcame the obstacles, triumphed over the odds and showed us they were "miracles".

Some athletes could find excuses for not achieving, winning, or reaching their dreams. They could blame it on their position in life or everything and anything outside of themselves. The underdog doesn't always walk away with the championship but their ability to apply themselves and reach for the stars is within their control. Derek Jeter, one of the greatest New York Yankees players stated, "There may be people who have more talent than you, but there's no excuse for anyone to work harder than you do – and I believe that." As with athletes that accomplish more than others expect, Derek Jeter found strength in other people's negative expectations. "I love it when people doubt me. It makes me work harder to prove them wrong."

Take Away for Step Ten:

A Champion's Mindset© focuses on what he can control. He never quits and never gives up. He focuses from start to finish and remains positive while putting forth his best effort. Luck is not what brings him to greatness. The Roman philosopher Seneca believed, "Luck is what happens when preparation meets opportunity."

Continue to fight till the whistle is blown. Doing your best is not an outcome. Being prepared physically and mentally is what makes the difference between winning and losing. That's not luck. Miracles do happen when you have committed yourself to the herculean effort to practice, learn and grow, compete with unwavering passion, and remain positive.

Step Eleven: The Unmentionables

Outline

1. **What is choking?**
2. **The "Yips"**
   Steps to handling the Yips
   Review nine evidence-based steps to address the Yips
   Review three clinical steps to handle the Yips

Unmentionable #1 - Choking

"Make sure your worst enemy doesn't live between your two ears."
Laird Hamilton

Have you ever heard an announcer say, "He choked"? When an athlete possesses the physical attributes along with the competitive strategies, yet succumbs to the perceived pressure of the moment, we all witness the sudden drop of his skill set. Superman becomes unmasked. The vaunted champion becomes human. The professional athlete looks more like an average Joe. Even at elite levels of sport, it's all mental.

The following story illustrates this point. The year was 1988, Dan Jansen had just won the World Sprint Championships Speed Skating. Years of effort, training, planning, preparation, coaching, competition unified into that glorious moment of attaining his dream to compete for the United States in the Winter Olympics as one of the favorites to win. He was the odds-on favorite to the 500 and 1000-meter races. However, the unthinkable happened. He fell in the 500-meter (after hearing his sister was diagnosed with Leukemia) and a few days later fell in the 1000-meter races. Putting these tragic events behind him, he again pursued the four-year arduous pursuit of the 1992 Winter Olympics, but unfortunately, he did not medal. At the 1994 Lillehammer Winter Olympics he finished 8th in the 500-meters. But in his final attempt to reach the podium, Dan Jansen reached his dream and won 1st place in the 1000-meter event for his only Olympic medal. How do the best not perform up to their abilities?

How does this happen? Obviously, someone didn't sneak into their room in the night and remove their calf muscle. No one clubbed them on their head and caused them to forget how to hold a ball. What had been practiced for years and become second nature and automatic, for a brief moment in time, suddenly disappeared.

- Imagine that you were in position to win the Masters Open in golf. You had just shot a course record 63. All was looking good until the weight of the moment kicked in. In 1996, Greg Norman can personally attest to what Lemony Snicket would refer to as a, "Series of Unfortunate Events" as Nick Faldo won. In this case, Nick didn't win, but rather the Great White Shark lost. He clearly possessed the skills and had proven he could dominate. What Greg Norman experienced was not a complete loss of functioning but a situationally specific change in performance based upon the self-imposed perceived pressure of the moment.

- One of the most hallowed stadiums in the world would be arguably Wimbledon. To reach the finals of this Grand Slam major event is a lesson in consistency and domination. Jana Navatna was on the verge of capping off an incredible run in 1993. Tied with Steffi Graf with one set apiece. Jana leaped to a 4-1 lead in the final set. All she needed was to continue exactly what she had accomplished for the last two weeks. Instead one double fault opened the flood gates to a disintegration, losing the next 5 games and the championship to Graf. Many can remember the heartfelt moment during the awards ceremony in which the Dutchess of Kent consoled Jana who wept uncontrollably.

- One of the elite divers I coached was referred to me because during "Big" name meets she struggled to complete the dives she had already mastered. Her coaches began referring to her as BMC, short for Big Meet Choker. This label did not help her feel secure. She internalized this negative label and began to think about herself as the BMC. Her self-talk became her reality and her tendency to focus on the name of an event and internalize the belittling comment became a roadblock to her success.

Occasionally, you will be watching the NBA and see one of the best players approach the free throw line in a pivotal moment in the game. The perceived "pressure" of the moment becomes too significant even for the seasoned professional. In the blink of an eye and in front of all fans, he misses everything. Inevitably, the crowd chants in unisome, "Air Ball."

Choking is the tendency to become distracted by the "gravity" of the moment. Some people refer to choking as a "Brain Hiccup" or the momentary suspension of an exceptional ability due to "freaking out."

This not only happens on the competitive field but also in the corporate boardroom. I was brought in as a consultant to a large major corporation in Chicago to work with a highly competent young man who was on the verge of a major promotion to V.P. of Sales. His pattern was predictable and consistent but this superstar would freak out when interacting with his superior. Even though he had graduated with honors, mastered the technical requirements within this business, was the annual top salesman and was required to train new and early career professionals on the job, he still freaked out. Whenever he was in the presence of the decision maker for his potential promotion, he would become a tongue-tied pre-teen. Though he possessed the skill sets for advancement within this corporation and reached his annual goals, this young man feared embarrassment or rejection. As we discussed his pattern, it became clear he would become lost in his own thoughts and feelings. Once he learned to focus on things within in his control (e.g. the task, his recent projects, the development of a highly accomplished team) rather than becoming consumed with aspects beyond his control (e.g. his supervisor's opinion, the decision to promote him) he was able to remain focused and stay calm and shine. Once he focused internally on the tasks within his control, his boss was able to appreciate his capabilities and realized he would be an asset to the corporation as their new V.P. of Sales.

- In 2004, Major League Baseball was the setting for one of sports' greatest display of choking. The mighty New York Yankees were up 3-0 in the ALCS championships. They had just beaten their arch rivals, the Boston Red Sox 19-8. In game 4, the Yankee's had the lead going into the bottom of the 9th with their ace closer, Mariano Rivera. Then something happened that had never happened in the entire history of major league baseball, losing the chance to become champions after amassing a 3-0 lead. Headlines read, "Shocking collapse", "Champs to chumps", "Choke city" and more. The Yankees have won 27 World Series Championships throughout their illustrative history and lose to their most despised adversary revealed even the greatest can occasionally struggle with the significance of the moment. The following front-page headline image from the Daily News sums up this moment in time. (photo from The Daily News front page October 21, 2004)

- One of the tennis players I coached told me that every time she played against a certain lower ranked opponent in the latter stages of a tennis tournament she would choke. She possessed every stroke and even developed a powerful weapon in her forehand. However, whenever she faced this opponent she would play like a novice. The writing was on the wall. I mean literally. When she saw her name listed on the brackets displayed on the wall of the country club tennis facility, she would anticipate failure. She stated, "I'm gonna choke again." We discussed her assessment of her opponent and she claimed that because her opponent was from an eastern block country she "must" have received some "specialized" training. Her irrational perception caused her to change her own level of performance. I reinforced three major points with this athlete. 1) Less is more. She needed to work on the basics to increase her probability of success. Hit her ground strokes deep, take advantage of her opponent's second serve and don't try to rush, force and create anything. Just remain in the point and be consistent. 2) Challenge her irrational internal dialogue that pertained to her opponent's "specialized" training. We had her talk with several other competitors who were also trained in the same program as her opponent. She discovered there never was any specialized training. 3) She was a higher ranked player than her eastern block opponent. She had amassed more wins covering more tournaments, against more skilled opponents. She needed to internalize this reality and accept the fact she possessed more quality to her game, and if she got out of her head and focused on the moment, she would prevail.

- Research shows believing in stereotypes can lead to thinking they are truths and acting on them based on false beliefs. (Sports Psych Journal). This is best illustrated by my team, the Chicago Cubs. To know them is to love them, "The Loveable Losers." For those of you who are not up to date on baseball history, the Chicago Cubs had not won the World Series since Robert Peary set sail for the North Pole, Henry Ford produces his first Model T car, and Theodore Roosevelt was President of the United States. These and more wonderful world events took place in 1908. That's not a typo. Over one hundred years had passed since the Cubs won the World Series in Baseball. Establishing the longest drought since their last championship compared to every professional sports teams can lead to a "losers" mentality. To explain bad outcomes, we create false associations called superstitions. Superstitions often become part of the identity, and false beliefs become associated with the eventual outcomes. Fans even came up with false, irrational and magical excuses for the Cubs inept play including in 1945 Curse of the Billy Goat, in 1969 the Black Cat and even cruelly blaming a loyal fan (Bartman) in 2003 for the continuing futility. Even Bartman's interference didn't stop the Cubs from making the next out or prevent them from scoring again in the 9th inning. Blaming adverse outcomes becomes part of the identity, "The Loveable Losers." Unfortunately, the running misconception of my Chicago Cubs is they have the exceptional ability to snatch defeat from the jaws of victory. On an unconscious level people might begin to internalize the inevitability that the losing history will invariably repeat itself. Fortunately, the Baseball Gods determined the long-suffering experience of generations would finally end in 2016 as my baby bears triumphed to raise the World Series trophy. The sweet taste of victory was finally ours. Well, anyone can have a bad century.

Most athletes have experienced or can relate to choking under pressure in competitive sport (Wang, Marchant, & Morris, 2004). They studied athletes coping style and susceptibility to choking. Wang et al. (2004) note many of the most talented and experienced athletes speak candidly about choking. Pete Sampras, for example, the 14-time singles Grand Slam Champion in tennis, admitted after winning his seventh Wimbledon title, "We all choke....No matter who you are, you just feel pressure in the heat of the moment" (Sampras, 2000, p. 68) Sampras, (2000). Historic win for Sampras, The Advertiser, July II, pp. 68.

Dr. Sian Beilock (Professor of Psychology at University of Chicago, wrote *Choke: What the Secrets of the Brain Reveal About Getting it Right When You Have To.* (Beilock) Choking is defined as, "Worse performance than expected because of perceived pressure. A variety of body reactions such as heart racing, palms sweating, mind racing off task, and thinking too much." She recommended that athletes focus on the moment versus over-analyzing or over-thinking on minute details. This is commonly referred to as paralysis through analysis. Dr. Beilock also discusses performance failure and what happens in the brain. Specifically, observed a malfunction of the pre-frontal cortex. When automatic activities become analyzed in too much detail the ability to perform these skills decrease. We all experience pressure situations in life (e.g. Olympics, speaking in class, interviewing for a job, pitching in the World Series) and our brains react similarly. Also, false perceptions and stereotypes can interfere with a performance. If you personalize false perception you begin to think of the negative stereotype rather than performing at an optimal level. She encourages becoming use to mild stressors in order to improve performance for future stressful situations. Create practice situations that mimic the real world competitive situations. Additionally, visualization helps prepare you for managing your physiological reactions to the perceived competitive situation. You can watch a wonderful video of Dr. Beilock discuss The Science of "Choking" at https://www.youtube.com/watch?v=zcr4ZD-Vrsg.

In life, we all react to how we perceive our world. Reacting leads to choking. Top athletes have learned to control how to react and how to response. Wang et al. (2004) investigated the relationship between coping style and choking susceptibility in college basketball players. 66 undergraduate basketball players filled out the Coping Style Inventory for Athletes approximately one week before participating in the experiment. The inventory had 8 items related to "approach coping" and

8 items related to "avoidant coping." Wang et al. (2004) stated that approach coping style refers to coping strategies such as, "I quickly became more aggressive or enthusiastic for the purpose of improving my performance." I refer to this style as, emotionally "Reactive." Whereas avoidance coping style refers to strategies such as, "I did not let the unpleasant experience bother me" and, "I reasoned that it was just part of the game." I refer to this style as "Responding." The experiment consisted of the participants taking 20 free throw shots in the low pressure condition with only a research assistant present to record the score, and 20 free throw shots in the high pressure condition which included an audience, videotaping, and monetary incentives. Prior to each condition, participants completed another form, the Competitive State Anxiety Inventory-2 which assesses the level of anxiety during competition. Results show participants displayed a decline in performance under the manipulated high pressure condition. In "real competition" the athletes' perceived pressure would likely be higher than in the study and the effects of the pressure would likely be magnified. Consistent with previous research an approach coping style is related to high perceived anxiety. Again, I refer to this style as, emotionally "Reactive." In contrast, the avoidance style tended to reduce the intensity of perceived pressure. Again, I refer to this style as "Responding." Results also showed an approach coping style is a significant contributor to poor performance. Wang et al. (2004) suggests those using the avoidant coping style under pressure may be less likely to choke. When I work with an athlete at any skill level, I have also found emotional reactivity is the kiss-of-death or as Wang calls it "approach coping style.

Think back to the quintessential golf movie, Caddyshack (1980)There is a moment in the movie when the entertainingly obnoxious Al Czervik (Rodney Dangerfield) bets the blue blood Judge Smails (Ted Knight) that he would slice his tee shot. Judge Smails replies, "Gambling is illegal at Bushwood sir and I never slice." As you may recall, Judge

Smails becomes so flustered by the pressure, he slices his tee shot into the trees.

As Dr. Beilock posed, even at the most elite level of sport an athlete suddenly experiences performance failure and does not perform up to his physical abilities. Examples in sports range from Isiah Thomas throwing an inbound pass away to Larry Bird in the 1987 NBA Eastern Conference Finals; Chris Webber calling an ill-advised timeout without any remaining timeouts which cost the University of Michigan Fab Five a chance to win against their vaunted rival UNC Tarheels in the 1993 NCAA Championship; In 2008 Chelsea's John Terry was in position to win the UEFA Champions League during penalty kicks only to slip and drive the PK off the side post leading to their loss to Manchester United; and the Dallas Cowboys' starting quarterback Tony Romo bobbles the hold for a 19-yard field goal which led to their loss against the Seahawks in the 2007 Wild Card game.

Everyone has had the momentary strangle-hold of perceived pressure which inexplicably causes the simple to become overwhelming, triggers a brain hiccup, and leaves everyone scratching their heads in total disbelief.

Unmentionable #2 – The "Yips"

Steve Sachs, 2nd Baseman for the MLB Los Angeles Dodgers suddenly couldn't throw the baseball from his position at 2nd base to his 1st baseman. What was once automatic had shifted to a robotic, step-by-step painful motion. This dilemma has been referred to as "Steve Sax Syndrome." Fortunately, he was able to address these motor struggles and regain his skills and compete in the major leagues.

In all of sports there is one word athletes avoid discussing like it is the plague, the Yips. The Yips are more than choking. The Yips is an elite athlete loses the well-honed physical ability to perform some specific maneuver. This is not a one-off. The loss of muscle memory and the sudden inability to control his movements becomes his new normal.

There are two types of Yips, 1) impaired motor-movement and 2) performance anxiety-related symptoms or fear of failure.

Examples:

- An NCAA Catcher could no longer throw the baseball back to the pitcher and would question every minute step of his throwing motion. He would ask himself, "How much pressure do I put on the ball?", "Do I throw from 3/4 or over the top?", "Where is my release point?" Curious as it was, as I coached him, we discussed all the moves he still could do. He had a great gun and could throw a rope from home to 2nd base in order to tag out a runner who attempted to steal. He was a great batter. He could call a solid game for his pitchers. He just became fixated on this singular motion. By the time we met, he was dreaming about the lost ability, thinking that there was no way he would ever get it back and his future pro career was over before it began. We discussed his automatic throwing motion. I had him toss several stress balls to me in my office. While we were tossing the stress balls, we would joke about life and regale in stories about his baseball experience. I asked him to NOT think of a big purple elephant, especially the one with pink polka dots. He giggled and said, "The only thing I can now think about is that doggone purple elephant with the pink polka dots." The brain doesn't care what it chooses to focus on, it will focus on whatever you tell it to. Again, that means no one CANNOT tell the brain what NOT to focus on because then it is the only thing your brain will focus on. Though he felt he couldn't throw to the pitcher he knew he still could throw to 2nd base. So we practiced having him gun the ball towards 2nd base but have the pitcher intercept it. We rehearsed visualizing the ball going back to the pitcher and practiced muscle relaxation skills. When he was relaxed, we spent the next 15-20 minutes chucking the ball back to 2nd base. We returned to visualizing the desired motion, rehearsed relaxation training, and then brought the pitcher out. Over the next 10 minutes, he fired the ball to 2nd base and his pitcher would snag the ball in mid-flight. Two days later, he called me and expressed embarrassment for taking up my time as the issue had seemingly disappeared. His overall ability to shine had returned.

- I coached a PGA Golfer who would suddenly stop his swing on the downward motion. He discussed watching a videotape of an NBA Basketball player, Charles Barkley, who developed a hitch in his downward golf stroke. Suddenly, he was bitten by the same golf stroke bug. When we met, I asked him to bring his club with him. His focus was on his downward motion. He would repeat to himself, "Don't lock up, don't lock up." (Remember, that you CANNOT tell your brain what NOT to do.) We discussed his love of the sport, his previous playing experience, and fond memories of golfing with his father. Then we worked on focusing on the full stroke. We did this with visualization and guided imagery. (Remember, muscle memory can be impacted by using your mind's eye.) As he focused on the fluidity of his visualized golf swing, he practiced remaining physically calm and relaxed. We practiced deep breathing, muscle relaxation, visualizing the swing, and his relaxation training. Then I had him practice his swing with a different internal chatter and I asked him to show me his follow-through. I held a stick up in front of him and asked him to hit it out of my hand as his followed through on his swing. The stick went flying. I asked him how he was able to do this and he replied, "It wasn't that I wasn't thinking about locking, I was thinking about my follow-through and knocking that darn stick out of your hand."

- One play could determine the reputation and identity of a player. A player spits, another stomps on a player, or runs into the crowd to challenge a fan. In 1971, the MLB Pittsburgh Pirates won the World Series. A key element was their stellar pitcher, Steve Blass.

By the next year he was out of MLB, and out of all baseball by 1975. He lost the ability to successfully pitch a baseball. The disappearance of his ability has become synonymous with the yips and is sadly referred to as "Steve Blass Disease" (O'Neill).

- Amazingly, even after achieving magnificent accomplishments, a professional can succumb to this debilitating condition. The New York Yankees' second baseman, Chuck Knoblauch was Rookie of the Year, and had been a part of several World Series championships only to be bit by this malady. He suddenly was unable to make the routine throw from second base to first base.

- There might be something in the water in NYC as the New York Mets catcher Mackey Sasser surprisingly could no longer throw the ball back to the pitcher. After six years and several team changes Sasser retired from baseball. This pattern became brutally known as "Sasseritis". As a post-note, after leaving professional baseball Sasser did work with a therapist, regain his ability, and coached at the college level helping others with this struggle.

Philippen and Lobinger (2012) interviewed 17 yips-affected golfers to record the thoughts and feelings they experienced when the yips occurred, as well as record the focus of their attention right before putting the ball. (The yips in golf manifest as involuntary jerk or freezing of the arm causing a disruption in the putting movement.) All participants had golf experience ranging from 4 to 60 years and had tournament experience ranging from club level to national championship tournaments. The results suggest golfers were primarily occupied with negative thoughts such as perceived loss of control, loss of confidence in their putting skills, and worries about mistakes due to the yips. Feelings associated with the yips were entirely negative and included disappointment, frustration, anger, and especially anxiety about having to take a putt. Eleven of the participants reported a focus on technical aspects, or a focus on the yips and its negative performance outcomes.

These results could be a consequence of the inability to perform a smooth putting stroke, however, assuming the psychological factors have an influence on the yips, the negative experience of the yips may explain its long-term nature.

As mentioned earlier, there are two types of Yips, impaired motor movement (Type I) and performance anxiety-related symptoms (Type II). Stinear et. al., (2006) found under experimental conditions of putting of low- versus high-pressure situations, two types of Yips were identified. The high-pressure condition used monetary incentive, video-taping and a person (part of the experimental team) giving negative feedback. The muscle movement-related group (Type I) exhibited great muscle activity during the putting while the anxiety-related group (Type II) experienced changes in cognitive/performance anxiety or fear of failure. The Type I struggled to quiet the firing of forearm muscle fibers. Remember, this was not a problem of one situation but became a pattern. Some might refer to Type II as "choking" but I would refrain from that definition. To me "choking" is being overwhelmed by the perception of this situation, while the "Yips" are a pattern. The Yips which are involuntary muscle twitching or activation (also known as "dystonia").

Steps to address the Yips

Following are nine options for those struggling with the Yips:

<u>Less is more</u>. I worked with a tennis player who reported after missing several months due to an injury, she had lost muscle memory in her forehand. Rather than forcing the continuous failure, she focused on hitting non-competitive forehands against a wall and on basic form without worrying about winning points. This liberated her from negative thoughts and rebuilt her muscle-memory and technique.

<u>Understand the underlying fears</u>. Athletes that focus on external factors may unintentionally create an internal panic leading to the

Yips. One of the gymnasts I coached had lost the ability to perform her maneuvers on the balance beam. Suddenly the four-inch-wide beam became impossible to walk across. She had reached a point in her competitive career the expectations to perform at the most elite levels on a consistent basis was too much for her. Her fears of disappointing her teammates and parents began to consume her on a daily basis. She began to dread the opportunities to compete in tournaments. Together, we discovered her self-worth was tied to her parent's reactions to her performance. Her parents provided conditional love. If she struggled they would be cold to her and her father would verbally belittle her. We needed to help her develop a better sense of self based on factors within her control. She had spent her formative years trying to please in order to receive affection. Once she started to realize her own self-esteem was a function of her ability to apply herself, do her best, be in the process and take pride in her commitment towards excellence, her focus became less on winning awards, and less on what her parents would say. Her focus shifted from emotional fear of worst case outcomes, rejection and negative evaluations, to doing her best, knowing she had mastered these advanced skills, and to value the feedback of those who loved her unconditionally. Her magnificent athletic abilities returned.

Immobilize the affected hand or limb. (Priori, et. al., 2001) A golfer wore a splint on his right wrist, allowing him to continue to move like a pendulum without experiencing the twitching.

Changes in the equipment. This logical intervention makes perfect sense. If an athlete uses different equipment he needs to develop different muscular controls and techniques. The shift from the previous form requires slightly different regions of the brain to acquire new bodily motions. Physical posture becomes different thereby making visual analysis different. The involuntary twitching tends to disappear with the new equipment.

Changes in technical motor skill retraining (Zeuner, et. al, 2005) Learning new cross-training skills to improve the existing techniques can help athletes overcome the Yips. NFL and MLB players turn to ballet or karate in order to counter their struggles on developing a new pattern of motor movements and muscle control.

Changing sensory training (Zeuner, et. al., 2002) Training an athlete to focus on a different sensory experience can help resolve the Yips.

Acupuncture has been reported in case studies (Palle-Rosted, A. 2005). Many of the non-traditional interventions become more acceptable when addressing these struggles. An Olympic fencer found by using acupuncture, she stopped the involuntary muscle contractions. The acupuncture of specific muscles sent a message to her brain that inhibited the muscle twitch of those muscles.

Pharmacological interventions have been used, but come with potential unintended consequences.

Social-Focused Guided Imagery (SFGI) strategically walks the athlete through multiple visualization steps. 1) a self-assessment of the severity of the problem is rated by the athlete, 2) then he focuses on positive outcomes during visualization, sensory awareness with positive outcomes, 3) re-assessment of the perceived severity of the problem after social-focused imagery was rehearsed; 4) the athlete writes a letter to themselves describing the positive sensation and perception of successful visualization outcomes (Bell, RJ and Thompson, CL).

In addition, following are more recommendations I have found to be helpful:

<u>Change in motor coordination</u>

Golfers have switched their high hand versus low hand on their grip. <u>The change in motor coordination</u> helps the brain to relearn new motor skills and techniques. Most players experience the "yips" in one limb or hand hence changing some aspect mechanically could help. I have coached several golfers who lost their short game found that by switching their high and low hand, grips helped overcome their involuntary muscle twitching. One right-handed golfer actually retaught himself how to chip as a left-handed player. This resolved his involuntary twitch but required almost a full year to develop competitive accuracy. One of the Dartists I coached found his "yips" resolved when he change his grip (tip of middle finger holding the dart rather than his index finger and leaning slightly more forward). Also, one of my NCAA 2nd Baseman practiced throwing from a three-quarter release point rather than his traditional over the top.

<u>Altering focus.</u>
1) A catcher who struggles throwing the ball back to the pitcher now focuses on launching the ball to second base.
2) A golfer I coached froze on his downward swing toward the ball. We went to a local chipping green and practice focusing on hitting a yard stick out of my hand. I stood in front of him and just passed his follow through point. I held the yard stick horizontally at his follow through point. His task was to knock the yard stick out of my hand. No ball was initially involved so he could focus specifically on knocking the yard stick out of my hand. Once he refocused, he was able to successfully practice full swings.

I also coach athletes to implement three additional interventions.

1) <u>Physiological</u>

> Practice Deep Breathing to increase oxygen to the brain and body.

> Perform Muscle Relaxation techniques to burn out the muscles in order to voluntarily take control of the muscles.

> Visualize a positive mindset of successful motor performance

2) Rehearse <u>Cognitive-Restructuring</u> by stopping the intrusive negative thoughts and inserting positive, constructive, productive phrases based on reality.

3) When worried about worst case scenarios and external judgement, work on <u>Mindfulness and Acceptance</u>, focusing internally and on the process.

Take Away for Step Eleven:

The two most feared words, Choking and the Yips can be addressed and resolved. Choking occurs when the athlete focuses on external factors. Taking personal responsibility and focusing on the process helps athletes maintain optimal athletic ability, keep a healthy perspective and refrain from blaming negative outcomes. There are numerous research-based steps to successfully challenge the Yips and keep you in the game.

Step Twelve: Recover from Injury

Outline

1. **Injury and when to return from Injury – The 2/3rd Rule**
2. **Four-steps of mental toughness during injury recovery**
3. **Three-phases of rehabilitation**
4. **Fear of Re-Injury**
5. **Signs of poor adjustment to injury**
6. **Review statistics of youth injury**

Injury and when to return from Injury – The 2/3rd Rule

Though I am not a medical rehab specialist, I did stay at a Holiday Inn Select last night. Unfortunately, I have experience from the other side of the coin. I have been a frequent flyer in the medical rehab programs as I have torn my right knee nine times and had seven knee surgeries (2 ACL reconstructions and 5 Arthroscopies).

While completing my training at The Johns Hopkins University School of Medicine, I had my first ACL reconstruction which was performed by the preeminent orthopedic surgeon, Dr. Charles Silberstein. When I asked the post-operative question about my return to competitive sports he replied, "Take the 2/3rd Rule" (Silberstein,1989). He reassured me with proper medical rehab I would be able to return to athletics. He clarified that every person and every injury is different, but I should not be impatient with my recovery and consider returning after 2/3rd the amount of time I was away from the sport.

In other words, don't rush it. I love the question, "Hey Doc, when will I be ready to get back to playing?" The answer is surprisingly simple, "Longer than you want but shorter than you fear." Every athlete wants to get back into competition NOW! The reality is she will not be returning as soon as she would want. And, every athlete has a fear that she might never be able to compete. She again asks, "When will I be able to return?" My reply is the same, "Longer than you want, but shorter than you fear." Think of Chicago Cubs' second-year player, Kyle Schwarber, who tore his ACL in the fifth game of the regular season. He quickly underwent repairs and rehabbed across the entire summer. Miraculously, Schwarber returned in the middle of the World Series and played an instrumental role in helping the Cubs become World Champions.

As a football player once told me: 'The very first day of training camp, is the first day of playing injured'. The drawback of developing the warrior mentality is many athletes develop an incredible pain threshold. This might lead an athlete to re-enter too soon and make his injury worse. In the short term, coming back too soon may make sense because the athlete does not want to lose his position on the team but coming back too quickly may sacrifice his ability to perform up to expectations, causing re-injury and thereby harm the team.

Think of Robert Griffin, III (RG3), a spectacularly gifted physical specimen. He sustained a knee injury and his quick return was applauded like being a true gladiator. However, he re-injured his knee against the Seattle Seahawks in the NFC Wild Card game. Controversy still remains, as reported by Robert Klemko in USA Today, "Dr. James Andrews says he never cleared Robert Griffin III to go back to the game after injury" (USA Today, January 6, 2013, Klemko, Robert). RGIII has never returned to his pre-injury performance level.

Worse than that is being vilified and presumed guilty in the court of public opinion. Think of the Chicago Bears Quarterback, Jay Cutler, a recognized team leader and competitor. When injured, he should have acted as a mentor and supported the active players. Instead, he appeared to sulk on the sidelines, acting disinterested and non-emotionally invested in the game or his teammates. Cutler could've continued to contribute by remaining connected to the team, players and strategies. The negative image projected by Cutler did not help his reputation. What he may have felt internally, did not translate to the fans.

What Cutler did not accept is that no one wants to sit out for an injury, small or big. When a responsible athlete is injured, she does not discontinue being a member of the team or stop studying and preparing. She can be a fantastic supporter of the team or the new player who is filling in for her. Her teaching wisdom can translate to a form of coaching. Mentoring the younger, newer players (as displayed by injured Peyton Manning), makes him an indispensable asset to his teammates, the team and adds credibility to his future status.

The professional athlete should make good use of her time while recovering by visualizing perfect form. This concept is referred to as the "Theory of Reminiscence". Her brain only knows what she focuses on. If she focuses on perfect form, she can improve her muscle memory *and* improve her skill set by the time she returns from rehab.

Besides the chapter on eating disorders and athletes, this will be the only time that I will encourage using a carbohydrate, R.I.C.E. R.I.C.E. is an acronym that stands for Rest, Ice, Compression and Elevation.

If she is unable to perform her sport during his injury rehabilitation, she could consider what activities and exercises would be able to participate in during this time. Not exercising her sport's specific movements is referred to as "deconditioning." Ask a physician or physical therapist for recommendations. Train through recovery in a safe and effective way by doing pool work, stationary bike, etc.

Coaches always say, "The best ability is availability." Top athletes compete at their best when they are playing. Elite athletes that are injured are not helping their team to the best of their abilities. An athlete that is not in the best possible physical condition when returning after the off-season puts her teammates in a difficult situation. So, make good use of recovery time! Additionally, if an athlete engages in behaviors that are illegal or violating policy they earn the right not to compete. Lastly, if a player has too many distractions in their life, they will not be mentally focused and may become a liability to their team.

Four-step Protocol of Mental Conditioning during Injury Recovery

The athlete needs to develop the capacity to be fully and completely ready to re-enter the sport when her medical specialist or orthopedic surgeon gives the go-ahead and signs off on her restrictions. It is a mindset. It is about planning and preparation. It places the athlete into the best possible position for return to competition.

The Four-Step Protocol:

1. Come back Stronger
2. Faster
3. More Flexible
4. Full Anticipation of Return to Competition.

Too often a player goes through physical rehabilitation from an injury but never focus on her mental preparation for re-entry into their sport. Most rehab specialists report an athlete will go through the routines of physical therapy until released. This is a passive process that relies on an authority figure releasing her from their treatment. Most rehab specialists want athletes in recovery to be highly motivated, driven, self-reliant, and follow treatment plans to the fullest. They want to bring the athlete back stronger than she was previous to the injury and improving quickness, agility and speed. Most sports do not require long distances to be run in competition. They do require spurts, short bursts, sprints, darts, flashes and quick step footwork.

Additionally, the elite athlete realizes that re-injury or pulling another muscle when returning to competition is one of the worst experiences of a sports career. She stops just as she gets started. In light of this reality, the athlete wants to make sure he is working on becoming more flexible than prior to the injury with greater range of motion. Lastly, it is not being physically ready that gets the athlete back into the game, it is her mental attitude. The fears or apprehensions that sit quietly in her memory bank of re-injury, lost performance or not returning to the level of competition linger, and can interfere with his recovery. Therefore, maintaining a highly level of excitement and anticipation about returning to the competitive field is a must throughout her rehab.

One of the football players I coached came to me after tearing his anterior cruciate ligament (ACL). Terrified that he would not receive acceptance to any college football program, he began his long road to recovery. This young, talented athlete had always believed that he was invincible. His serious injury brought him to me to forge a path that would bring him back to the gridiron. When he applied the four-step protocol, and used his recovery time to become a more physical specimen. He surpassed his squatting records, decreased his time in the 40-yard dash and improved his range of motion. He utilized the combination of Diaphragmatic Breathing, Muscle Relaxation and Visual Imagery to develop a positive perspective and an internal mindset of optimism about his triumphant return. After signing his Letter of Intent for a college football opportunity he expressed his gratitude for engaging in the mental four-step protocol. This was even more notable since one of his high school football teammates had gone through the same procedure, but was well behind him in his preparedness and was not being picked up by colleges.

A former nationally ranked soccer player told me he wished he had met me years earlier when he sustained a major leg injury. His rehab was passive. He never returned to full physical capabilities and was filled with negativity throughout his recovery. He was not taught the four-step protocol (Stronger, Faster, More Flexible and with Full Anticipation of Returning to Competition). He believed his confidence in achieving his competitive ability and functioning upon returning would have been attained. His internal dialogue would have been positive, excited, upbeat and primed for the opportunity to return to the field of play.

In possessing these four steps (Stronger, Faster, More Flexible and Full Anticipation of Returning to Competition) the athlete will come to realize that her recovery is based on the team of professionals that performed surgery and/or provided rehabilitation. These professionals hopefully have instilled confidence in her ability to execute her skill set. Just like in any other athletic endeavor the athlete needs to have a strong belief in his coaches, trainers, providers and nutritionists.

Lastly, the athlete needs to have faith in herself. She needs to hold herself up to her highest standards and never lie to herself. She might not apply herself every day and do every activity recommended but she realizes if she wants to return to full speed and capability, she needs to be leading by example. She needs to have integrity which is best described by, "Say what you mean and mean what you say!" Her rehab is not a passive process that is done to her, but rather an active process with her at the center of the program.

I met an elite high school golfer several weeks into his rehab from a shoulder injury. He was given a choice to either have shoulder surgery which would entail a lengthy rehab period or he could initially implement an aggressive physical therapy regimen. He opted for the aggressive physical therapy approach. Six weeks later he was referred to me by his physical therapist because of his slow rate of recovery. He informed me he was lifting the weights but not doing the stretching at home. His excuse was, "I'm already flexible." We talked about his decision-making process. His belief was that he was a young, virile athlete, but this perspective clearly violated his long-term best interest. His youthful exuberance was leading him down a path that did not satisfy the four-step protocol. Once he began to implement it, recovery and rehab helped to attain his desired outcomes and returned to competition.

Three Phases of Rehabilitation

When working with a sport psychologist during medical rehabilitation there are three phases to be addressed:

1)   <u>Initial Pain Management</u> is a process in combination with the physician pharmacological intervention, physical therapist, rest and a sport psychologist. This process integrates numerous techniques to decrease the perception of pain. Specifics techniques include: Diaphragmatic Breathing, Muscle Relaxation and Visualization. By altering blood pressure, muscle tone, and increasing oxygen levels the patient can manage the pain easier which leads to more compliance, increased physical effort during rehab and improved engagement by the patient throughout her rehabilitation.

2)   <u>Functional Muscle Rehabilitation</u> is a process in combination with a physical therapist, pharmacotherapies and a sport psychologist. This process utilizes the pain management techniques while increasing focus on the mental aspects required to push through the discomfort of physical therapy, aqua therapy, stretching, range of motion protocols, etc. Maintaining a healthy perspective, implementing realistic expectations, decreasing the expenditure of negative thoughts, as well as not wasting emotional energy dwelling on the past are also keys to successful rehabilitation.

3)   <u>Returning to Competition</u> is conducted along with rehab specialists and trainers. The mental aspects are used in a step-by-step progression. They are minimal during the pain management phase, moderate during the functioning muscle rehab phase, and intense during the return to competition phase. The concept of returning to athletic competition is best determined by the two-thirds ratio. Based upon the time away from competition, a two-thirds ratio is a realistic benchmark for an elite athlete to return to full speed, strength, and optimal mentally conditioning.

The goal is to take an active role throughout the rehabilitation process. All too often athletes assume a passive role and engage in mediocre rehabilitation based solely on the minimum expectations while awaiting the medical discharge based upon basic functioning. When an elite athlete participates with a sport psychologist while in orthopedic rehabilitation, she takes a more active role throughout the process. The four aspects to psychological rehabilitation are to return to competitive play 1) stronger, 2) faster, 3) more flexible and with 4) full anticipation to return. Rehabilitation for the elite athlete is not to attain basic functioning, but to use this time to come back better than before the injury both physically and mentally.

Additionally, there are other areas utilized by sport psychologists to help athletes recover during the three phases of injury rehabilitation. Visualization during all three phases (Initial injury, Strengthening, and Returning) has been shown to have significant benefits (Hamson, J. 2006). Addressing fears and worries to prevent muscle locking which could lead to rigid muscle movement is important. When an athlete focuses on factors outside her control, she increases the probability of re-injury. Lastly, addressing other life issues which interfere with optimal functioning due to distraction. The ability to recover from injury is both physical and mental. Unfortunately, the mental aspect of rehab is often forgotten.

Multiple factors make up an individual's character, and it is these factors that play a significant role when coming face-to-face with adversity. An athlete's frame of mind is a key component when traveling down the road of recovery. In the past, psychological aspects of injury and athletic rehabilitation have often been overlooked. Health care professionals typically focused on the physical state of the athlete (Andrews & Harrelson, 1991). However, it is now understood, the psychological state of an injured athlete is equally important, if not more important than the physical state. Both athletes and coaches commonly believe the mind is equally important to overall sport performance as is physical abilities and talent.

Shuer and Dietrich (1997) were the first to study the relationship between chronic injuries and psychological ramifications. They concluded chronic injury in athletes correlates with the trauma of a natural disaster. Other researchers have found that athletes struggle with mood disturbance after chronic injuries (Granito, 2002, Storch, 2005, Wiechman and Williams, 1997, Manuel, J.C., 2002, and San Jose, A., 2003). This is a reality that cannot be stressed enough. With the fear of physically not being able to return to sport comes the panic of losing one's identity and other adverse emotional stressors. In two studies, Tracey (2003), and Weiss and Troxel (1986), identified a range of responses by injured athletes which included disbelief, fear, anger, depression, tension, frustration, and lower self-esteem. Athletes reporting frustration and fear of "missing practice", "losing fitness", missing out", "playing catch-up", and worrying over, "how long they would be unable to participate in a given sport."

Ballerinas and danceurs from major ballet companies frequently disregard physical injuries out of fear of losing their lead spot in the company. We know the great majority of injuries in dance result from overuse, (Caine & Garrick, 1996, Kerr, et. al. 1992) which tend to be accompanied by pain and discomfort and a lack of understanding. The psychological ramifications typically are unrecognized or ignored (Liederbach, M. (2000). Theatrical dance evolves a "culture of tolerance" concerning injury and pain that encourages dancers to dance through, around, and in spite of injury. If the physical injury is ignored, the psychological impact of an injury will not be addressed. The article "And the Dance Goes On: Psychological Impact of Injury" discusses the increased focus on the nature and prevalence of dance injuries in accordance with the research on psychological aspects of athletic injury. Ultimately, it illustrates a concern for the emotional side of injury thriving in the dance science community. Consider the old adage "Break a leg." We may need to discover its origin for this point. Who would wish for this outcome?

Fear of Re-Injury

Kinesiophobia, *the fear of re-injury*, is defined as a disturbing thought which reoccurs in an athlete's mind. Tied into this is the "Self-fulfilling prophecy" idea, when the outcome is caused by the athlete's own fear. That's right, we have created a word for the fear of re-injury, Kinesiophobia.

If an athlete, is apprehensive of her recovery and rehab and fears re-injury, she will protect herself by guarding the injured area. She will hold her arm closer to her body or tense out the muscle to protect herself from contact. By changing her natural abilities because of fear, she moves in a less fluid matter. When she uses poor form, she puts herself at greater risk of physical injury. Additionally, if she is focusing on protecting her injured area she is not focusing on the moment, the play, or her opponents and will leave herself open to being catastrophically hit by her opponent.

Several studies support the findings of athletes struggling to return to competition due to fear of re-injury (Flanigan, D., 2013), Kvist J. et al. (2005) and Thomee, P. et. al. (2008).

Recovery from injury has been correlated to social support. This is not a time to tough it out on her own. Sufficient social support is associated with decreased levels of stress, anxiety, depression and negative emotions, while inadequate social support causes a delay in rehabilitation and inverse levels of stress (Barefield, S. and McCallister, S. 1997). Team sport athletes have had more social support and encouragement which positively affected their recovery from injury. Overall, it appears social support similarly affects elite, recreational, individual, and team sport athletes. (Green . S.L. and Weinberg, R.S. (2001).

There is a concept called, Self-Efficacy (Bandura, A., 1977) which has two vital parts contributing to a successful outcome. First is the awareness behavior "A" leads to desired outcome "B". Second is the realization that you possess said behavior "A" or you have the ability to acquire behavior "A". According to Albert Bandura, self-efficacy is "the belief in one's capabilities to organize and execute the course of action required to manage prospective situations." As Bandura and other researchers have demonstrated, self-efficacy can have an impact on everything from a psychological state, to a behavior, to a motivation. Regardless of acquiring a new skill or recovering from injury, elite athletes want to possess both parts of Self-Efficacy.

Fear of re-injury was the most common reason cited for a postoperative reduction in sports participation. Adern (2011) concluded psychological factors vastly contribute to the return to a sport. As more people involved in athletics recognize the importance of sport psychology in sports recovery, they could help erase the stigma surrounding psychological assistance (Ardern, et. al., 2013). The Chicago Cubs' Kyle Schwarber, suffering from a knee injury in April, was able to miraculously return to the lineup in October. His 400+ batting average as a designated hitter in the 2016 World Series was due to both his medical treatment and his psychological toughness.

Ask yourself, "What can I do after an injury to help my recovery?" There are several possible directions. Consider what Driediger et al. (2006) analyzed exploring the use of imagery by injured athletes receiving physiotherapy. These athletes strongly emphasized that imagery served cognitive, motivational, and healing purposes in rehabilitating their injury. Whenever we imagine ourselves performing an action in the absence of physical practice and conditioning, we are said to be using imagery. The more specific strategy of motivational imagery encompasses thoughts of 100% positivity- e.g., picturing whipping that slap-shot into the left side of the goal, hitting that ground ball past the second baseman, making that foul shot with two minutes left in the fourth quarter. Motivational imagery was applied to amplify mental toughness, help maintain concentration, nurture a positive attitude, and goal setting (imagining being fully recovered). Imagery during rehabilitation was concluded to aid the healing experience and accelerate the recovery time of injured athletes.

Correspondingly, Evans et al. (2006), used imagery at three phases during an athlete's rehabilitation - early, mid, and late. These athletes primarily used cognitive, healing, and pain management imagery. Cognitive specific imagery, which involved the repetition of specific performance skills, was used prominently to enhance self-confidence. In the later phases, healing and pain management imagery was used to advance healing and deal with pain. The study provided support for the effect of a number of variables on an athlete's responses to injury, proposed by Weise-Bjornstal et al. (1998) an integrated model of response. According to the model, pre-injury factors (e.g., personality, a history of stressors, coping resources) (Williams & Andersen, 1998), as well as both personal and situational factors influence an athlete's mindset facing a sport injury.

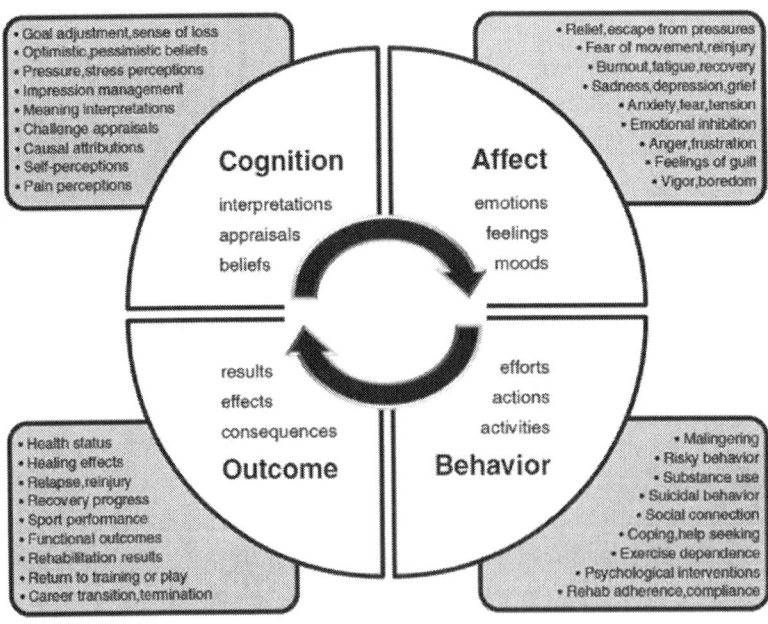

Fig. 1. Biopsychosocial model of post-sport injury response and recovery (Reprinted by Wiese-Bjornstal, 2010).

The model illustrates these "thoughts" of sport-related injuries then influence both emotional and behavioral responses in a reciprocal and ongoing process to, ultimately, impact (positively or negatively) physical and psychological recovery outcomes (3) *The Handy Tool of Imagery During Injury Rehabilitation.*

It becomes apparent, fears of re-injury can lead to an overprotective tendency by athletes which unwittingly can lead to the exact opposite outcome. As an athlete "braces" her muscles in order to prevent re-injury, the tightening of the muscle group prevents the athlete from moving fluidly. Movements are no longer smooth. The restricted motion can lead to awkward movements, off-balance maneuvers, evolving in a body fighting against itself. The unintended consequences of the self-preservation mindset unfortunately place the athlete at risk of re-injuring herself.

Excessive injuries and surgeries can lead to an absolute fear and dreaded experiencing residual pain, fears of lost function, and worse, Post-traumatic Stress Disorder (PTSD). Athletes state they are experiencing intrusive thoughts of the worst outcome possible. The ongoing experience of pain can lead to the avoidance of rehab due to the level of discomfort. Some athletes have told me they experience nightmares that awaken them with visions of the horrifying injury as though they were back at the exact moment of the occurrence. For these athletes, their fears might lead to avoiding rehab and their sport. Slow and steady is recommended by many trainers and physical therapists to quiet their fears. Quite often, the recovery needs to use a multi-modal approach, a team approach that has the athlete, orthopedic surgeon, rehab specialist, sport psychologist, even family members all working together as a collaborative team.

Many athletes from every skill level (middle and high school, college and pros) have shared with me their experience of intrusive, wake-inducing dreams. When an athlete's identity was associated with their athletic performance, they might experience dreams/nightmares of negative future. Therefore, when they suffer a major injury, not only are they physically injured but they are injured psychologically as well. Fears of a lost future are suddenly challenged. Hope becomes threatened and the vision of life is assaulted due to the physical injury. Therapy often provides the perfect forum to vent and release these worries, fears and concerns. If fear-based dreams keep waking them throughout the night, it is wise spending time discussing their fears and fully processing through their concerns. Finding a safe and supportive therapist to discuss any and all concerns can be a vital step towards working through arousing dreams. Once the athletes have released the emotions, they will find the intrusive dreams begin to dissipate. Investing wisely in athletes can prevent dangerous and adverse impacts physically and mentally.

Signs of Poor Adjustment to Injury

Monitoring for poor adjustment to injury could include the following symptoms (Klenk, C., 2006, ACSM, 2006, Rodriguez, C, 2005),

- Denial (considers the injury to be no big deal)

- Dwelling on minor physical complaints

- Exaggerating, bragging about accomplishments

- Fatalistic thinking (whatever I do, things are not going to improve)

- Feelings of anger and confusion

- Obsession with the question of when to return to sport

- Rapid mood swings

- Withdrawal from significant others

Review statistics of youth injury

Just to reiterate, athletes are at risk of getting injured.

Many people ask about the frequency injuries take place in youth sports. Following are the latest findings from the U.S. Center for Disease Control (CDC). Youth Sports Injuries Statistics (http://www.stopsportsinjuries.org/media/statistics.aspx) which revealed participation in organized sports is on the rise. Nearly 30 million children and adolescents participate in youth sports in the United States. This increase has led to other startling statistics about injuries among America's young athletes:

   o   High school athletes account for an estimated 2 million injuries and 500,000 doctor visits and 30,000 hospitalizations each year

(Powell, J.S & Barber Foss, K.D., 1999). Injuries in sport are a fact. The amazing reality is the frequency by which they occur.

o   More than 3.5 million kids under age 14 receive medical treatment for sports injuries each year (Powell, J.S & Barber Foss, K.D., 1999). Under-developed physical structure, developing coordination, and limited interpersonal teamwork lead to unintended injuries.

o   Children ages 5 to 14 account for nearly 40 percent of all sports-related injuries treated in hospitals. On average, the rate and severity of injury increases with a child's age (Preserving the Future of Sport: From Prevention to Treatment of Youth Overuse Sports Injuries., AOSSM 2009).   As mentioned above, under-developed physical structures lead to sports related injuries requiring hospitalization. As the athletes ages, her injuries continue. Athletes generating greater physical contact, leads to more dramatic consequences.

o   Overuse injuries are responsible for nearly half of all sports injuries to middle and high school students (Safe Kids USA Campaign Web site. 2009).   The main reason this occurs is youth sports specialization. There was a time when a child participated in several sports. The most athletic player could excel in many sports. Now a player is encouraged to select one sport and spend his time and resources perfecting that sport. Unfortunately, an athlete specializing in a single sport might experience overuse injuries. Additionally, using poor form or doing rotational motions beyond his ability level will contribute to overuse injuries. Since 2000 there has been a fivefold increase in the number of serious shoulder and elbow injuries among youth baseball and softball players (Preserving the Future of Sport: From Prevention to Treatment of Youth Overuse Sports Injuries. AOSSM 2009).

o   Although 62 percent of organized sports-related injuries occur during practice, one-third of parents do not have their children take the same safety precautions at practice as they would during a game (Safe Kids USA Campaign Web site. 2009).

o   Injuries associated with participation in sports and recreational activities account for 21 percent of all traumatic brain injuries among children in the United States (Preserving the Future of Sport: From Prevention to Treatment of Youth Overuse Sports Injuries. AOSSM 2009). This fact needs to be addressed by long-term research to discover the association between early childhood sports related head trauma and later neurological consequences. According to the CDC, more than half of all sports injuries in children are preventable.

o   By age 13, 70 percent of kids drop out of youth sports. The top three reasons: the attitude of adults, coaches and parents (Safe Kids USA Campaign Web site. 2009). 1) Negative adults surrounding them in their sport of choice. 2) Coaches who are hyper-reactive, emotionally castrating the athlete, or 3) Misguided over-involved, judgmental parents. Think about this fact: the top three reasons youth athletes stop playing sports is because of the adults surrounding them. (Not to make too much of a point out of this but if you are one of these three listed you might want to take into consideration the feedback that you have received and begin to personally address your style before you devastate a young athlete before they ever reach their potential.)

o   Among athletes ages 5 to 14, 28 percent of football players, 25 percent of baseball players, 22 percent of soccer players, 15 percent of basketball players, and 12 percent of softball players were injured while playing their sport (Preserving the Future of Sport: From Prevention to Treatment of Youth Overuse Sports Injuries. AOSSM 2009).

Take Away for Step Twelve:

I learned many valuable lessons from my patients at Johns Hopkins. Anyone suffering a major loss in functioning experiences a psychological impact. Any athlete that focused on what she could no longer do, tended to become depressed. However, any individual who focused on what they could do, tended to be more satisfied with her life. I have found that this same philosophy applies to an athlete that is recovering from an injury. If she focuses on the fact that she is not playing, she tends to be depressed. If she focus on using this rehab time to achieve better fitness than she had pre-injury, she is more likely to be optimistic.

The athlete should use the time to be active in rehab and push herself by attaining the four-step protocol of being 1) Stronger, 2) Faster, 3) More Flexible and 4) Full Anticipation of Returning to Competition. This breeds a positive motivation to an athlete's recovery.

Also, during an athlete's rehab, she could be productive by:

1) learning and developing better tactical strategies.

2) studying opponents and determine their weaknesses.

3) watching other exceptional athletes and learn from their tactics.

4) visualizing to develop greater mind-body linkages.

5) improving her technique and skills by visualizing the proper form during rehab, so upon returning to the competitive field he is better than before his injury. Being active not passive during rehab is the best advice I can give!

Step Thirteen: Avoid These Roadblocks

Outline

1. Superstitions
2. The Entitled Athlete: You're All That and a Bag-of-Chips
3. Eating Disorders and Athletes
4. Celebrate Safely: Don't get injured celebrating
5. Sabotaging yourself and your team: Legal or Illegal
6. Maintaining Humility: Act like you've been here before
7. Olympic-itis

Roadblock One: Superstitions

An athlete I coached said, "We are on a winning streak so we decided not to shave our beards while we continue to win." Another athlete that I worked with wore his girlfriend's underwear as he believed it magically brought him good luck.

Everyone is familiar with the superstitions, Beware of Friday the 13th, don't walk under a ladder, don't let a black cat cross your path, don't break a mirror or open an umbrella indoors. In reality, it's probably the rare professional athlete that does not have a superstitious ritual.

Superstitions apply to athletes and fans alike. Rabbits foot, repeating specific chants, wearing specific clothing, all believed to provide some advantage to the athletic endeavor. In a recent movie, Silver Playbook, Robert DeNiro's character believed in order to increase his favorite football team's chance of victory, numerous specific actions, steps and behaviors had to be followed exactly. If there were diversions from these beliefs not only did he fall apart, but his beloved sports team would suffer the consequence of losing to their opponent.

Hall of Fame inductee, one of the great second baseman in Major League Baseball by the name of Joe Morgan, excelled in fielding and hitting and had a unique batting routine. Joe repetitively displayed an elbow twitch. It was said that when Joe felt uncomfortable or not ready, he would snap his elbow down an odd number of times. When he was ready he would snap his elbow down an even number of times.

Since an elite athlete must perform his sport at the highest level and on a consistent basis, many employ any form of repetitive behaviors/superstitions in order to gain an edge he believes magically making behavior more on target and eventually more successful. The superstition occurs when an athlete experiences some success or failure to which they attribute the repetitive behavior.

Let's not lose sight of the difference between a routine and a superstition. A routine gives a sense of comfort or a home court advantage regardless of where competing. A specific bedtime, bringing fluids, bananas and power bars to a competitive match to replenish fluids and refuel is a wise routine. A superstition is a ritual that when it doesn't occur, the athlete may experience distress. A sense of panic and dread appears if the ritual is not followed to the letter.

Nomar Garciaparra use to display a peculiar re-tightening of his batting glove in-between every pitch. This compulsive behavior provided him with a sense of control, comfort and predictability. Big Pappi wasn't purposefully trying to be gross when he spat into his batting glove prior to stepping into the batter's box. His repetitive behavior or superstition, was his physical prompt to stay focused and ready for the 95mph projectile heading his way.

To believe some power outside of us is specifically invested in our positive outcome is primitive. After a victory, you will always find an athlete who thanks God for the outcome. To this date, I am still waiting for a reporter to go into the losing team's locker room and interview a dejected player with the question, "Why has God forsaken you? Apparently, you did not pray enough? Clearly, God prefers the others more than you."

Superstitions develop because of the process called conditioning. Not the conditioning associated with running sprints but rather associating one event with another event. The classic study by Pavlov (Pavlov, I. P. (1928) in which he brought food to a dog, and the dog would salivate. Food is the trigger (Unconditioned Stimulus). Salivating is the normal reaction (Unconditioned Response). Then he paired the introduction of food along with the sound of a bell. The bell becomes conditioned/associated with the presentation of the food and the expected response of salivating occurs. Interestingly, when you remove the food and only ring the bell the dog continues the salivating reaction (Conditioned Response). You are a living, breathing animal, a person. And yes, you react in similar manner as a dog. The association with some unrelated behavior, clothing, or chant becomes tied to the potential outcome.

You might have seen a recent BMW X1 commercial where four men are about to drive to the big game. They go through a checklist of magical superstitions, supposed to help their team win (eg; rabbit's foot, lucky socks). One guy switches to the driver's seat because that's what they did when their team won, but the driver refuses to switch. The frustrated man standing outside of the vehicle yelling, "Ok, we gonna lose."

Most sports fans have a friend who keeps wearing his "Rally Cap". For the less informed sports fan that is when a fan wears an inside-out Baseball cap (see picture below). He either saw someone else engage in this behavior or was told by a friend to "Put on your Rally Cap. It's comeback time in the bottom of the 9th Inning."

People don't like to feel powerless. Superstitions give them a magical sense of control. Just like worry is an illusion of control over situations we don't have any control, superstitions provide us with a belief that in some small way we influence the universe and therefore we can impact our favorite team's performance.

One collegiate Baseball player who I coached was struggling in the outfield. His coaches were surprised at how slow he reacted to balls hit in his direction. It turned out that he developed a "Joe Morgan" type of superstition which was displayed by eye-blinking. If he felt ready for the next play he would blink once/odd number. If he didn't feel ready he would blink a second time/even number. The main problem is that blinking is also an involuntary behavior. So, when he was ready he would purposefully blink once and then unfortunately his eyes would need to be refreshed and he would involuntarily blink a second time. Do you see the dilemma? He would blink purposefully once and then involuntarily blink a second time. So, what would you have to do if you were ready but now blinked a second/even amount? You would of course teach yourself to blink a third time/odd amount to be ready. And so went the cycle. His coach videotaped him one game and you could see this repetitive, compulsive, superstitious behavior of blinking. Once, we began to address his irrational belief system and accept that his state of mind (readiness) was not dependent upon an external or behavioral act, he was able to let go of this repetitive, self-created superstition.

Jason Terry of the Dallas Mavericks began the practice of wearing team shorts the night before a game. In college at Arizona he wore his team's shorts. As a Maverick, he began wearing the shorts of his opponents. Every night before a game, Jason would wear a pair of opposing team shorts in a ritualistic manner. He also wore five pairs of knee-high socks during every game. Not five individual pairs throughout the game, but five pairs at one time in order to feel comfortable.

Everyone has seen Baseball players superstitiously step over the painted white lines. In some way the athlete feels he is magically protecting his mother from the unfortunate medical consequence of a broken back.

Bruce Gardiner of the Ottawa Senators use to dunk his hockey stick in the toilet. Based on the advice of one of his teammates on how to get out of a scoring slump, he implemented this strategy and miraculously the slump ended. He would revisit this superstition whenever he felt that he needed to end a slump.

I have worked with race car drivers and they all avoid bringing peanuts (still in the shell) to the race course. Each one shared they were taught this superstition from one of their mentors.

The winningest female pro volleyball player in the history of the AVP is Kerri Walsh. She kicks the sand with her left foot before every point. This habit has become so engrained that it is second nature. If you were the winningest female pro volleyball player in history, it would certainly lead you to continue doing whatever it is your doing.

Perry and Kristi (2008) designed a study to test the ideas of Gmelch (1974), a study involving baseball superstitions. In it he hypothesized the amount of superstitious behavior was dependent on the level of difficulty and uncertainty of the task. Perry and Kristi (2008) hypothesized that participants (26 male and 14 female undergraduate students) would show more superstitious behavior when completing a difficult golf-putting task as compared to an easier putting task. Golfing skill was not required for participation and each participant was given $5 and the chance to win $50 for making the most putts. Each participant used 4 colored balls to complete 20 easy putts from 3 feet, and 20 difficult putts from 9 feet. Superstitious behavior was defined as choosing the same color ball after making a putt. The participants were told they were being assessed on how one's attitude positively or negatively affected their putting ability. Results showed there was no significant difference between the difficult and easy conditions for all participants combined, however, low skill participants were more superstitious in the easy putting task than the difficult putting task, and high skill participants were more superstitious in the difficult putting task than the easy putting task (Perry and Kristi, 2008). If you think about Perry and Kristi's findings, non-skilled individuals would certainly not expect to perform well on the more advance tasks. Therefore, they have no perceived pressure. However, tasks requiring basic skills the non-skilled athlete would perceive this situation as a source of stress and at this point the less skilled person would begin to display a superstition. The opposite was noted the more skilled individuals felt extremely confident and comfortable with the basic tasks. Yet when exposed to the more challenged task their expectations increased and they displayed a superstition to provide them with a sense of control to increase their performance. In essence the player is saying, "I'll use the 'good' ball."

In a study by Bleak and Frederick (1998) superstition use in three, NCAA, Division 1 collegiate teams were examined. Athletes (87 men and 20 women) on football, gymnastics, and track teams were given a survey measuring use of superstitious rituals and their perceived effectiveness, importance of sport success, sport anxiety, locus of control and religiosity. Results indicated that gymnasts reported more superstitious behaviors than did football or track athletes. This was supported by previous research indicating the focus and importance placed on each individual performance in gymnastics leads to more rituals being used to increase one's chance of success (Bleak & Frederick, 1998). Although commonalties existed in superstitious rituals across sport, results indicated that each sport also had rituals specific to it. Attire and prayer were the main focus in football rituals. Gymnasts also emphasized clothing rituals, however, team rituals and pregame food rituals were also very important to these athletes. Track athletes also had clothing rituals, but they were the only athletes that mentioned lucky items of clothing or lucky markings on shoes. This study also looked at ritual effectiveness which was rated on a five-point scale (3=neutral, 1=low effectiveness, and 5=high effectiveness). Survey results indicated that even the most widely used rituals vary in their perceived effectiveness from a low score of 2.64 to a high score of 4.43. Prayer rituals had the highest effectiveness scores across all groups, whereas clothing rituals had the lowest effectiveness scores across groups. These results indicate it is not ritual or superstition that indicates popularity of a superstition or ritual (Bleak & Frederick, 1998). The results of this study also suggest that religiosity, sense of personal control, importance of success and anxiety do not contribute meaningfully to total level of superstitious rituals. Overall, it appears superstitious behaviors are much more personalized in nature, including what sport the individual plays and the effectiveness of the ritual. Athletes may develop rituals that correspond with their personalities and individual belief systems (Bleak & Frederick, 1998).

You might be asking, "So what's the big deal?" If you develop a pattern that provides you a sense of comfort or confidence, there is probably nothing wrong with that behavior. Superstitions are more entertaining when you discover the crazy range that fans and athletes create in order to increase their belief that this behavior will somehow influence the outcome. Clearly when a behavior becomes compulsive, or a superstition has intensified an intervention might be needed.

Superstitions are a form of magical thinking. The individual is ascribing their athletic performance or the eventual outcomes of their sport with magical association. If an athlete's behavior doesn't adversely impact himself or others, and if he isn't freaking out when his superstition is prevented, it's all good. Have at it and may your team succeed because of put your rally-cap on.

Roadblock Two: The Entitled Athlete

I coached a golfer who had the potential to be the best in his state. His name was well established in local sports pages and he had become a big fish in a small pond. His minor fame had begun to unduly influence those around him. Not only were peers treating him with high regard but his teachers were taken with his celebrity status. The constant praise and privileges afforded him became so routine he began to think that the rules didn't apply to him. Every day he arrived late to school, but his instructor never reported him being late. He felt rules didn't apply to him. At our first meeting together I told him I had read numerous articles relating his successes but I had also heard from his golf coach he never applied himself because his natural talents were leading him to victory. I told him that I thought, "He was a dime-a-dozen" and that his first period teacher was doing him a disservice by not holding him accountable to the rules. I told him he possessed tremendous potential but due to his lack of diligence he might never reach it. If looks could kill, I'd be dead right now. He claimed that he had never been spoken to with such a dismissive attitude. Prior to our meeting, he had, "drank his own Kool-Aid" and believed all of the write ups about how amazing he was. He felt that he was "All that and a Bag-of-Chips." After reflecting on my feedback, for the first time in his life, he began to apply himself and live up to his potential.

Athletes who are taught at an early age rules don't apply to them begin to develop a grandiose sense of self. This is a slippery slope unwitting peers and adults feed into. The young athlete that is treated "special" will begin to believe that he is "special" and not be required to follow normal age appropriate expectations.

At a young age some individuals who are treated preferentially and don't have to follow rules develop the belief system that rules don't apply to them. They are special because of the unique advantages they have received from teachers, bosses and friends.

Most people develop moral decision-making abilities. They make up their minds based upon the reality that a behavior/choice/action is either good or bad, right or wrong. However, there is another group who don't experience the same consequences as the rest of humanity. These individuals develop, "Consequence Driven" abilities. They make up their minds based upon two questions 1) What are the odds that I am going to be caught? 2) Will the consequences be great enough that I should care? If I speed, what are the odds that I will get caught by a police radar? If I fudge a few numbers on my taxes, what are the odds that I will get caught? Will the consequences be great enough that I should care? In Football, if I get caught with PEDs I will get suspended for only a few games? In Baseball if I get caught using PEDs I get a major suspension.

This type of individual is always testing the limits and only considers how a rule does not apply to him. While a rule follower understands a behavior is either good or bad, right or wrong. They don't play out elaborate mental gymnastics that talk them into bad decisions, or have poor impulse control that puts them in harm's way.

I encourage athletes that play on teams to understand how the intricate web of personalities and skill sets are required to dominate. However, an athlete who thinks he is the most important, the best, or above the necessity to play as a teammate turns into a liability for the team. In today's climate of grab-as-much-money-as-you-can, all too often players forget the unity required to achieve greatness in team sports. The player who believes he is more important than the team begins to destroy the team from within. Usually teams defend themselves from opponents that compete against them, but in this case the opponent is among them. These players are referred to as, "Cancer." They cause great teams to fall apart because they don't fight for the best interest of the team, but instead for their own needs.

A young athlete said at the beginning of one of our sessions, "Dr. Shinitzky, it's really hard to make the right choice." I agreed with him, "Yes, it is hard to make the right choice when the wrong choices are still 'acceptable' options." Some athletes become too grandiose and believe once they have achieved greatness they no longer need any coaching. They ignore, trivialize and minimize the wisdom of their coaches. "It is easier to build strong children than to repair broken men." Frederick Douglass. We are all aware of the old adage, "An ounce of prevention is better than a pound of cure." Invest upfront rather than waiting for the consequences.

In college, some players who earn a scholarship walk around campus like the "BMOC", Big Man on Campus, with the inclusion of the word, Man, which implies maturity. In reality, these chest pounding, brash, ego-inflated athletes have bought into the hype that valued skills allot them special status (entitled).

Some nationally ranked, world-class and professional athletes have received special treatment for years from their families, teachers, fans and the legal system. They become their own worst enemy by creating self-imposed barriers (illegal, selfish, disrespectful or aggressive behaviors) by not accepting feedback, coaching or helpful advice.

Being your best is a life-long pursuit. You are never too good, too successful or too accomplished not to continue developing, improving and perfecting your craft. Take a moment and think of the greatest athletes. Have the athletes ever gone through a period of time in which they struggled? Did they develop any new skill sets to make them more competitive, to address any weakness in their game or retool their mind and body in order to compete over the years? To believe they have learned all they can learn is a myth, a delusion, a roadblock. Achieving success at one level is merely a stepping stone for greater and future successes.

Nick Saban, who is arguably one of the greatest college coaches of all time, discussed how many of today's athletes have the illusion of having many choices. "Actually, they are misguided. When an athlete thinks he has many choices he is at risk of making bad choices." Coach Saban feels, "Too many of today's players are not accustomed to being told 'No'. When an athlete is treated to feel excessively special by their parents, community or school, we do them a disservice."

When an athlete violates a rule he needs to learn there are consequences. Grandiose mindsets invariably leads an athlete to believe he doesn't have to listen to critical feedback. Since he excelled in the athletic arena he has felt that he doesn't need to reflect on his behavior. He externalizes personal responsibility and blames his circumstances on everything and anything besides himself. After benching and then sending the player to the locker room for intolerable behavior during a football game, Coach Mike Singletary in the postgame interview called out his player for selfish behaviors. Coach Singletary stated, "Cannot play with 'em. Cannot coach with 'em. Cannot win with 'em. Can't do it!"

Since you are the one person you can control, start by looking at yourself. No matter how good you think you are, there is always room for improvement. Consider the feedback from coaches before you simply reject their comments.

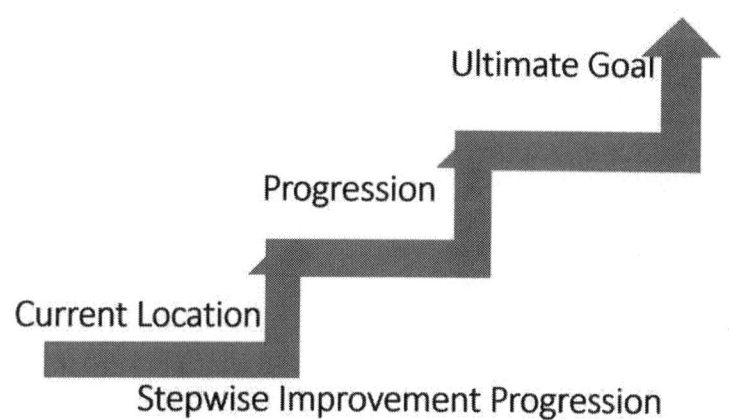

If you think all of feedback is beneath you, you will never advance to your ultimate level of athletic achievement.

I came across a wonderful picture that perfectly depicts the classic rephrase there is no "I" in Team. This picture and description truly expresses this point.

THERE IT IS
THE 'I' IN TEAM
HIDDEN IN THE 'A' HOLE.

Humorous as this picture might be, it is extremely accurate.

Individuals that place themselves above the team become a distraction. When a star athlete behaves like an impetuous child he draws the attention of other players on the team and throw them off their game. More times than not the selfish athlete needs to be removed from the team in order to save the team. This leads to a bizarre mathematical concept, "Addition through subtraction." As I say to my athletes, "Sometimes the best thing to do when you are in a dysfunctional relationship, is not be in it." By getting rid of the negative you improve the overall team. Hence, addition through subtraction.

A few other examples of the entitled athlete:

- There was a major league baseball player who was kicked off the Tampa Bay Rays for numerous reasons. While in New York he made disparaging comments to a person who was Jewish which lead to him being kicked off the team. When a team is willing to pick up an athlete who has a habitual pattern of negative behaviors, they reinforce the negative behaviors.
- A NFL star was convicted of double murder. Somehow he thought that he would get away with this action. He had a history of assault while in college. His head coach could have released him but instead helped keep him on the team. As a professional, his behavior escalated to murder.

When schools and teams value the importance of winning a championship at the expense of enforcing appropriate logical consequences it is bound to lead the athlete down to tragic consequences. The schools and society could have nipped this in the bud at an earlier stage. What consequences were not imposed by his coach or the university? Does no-action do the athlete any good by repeatedly rescuing him? Is the NCAA or NFL valuing winning a championship over the growth and development of young athletes? Would this terrible situation have occurred if he was stopped in high school or college? What would have happened if someone would have intervened earlier?

- An NCAA Division One football player was attending his school on a sports scholarship. Needless to say, it was surprising he graduated high school let alone that he was accepted into one of the top football powerhouses in the nation since he did not attain the minimum standards for admission. One day he was administered a random drug test which proved positive for an illegal drug. He was told the school policy was, "Three strikes and you're out." At this point, he was suspended from the team and offered assistance to address behavior. He was told he would need to take another "random" drug test in 3-4 weeks. Again, the results were positive for the same illegal drug. His suspension was turned into a potential release from the school if he continued. He was again told that he would need to take another "random" drug test in 4 weeks and reminded of the school "Three-Strike" policy. He was told he would be dropped from the program if he failed the drug test and would lose his sports scholarship. He was referred to me before the results were obtained. I asked him what the results were going to show. He replied without hesitation, "Positive." I asked him for his reasoning in light of what the potential ramifications were going to be. He shared, "It's a stupid law and a dumb policy." We discussed how he allowed himself to be talked into a bad choice and out of a good decision. He felt that he was above the law and that no consequences would truly occur. His sense of entitlement ended his future in sports because he was never accepted to any colleges or professional teams.

Often, Commissioners of professional associations and coaches of Olympians say to me when referring an athlete, "Doc, I don't want you to make him a better athlete, I want you to make him a better person." In making someone a better person we invariably make them a better athlete.

All too often, elite athletes have been provided "special" treatment. This systemic problem is a societal issue that should be addressed. Parents need to be aware of the lessons they are teaching their children. Most of all, it is extremely important to proactively help young adults keep their successes in perspective and foster the development of a healthy sense of self.

Roadblock Three: Eating Disorders and Athletes

Eating Disorders are running rampant in the US as we are the most obese industrialized country in the world. Type II Diabetes has become common among today's youth. Our media projects an unrealistic image of what beautiful looks like. These recurring commercial messages adversely impact people from all walks of life.

Team doctors, nutritionists and trainers consistently point to the importance of maintaining good health in order to reach your greatest potential. Health must come first. Many athletes struggle with the problems associated with their diet, desperately want to avoid talking about this subject. This roadblock can have catastrophic consequences for an athlete.

Over the years I have found the need to provide educational presentations not only to the athletes and coaches, but also the parents, trainers, team physicians, Human Resource personnel, commissioners and owners. This problem needs to be addressed both from the bottom up (athletes upward) as well as from the top down (owners down). There are great online resources that offer exceptional information. The National Eating Disorder Association (NEDA) website, www.NationalEatingDisorder.org is one such site. Following are facts you should be aware of:

- One-third of all female athletes report attitudes and symptoms placing them at risk for anorexia nervosa. Three risk factors for developing a problem with food include (Williamson, et. al. 1995).
- Social factors that emphasize appearance or have weight requirements (Gymnastics, diving, bodybuilding or wrestling)
- Performance anxiety
- Negative self-appraisal
  - The phrase Female Athlete Triad is "disordered eating." This is not a diagnosis, but a pattern. The style, amount, pattern of eating is problematic or disordered. These athletes often have injuries, lose time from solo or team sports, and lose their periods. Additionally, many mistakenly view their unhealthy medical conditions as "normal" yet they are not normal. The International Olympic Committee has published a manual with recommendations titled, Managing the Female Athlete Triad (http://multimedia.olympic.org/pdf/en_report_517.pdf). The American College of Sports Medicine has a document titled, The Female Athlete Triad Position Stand

(www.acsm.com).   Clearly the focus needs to be on health, both physical and mental and to internalize that Good Nutrition = Health = Performance.

- There are other risk factors for athletes (coaches, trainers, parents, team physicians, HR personnel, owners and commissioners) that need to be addressed regarding diet, nutrition and healthy decision-making. Certain sports are fraught with disordered eating possibilities:
  a) Sports that emphasize the athletes' appearance create a risky atmosphere (e.g.; gymnastics, diving or bodybuilding).
  b) Sports that have weight requirements place the athlete in a risk category. An example of this would be a wrestler. In order to make the acceptable weight for competition, he uses a rubber suit, spits, sweat box and diuretics to lose as much pre-weight as possible.
  c) Sports that focus on the individual athlete rather than on the team (e.g.; gymnastics, running, figure skating, and diving).
  d) Sports that require endurance (track and field, running and swimming).
  e) Athletes that believe lower body weight improves performance.

f) Athletes that have been training for sports since childhood and willing to do anything to win.

g) Athletes with low self-esteem, a perfectionistic tendency or a pre-occupation with body-image are also at risk of developing disordered eating. (Bachner-Melman, R., Zohar, A, Ebstein, R, et.al. 2006. How Anorexic-like are the Symptom and Personality Profiles of Aesthetic Athletes? Medicine & Science in Sports & Exercise 38 No 4. 628-636.).

h) Zucker et. al (1999) found athletes that participated in sports with judging (gymnastics) versus refereed (basketball) were at-risk.

i) Several researchers found athletes that participate in sports emphasizing leanness for performance success (runners, figure skaters, gymnasts and cheerleaders) (Hausenblas, & Carron, 1999, Klock & DeSouza, 1995, Hulley & Hill, 2001; Lundholm & Littrell, 1986; Szymanski & Chrisler,1990; Reel & Gill, 1996).

j) Lastly, athletes whose sport required weigh-in classification experienced an increase in disordered eating (bodybuilders, boxers) (Blouin & Goldfield, 1995; Goldfield, Harper, & Blouin, 1998).

Family history of eating disorder or family abuse were also at-risk of developing this pattern.

Not surprisingly, coaches that focus on outcomes/success rather than on the process or on the person create an unhealthy situation.

When an athlete is physically active he most definitely needs to refuel his engine. The ability to maintain his competitive weight is vital for many sports, but this need dramatically changes when his competitive life ceases. The simple equation of caloric intake vs. calories burned off needs to adjust once the physical demands change. No longer is the 4,000-10,000 calorie/day lifestyle appropriate. He needs to question and challenge his pre-existing relationship with food. For some athletes, this is the beginning of the end. I am not writing this for a dramatic effect but as a reality check. Disordered eating leads to obesity, joint damage, metabolic changes, and a myriad of other medical consequences which can contribute to a shortened life span. Though discussing how and what he might eat is a topic he would prefer to avoid, it remains one of the roadblocks that needs to be addressed!

Roadblock Four: Don't get injured celebrating

Clearly athletic endeavors can lead to an untimely injury. One of the NFL players often commented football is "Controlled violence." One study reported approximately 2 million physical injuries and nearly 500,000 medical visits and 30,000 inpatient hospitalizations occur in sport related activity on an annual basis. (Powell, JS and Barber Foss, KD, 1999. Injury Patterns in Selected High School Sports: A Review of the 1995-1997 Seasons. J Athl Train. 34: 277-84.). The sad reality is the majority of athletes do not retire by their own choice. Many professional athletes end up living in quiet obscurity. Sadly, all-too-often, a player is injured and is not able to regain his top performance level. He leaves his sport due to an injury well before his career was to end.

Winning championships is a feat that most competitors will never experience. Standing on the podium at a major athletic event is a privilege only for a few. Rejoicing in the revelry of triumph and wearing the championship ring, raising the trophy or wearing the laurels after successfully completing a competitive season is what dreams are made of. As athletes are often exalted on national sports television shows. But we need to encourage them to celebrate responsibly.

Imagine an elite athlete has competed at the highest level only to be sidelined not by his opponent, but by his very own celebration injury, a personal high-five, head-bump, jumping for joy, etc.

Some notable celebratory injuries include;

In 2012, MLB player Aubrey Huff sprained his knee when attempting to jump over the dugout railing to join his team on the field were celebrating the perfect game pitched by Matt Cain.

Imagine hitting the winning grand slam to send your major league baseball team to victory only to break your leg when jumping on home plate. Not the picture perfect ending to a life-long dream. That's exactly what happened to Kendrys Morals in 2012.

Nowadays, a pie in the face is the tradition for congratulating a teammate in baseball for helping the team achieve victory. Chris Coghlan of the Florida Marlins was the proud provider of the pie in the face of teammate Wes Helms, only to tear the meniscus in his left knee while performing the pie-in-the-face maneuver.

Celebrating victory at the 2011 French Open Golf tournament has led victors to jump in the lake at the 18th green. Thomas Levet joined the ranks of the self-inflicted injury group by taking a plunge without realizing the lack of water depth and injured his leg in the pursuit of tradition.

Even when you feel safe and have waited to celebrate with friends does not prevent unplanned consequences. A rare athletic accomplishment of winning both the Super-G and Downhill skiing world championships was attained by Lindsey Vonn. This was clearly a reason to let loose and cherish the combination win. However, Lindsey did not realize the dangers of toasting with champagne, and when the bottle broke, Vonn severed the right thumb tendon requiring emergency surgery.

Imagine kicking a football 43 yards during an NFL game. Pretty impressive! Unfortunately, Bill Gramatica in 2001 was so happy when he leaped into the air and fist pump his successful field goal kick. He landed precariously and tore his ACL.

Many athletes have fought through very physically demanding training camps and competitive seasons, only to be out done by their own impulsive celebration. In 1997, Gus Frerotte of the Washington Redskins decided he would head-butt the padded wall beyond the end zone after scoring a touchdown. In this moment of tough-guy behavior, Gus ended up spraining his neck. In this example, the wall won.

In 2007, Ted Ginn, Jr. of the Ohio State Buckeyes ran back the opening kickoff for a touchdown. The Buckeyes were competing to become the #1 team in the nation. Unfortunately, he ended up being injured by one of his own teammates when celebrating this glorious accomplishment in the end zone. I guess his Achilles Heal was his Achilles Heal.

Roadblock Five: Sabotaging yourself and your team

Would an athlete ever voluntarily put himself or his team at risk? Of course not!

Randell played baseball at a Division I University. This horror story could come from any state in the union. Randell's grades had dropped to the point that he was placed on academic probation. Randell had spent his entire life planning and preparing to play baseball at the highest level, and yet he was on the verge of losing his dream. His Guidance Counselor couldn't understand how his grades dropped so precipitously. He was bright and gleaned knowledge from classroom lectures without any difficulty. But it turned out that he was missing most of his classes. Randell had a history in high school of abusing drugs but denied any current illegal behaviors. The team required a drug test which turned out negative. He claimed he was just too tired to wake up and go to class or do his work. He was referred for a full medical assessment. It turned out that Randell was healthy as a "horse." When he was referred to me, we began discussing what the possible contributing factors were to his current situation. Even though Randell was a healthy young man, and not engage in any illegal behaviors, he was staying up all night playing multi-player videogames. He claimed he wasn't doing anything "illegal or wrong." This illogical logic put him in a position to voluntarily put himself and his team at risk. Staying up all night, not doing his work, sleeping through his classes added up to academic suspension. He claimed that he could control his gaming and that his "gaming was not a problem."

Athletes all too often sabotage themselves at an unconscious level by creating their own self-imposed obstacles that interfere with achieving their ultimate goal. On an unconscious level Randell feared that he would fall short of pro expectations and could not deal with the emotional pain of that potential rejection. So to prevent himself from ever experiencing his feared potential rejection, he sabotaged himself by making bad decisions. Once we acknowledged his fears, we addressed the concerns by creating a roadmap of steps to attain his aspirational goals. A more indepth discussion of how and why people sabotage themselves can be found in my first book, Your Mind: An Owner's Manual for a Better Life published by Career Press, 2009.

My discussion point with athletes is not whether something is legal vs. illegal but is it contributing to an adverse situation? Learn this simple phrase, "I know I CAN but SHOULD I?"

When presenting to the University of Michigan Football team many of their athletes expressed their appreciation of the benefits of choosing to attend this university. Several asserted they chose UM because of the education they would receive, others for the networking with alumni beyond the campus, and for the tradition and legacy of the football program. They understood how their behavior both on and off the field of play reflected their commitment to Michigan. These athletes were well aware that bad decisions do not only apply to the issue of legal vs. illegal. They openly discussed healthy decision-making to avoid obstacles to their goals.

Certainly any behavior that violates NCAA rules would be consider unacceptable. However, there are many more behaviors that don't violate any associations, rules or policies that could contribute to adverse outcomes.

Most people have a unique set of skills they employ to talk themselves into bad decisions, and out of good decisions. They provide the mental gymnastics that convince them that all is good despite the potential consequences, feedback and reality.

The array of mental skills frequently used by athletes to continue engaging in negative behaviors include:

Simple Denial – This is when you ask your child who happens to have a mouth full of cookies and chocolate smeared all over their face, "Whose been eating the cookies?" and they reply, "Not me."

Justification – An athlete emphasizes why she feels that she deserves to do this behavior.

Rationalization – An athlete comes up with excuses for his behavior.

Intellectualization – An athlete uses his intelligence to talk himself into bad behaviors by claiming that the majority of people he knows engages in this behavior.

Externalization – An athlete has a pattern of blaming someone else for his behavior.

Compartmentalization – An athlete acknowledges that she has done this behavior a few times in the past, but it is not a pattern.

Minimization – An athlete acknowledges that he has done this behavior but that it is not that bad or inappropriate.

How does an individual athlete or team improve? How do they learn not to sabotage? What do the coaches need to acknowledge? What does each individual athlete need to do in order to progress? The answer, Insight. But, this is only half the battle. Change is the second part of the equation.

What behaviors are counterproductive?

Marijuana in states where it is legal to use. We know there are negative impacts associated with the active ingredient, THC. Short-term memory problems, Amotivational syndrome, Respiratory issues from breathing in burning embers, learning and coordination issues.

There are many negative behaviors which need to be avoided. Several include: violating team rules, school policies, state laws, public intoxication, sexual assaults, or domestic violence.

Often, when I am consulting with an athlete or even discussing his case with his coach or parents, I have to share, "You're obviously a bright individual/athlete but I've got some good news and I've got some bad news. When the athlete or coach asked me what the good news is, I share that the athlete is bright. When asked what the bad news is, I share the athlete is bright. Both are correct. We have the intellectual fire power to talk ourselves into bad and out of good. As long as the bad is considered acceptable, the athlete will struggle with his choices.

A football player grew up in a lower socio-economic community of a major metropolitan city. He had maintained excellent grades throughout high school, took an active role in student government and had a long-standing relationship with his high school sweetheart. He was being recruited to play football from several colleges due to his physical attributes on the gridiron. He told me of a party he and the other recruits were invited to when they visited the university. He was happy to go but confused by the atmosphere. Alcohol and drugs were available, "friendly" young ladies were fawning over him, a few of the adults, alumni and university personnel, cavalierly discussed economic benefits for attending their fine program, subtle conversations about job possibilities for his father or uncle were mentioned, and one local car dealer laughed about the use of a vehicle to get around campus, especially during the cold winter days. He knew that both situations were wrong regardless if it was legal or illegal. When he got home, he made an anonymous report to the NCAA. They complimented him for not feeding into the potential violations, or being seduced by the situation, and not taking the bait. Instead he chose to attend a college that offered fatherly guidance from the coach, an atmosphere that sought to educate student-athletes, and opportunities to associate with young adults.

Roadblock Six: Humility - Act like you've been here before

The goal I encourage all parents to seek with their exceptionally gifted, athletic child is a sense of humility, perspective and gratitude. As one of my football players stated, "My natural physical abilities are God's gift to me. What I do with them is my gift to God." As an athlete strive to be your best. Strive to do your best. Hold yourself up to the highest standard. Volunteer. Reach out to those in need. Help make a difference in the lives of others. Be the shining light through the dark. The important factor is to keep your core values, be gracious and keep life in perspective.

All too often I have watched athletes display excessive celebrations. If an athlete will never have another opportunity to score, in that case, go for it! Party like it's 1999. But if the athlete's position is likely to score again, then let's keep the reaction in perspective. I encourage my athletes to, "Act like you've been here before." Additionally, rather than being penalized for excessive celebrating, merely turn to the official and tell him, "See you soon" or "I'll be back."

I have met many athletes who said when they make their millions they will become a better person. What I tell all of my athletes is that in reality, "Money doesn't make you a better person, it just makes you more of whatever you are." Money will make an ego-centric individual feel more special. A kind-hearted person will be more giving with more money.

To illustrate: One of the football players that I treated thought if he had the biggest house, drove the most expensive cars, hosted the biggest parties and threw money around in his community everyone would respect him. He had always dreamed of becoming an important person in his neighborhood. On one weekend, he cut down all of the beautiful shade trees on his property, even the ones that were required by the Home Owners Association (HOA) and were lining the tree-lined street. He enjoyed having his childhood friends hang out over the weekend and encouraged them to park their vehicles on his front lawn. When he did not receive the key-to-the-city and was told that the plans for his house violated the HOA code and deed restrictions for height and proximity to the sidewalk, he became frustrated and decided he would now purposely violate the rules and limits. He said that he felt "disrespected." His selfishness, grandiose expectations and demanding personality were always there, but only intensified now that he financially and economically was in a grand position in life. When I began coaching him, he shared his disappointment. With his dreams shattered, we discussed the false expectations based upon material wealth. He was truly in a better position in life with financial security and possessions. He was certainly within his rights to do many things that might merely challenge social standards, but there were rules and limits that were within the HOA's right to address, challenge and even take legal action to prevent. Once we got past his initial irritation to social reactions, we began to consider the numerous life challenges he had experienced. When he received an athletic scholarship to college, he did learn that the school had rules, grades and attend practice. He did get into a few fights and was suspended from the team for a short period of time. He blamed the other individuals for "not respecting" him and was tolerated through his graduation. Ultimately, he was "released" by a couple of professional football teams due to his struggles "getting along with his teammates." We discussed that each social and professional community have their own expectations, values and beliefs. As you can imagine we needed to spend a significant amount of time focusing on the topic of "respect." Once we worked through this issue, we began to visualize how his neighborhood was like a new team and how he fit into this new team. We discussed his ideal self-image and what personal areas of growth he wanted to pursue. One thing he wanted more than anything was to make sure young children had a role-model and father-figure that showed them respect. He started a non-profit foundation and partnered with the Police Athletic Leagues regularly visiting the facility, meeting with the neighborhood kids (in both his new community and in his childhood community) and offered lessons from his life. He developed a healthier way of reacting to perceived "disrespect." He propelled himself to become a leader in his community, made a huge difference in the lives of youngsters, and was no longer reacting with defiance to perceived "disrespect." As he said, "Now I am the man I always imagined."

If you consider negative behaviors acceptable you will likely allow yourself to do that behavior. One of the NFL Quarterbacks began celebrating in college after every touchdown by displaying the money sign with his hands. This behavior, though judged poorly by many in the sports world became his calling card. He apparently thought it to be entertaining and acceptable; however, his professional career was short-lived. This behavior has now become a personal foul. There is no need to taunt. There is no need to be grossly rude to your opponent. The goal is to rejoice in the glory of the moment.

The Cubs winning the World Series set off a chain of events equaling the power release from a tectonic shift in the mantel of the planet. As a lifelong Cub fan who has suffered from year to year, the 2016 championship was a celebration to end all celebrations. Five million Cub fans came out to share in the glory finally reaching the promised land. Every year the Cubs began the season tied for First Place. Usually by the second week we had accepted the mantra, "Wait till next year." The good news, fans did not torch cars or loot businesses. None of the players put themselves in harm's way, injured themselves or worse. The celebration was respectful elation, joyous pride and deliciously worth the wait.

An accepted celebration and one that is stylized after winning the Stanley Cup, after players exchange handshakes with their opponents, then hoist the Stanley Cup, skate around the ice and pass the cup to teammates.

Here is a new phenomenon that seems bewildering. Football players attempting to drop the ball just as they cross the goal line into the end zone for a touchdown. Question: How do you determine the winner? The team that scores the most points. So, dropping the football before crossing the goal line into the end zone might be counterintuitive. (www.sbnation.com). This misguided attempt to be "cool" is laughable. Players watched game film of their opponent, practicing and preparing for hours, and now the athlete jeopardizes his team's ability to be victorious. Back in 2009 DeSean Jackson of the Philadelphia Eagles football team famously dropped the ball at the one-yard line. In 2000 Chad Johnson of the Oregon State University football team displayed this brain hiccup when he released the pigskin before crossing the end zone.

Don't think it's just the prima donna offensive players that make this mistake. In 2013 the Denver Bronco's linebacker Danny Trevathan began his celebration one yard short of scoring his touchdown. My alma mater, the University of Iowa, in 2014 displayed the same cavalier fumble by John Lowdermilk as he dropped the ball while prematurely celebrating a pick-six in the Outback Bowl. For those athletes who plan on scoring touchdowns in football or helping your team win in other sports please consider this suggestion. Don't start celebrating too early. Don't showboat as you might become the next star on ESPN's Not Top 10 Plays. Act like you've been there before. Hand the ball to the official and tell them that you will be back.

Character is best described by the following. How you behave when no one is there to watch you. How you behave when alone. You might want to consider the word, Class. Consider your legacy and reputation. Consider how you carry yourself. Treat others in the manner that you would want to be treated. Athletes who display class are always respectful of others.

A past 'Dear Abby' newspaper advice column summarized this point:

What is class?

Class never runs scared. It is sure-footed and confidence in the knowledge that you can meet life head on and handle whatever comes along.

Jacob had it. Esau didn't. Symbolically, we can look to Jacob's wrestling match with the angel. Those who have class have wrestled with their own personal "angel" and won a victory that marks them thereafter.

Class never makes excuses. It takes its lumps and learns from past mistakes.

Class is considerate of others. It knows that good manners is nothing more than a series of petty sacrifices.

Class bespeaks an aristocracy that has nothing to do with ancestors or money. The most affluent blue-blood can be totally without class while the descendant of a Welsh miner may ooze class from every pore.

Class never tries to build itself up by tearing others down. Class is *ALREADY* up and need not strive to look better by making others look worse.

Class can "walk with kings and keep its virtue and talk with crowds and keep the common touch." Everyone is comfortable with the person who has class – because he (she) is comfortable with themselves.

If you have class you don't need anything else. If you don't have it, no matter what else you have – it doesn't make much difference.

Roadblock Seven: Olympic-itis

Olympic-itis is the term describing some athletes who return from the Olympics and no longer feel they need coaching.

"Why is it so difficult for champions to repeat their success?" Success can become an obstacle. When a coach helps develop greatness in a player or the team there becomes an expectation a successful outcome will be easy to attain for any athlete he trains. The path to success or greatness is fraught with many trials and tribulations. Champions are not created based upon a simple equation. One-part coaching + One-part experience = Champion. In the movie Avatar, the high priestess says to the main character, "It is hard to fill a cup which is already full".

Many first-year professionals who happen to be fortunate to play for a team that makes it to the championship game begin their career with the mistaken belief that this will be a common, predictable, annual experience. Later, in retrospect, to discover they might never return to the pinnacle of their sport.

Some athletes who ascend to the zenith of their sport may develop the belief they are now the omnipotent, all-knowing sage, developing the grandiose self-perception they no longer need the coach and wisdom can no longer be passed on to them. I share with all of my athletes, "The day you think that you are all that and a bag of chips is the first day you begin to lose as Number Two will be trying harder."

Many parents of elite athletes become frustrated with the coaching or the program because their child has not yet achieved greatness. These parents have high expectations for their child. They have invested money, time and family resources. They feel the reason their child has not won an Olympic medal or hasn't received Division I college scholarships or competed in their regional championships is the coach's fault and/or the program's lack of commitment to their child. Their misconception is that developing an elite athlete is like baking a cake. Select the proper ingredients (coach, facility) and bake for 30 minutes.

Parents can be a source of Olympic-itis. They often believe if they send their child to the same program that has produced previous champions, their child will be the next big Olympic hopeful. I was asked to meet with the parents of one figure skater who had tremendous potential. She had competed at every level and amassed a plethora of medals and trophies, and her mother fed her a constant flow of praise and unabashed grandiosity. Her mother was so fixated on the belief that if her child attended this training facility, worked under the tutelage of Olympic coaches, they could book their flights to the next winter Olympics. The problem with this logic is that this young lady frequently did not apply herself and regularly complained she had not received the preferential treatment she felt she deserved. After consulting with her coaches who shared with me she did not always apply herself. I met with the young lady and discussed the feedback I had received. Her coaches combined feedback shined light on her blind spots. Eventually, she was able to acknowledge her tendency not to apply herself. Once this bridge was crossed I met with her mother. In the course of an hour her mother went from denial that her "baby" could have possibly been any part of a problem, to considering the chance her child might be a factor. In time, we arrived at the reality that this athlete displayed an inability to accomplish the basic required moves. I shared with the mother that her love for her daughter, uncensored praise, might had the unintended consequence of contributing to an unrealistic expectation. The take home message was mom needed to allow the coaches to coach, and encourage her daughter to apply herself.

Athletes themselves can also suffer from Olympic-itis. One of the swimmers I coached performed better than anticipated in the Worlds, and returned to the United States only to trivialize the recommendations of his coaches. He felt he didn't need to hit the weights like he had before Worlds. He believed he was clearly in phenomenal shape and didn't need to workout as hard as those less talented than he. His misguided overestimation of his physicality would eventually be his downfall because he quickly fell behind the performances of the lesser athletes. When I finally got the request to meet with this self-praising, under-achiever, I needed to re-orient him towards the Post Championship Blues. Many great athletes have come down with this nasty mental condition. After attaining their ultimate dream, they can feel a sense of let-down or become exceedingly over-confident. Either way the Post Championship Blues can turn into Olympic-itis if not addressed in a timely manner. We discussed his accomplishments and sang glory to his honor representing the United States at the Worlds. We also discussed his loss of focus, over-estimation of his abilities and his lack of application which led to his substandard performance in subsequent meets. The singular factor that changed was his ability to apply himself to the levels he achieved prior to earning a spot on the US team. It took him a few sessions to shift from "It's not me, it's my coaches" to "It's me, not my coaches." Once he was willing to acknowledge there was an issue, we were able to approach this unhealthy thoughts and behavioral patterns. In addressing his Olympic-itis he was open to adapting his workout regimens and adjust his mindset towards new and more productive future goals.

US Olympic Figuring Skating Coach Lyndon Johnston has experienced this pattern with both athletes and parents of athletes. "Some parents think if they send their child to an Olympic training facility and have them work with a coach, they expect their child will be a guaranteed lock for making the Olympics" (Johnston, L. 2016). He also has seen Olympic athletes return with the mindset, "I no longer need to receive any coaching since I went to the Olympics" (Johnston, L. 2016).

Take Away for Step Thirteen:

There are many roadblocks that can be proactively addressed. Awareness of each roadblock can help you to create a game plan that fosters the development of healthy decision-making, humility, and maintaining a realistic self-perception. For the athlete who is challenged by superstitions, choking or the Yips, I have offered a range of steps to resolve these patterns. The information provided in this chapter will help you navigate competitive life and avoid roadblocks. Knowledge is power. Knowing what to avoid and how to handle these common issues will help you prevent experiencing greater problems down the road.

Step Fourteen: Being a Parent of a Champion

Outline:

1. **Attitude of Parents**
   Conscientious Neglect: Vicarious Pleasures and Unintended Consequences
2. **The 4 A's of Love**
   Four secrets of a loving parent
3. **Parents Have Three Jobs**
4. **Keys to Be a Supportive Parent**

Attitude of Parents

We all recognize parents who get ejected from a game because of the way they treat their child, yell offensive comments to the rivals, or berate the umpires. Some of these adults spew vial thoughts and feelings during every sporting event they attend. Their lack of emotional control creates a terrible environment for their child or the other kids. All too often I get a request from coaches, mentor or parents who are way too involved and live vicariously through their child's athletic success to offer counseling.

As I share with parents, "The day parents stop teaching their children their neurotic behaviors is the day that I'm out of a job." (Shinitzky) I have to remind the parents, "Your children are the best and the worst of what they are taught." (Shinitzky). Hopefully, this encourages parents to be the best role models they can for their kids. Though they provide love and assistance, they occasionally have unintended consequences from their behaviors.

I have been told by too many parents their job is to be "honest" and "no sugar-coating." Yet, based upon the temperament of their child, they might actually be using the wrong approach and causing irreparable harm to their child.

Parents can have a myriad of thoughts or feelings, but ultimately they have to learn to control their behaviors. If they freak out, cuss, give the silent treatment to their child based upon their perceptions, thoughts and feelings, they are out of bounds.

As former NFL Colts player, Joe Erhmann asserts our society teaches males three lies in determining manhood. 1) Who is the toughest in the sandbox, 2) Who beds the most women, and 3) Who has the biggest bank account (Marx. J, 2004). In a powerful, impactful book about Joe, he describes the painfully, sad family journey he experienced when his eyes were opened wide and discovered far more important lessons in life. Mainly, we need to teach our sons how to love themselves and each other. Which begins with our parents. A child is the best and the worst they are taught. The apple truly does not fall far from the tree.

Also, the impact of hovering parents on a young and developing athlete can be devastating. The young adult might seek to assert his own independence and therefore reject the help, suggestions and advice offered by the over-involved parent. The parent over-reacts, freaks out and the child under-reacts/minimizes.

The 4 A's of Love

Parents ask me what is required to be a good parent. During my training at The Johns Hopkins School of Medicine and Kennedy Krieger Institute I heard about the research conducted by Dr. Leo Kanner and Dr. Hans Aspergers which focused on children and their families (Edwin, D. and Denckla, M, 1995). There were four concepts consistently referenced which increased the bond between child and parent. I refer to these as the 4 A's of Love.

The 4 A's of Love are: Attention, Affection, Acceptance and Approval.

1. Attention – As a parent, I can spend time with you doing things you like. I can spend time with you doing things I like. I can

spend time with you doing things that we discover together and like doing together.

2. Affection – As a parent, I verbally and non-verbally, publicly and privately share with you how much I love you. I say the words and I behave in a loving manner. I do it at home and display this in public.

3. Acceptance – As a parent, I let you know how much I love you for your unique behaviors and characteristics. Knowing that is what make you a unique. I cherish you for being you.

4. Approval – As a parent, I will always be there to help you determine your goals and reach your dreams.

When parents display the 4 A's of Love, the child perceives his relationship with his parents as loving.

Let me share an important point for all parents. There is a difference between Intent and Impact. I was once asked to present at a church. As I approached the church I saw two little kids hopping and skipping across the grass, while their mother yelled at them to be quiet. I respectfully approached the mother and asked her in a perplexed inquiry, "Did I just hear you yell at your kids to be quiet?" Though her intention was to have her two little ones behave in a more socially acceptable manner, the fact is that these kids learned that whoever is the loudest wins, or do as I say not as I do.

If a parent asserts the belief, "Do as I say not as I do" as an acceptable form of parenting, I respond, by laughing hysterically. If you subscribe to the, "Do as I say not as I do" parenting style, please pass along my card to your kids, and I will look forward to treating them as young adults.

In addition, the parents who do not understand the difference between Intent v. Impact have unintended consequences to deal with. A parent using physical means as a way of parenting, teaches physical conflict resolution is acceptable. Might is right. One day your child might display what he has learned and the outcome will be ugly either at home or in society. You might offer hyper-critical and biting reactions to your child when they don't perform well. The unintended consequence might be you teach your child to be apprehensive out of fear of your reaction. He might be hesitant in competition out of fear of your volcanic reaction. You might notice he develops symptoms of anxiety both in sport and in life. Not paying attention to the difference between Intent v. Impact will invariably run directly into unintended consequences.

Now I want to preface this next section, "The following observations do not apply to you." You are an awesome parent who only wants the best for your child. The interesting thing is sometimes we, as the adult, might display certain behaviors which might contribute to his struggles. I never think you willfully would engage in any behavior to purposefully hurt your child.

- I coached a female athlete that was told by her family she needed to be more vocal. She tended to be a wallflower and vanish right in front of people. Though she possessed numerous accomplishments and can compete at the highest levels, she chose silence over conversation. Additionally, she had periods on the golf course when she became overwhelmed by her emotions after a bad shot. Her father, an extraordinarily committed parent had always been driven. During her youth, she remembers times on the golf course that her dad threw his clubs, cursed the gods on high and would have child-like temper tantrums after hitting a bad shot. More recently, after a tournament when her father expressed his perception of her struggles, the daughter in turn also asserted her thoughts of her struggles in this event. Her father became irate claiming she was being disrespectful, punished and gave her the silent treatment. We discussed how she was both the best and the worst of what she had been taught.

She learned at an early age that emotional meltdowns were normal and to be mute in response to her father. The father had never intended to hurt his daughter, but the unintended consequences created the very issues he now wished to stop.

- One of the athletes I treat has a high achieving father. He came to me with a fear that negative, painful events would occur during his sport. Interestingly, he had a history of nervousness in other arenas of his life, but had been able to overcome many of these challenges. On the other hand, his father perceived the world in a clear-cut manner with emotions not playing any part in sports or life. He was driven, focused, singular in commitment and had been his son's coach for years with his own athletic experience providing the knowledge to offer guidance to his son. The father never meant to create a home-life and athletic experience that contributed to his son's anxiety, but throughout the practice and competition his son would be scared and fearful of a negative outcome. He would anticipate his father's reaction of total frustration or the silent treatment. He only meant to help his son become the best athlete possible. When his son expressed his needs, father strongly insisted that was not the way he would do it. For the longest time, his father did not realize he was contributing to his son's anxiety. The great thing about the father was his was willing to address how he added to his son's anxiety.

- A basketball player I coached feared his father's reaction as he sat in the crowd. He would scan the crowd to find his father and watch the emotional frustration bounce off his father. The father was not willing to consider his factor in this equation. I encouraged the father to control or manage his own emotions because he was a distraction to his son. He finally decided he would address his emotional impact on his son.

The image below provides a guidepost for parents to truly appreciate what they should focus on with their child.

Your child's success or lack of success in sports does not indicate what kind of parent you are. But parenting an athlete that is coachable, respectful, a great teammate, mentally tough, resilient and tries his best IS a direct reflection of your parenting.

Whose goal or dream is it?

I coached a baseball player who had achieved much success throughout his high school experience even though he struggled in college. When we met and discussed his challenges (unresolved issues with father), we rekindled his interest in the legal field. Though he was voted the Most Improved Player on his team, he felt he was not playing with his heart.

When we followed up the next summer, he disclosed his inner thoughts and feelings. He had been playing baseball for his father who had previously reached the minor leagues as a young adult. But this athlete's long-term goal was to become a Supreme Court Justice. He was planning on turning down a pro contract to the minor leagues, only after he had taken the Law School Admission Test (LSAT) and had been accepted in one of the most prestigious institutions in the land. Yet he feared his father's disapproval. After he achieved top LSAT scores, the player, father and I met.

The athlete shared with his father how grateful he was for all of the years of playing baseball and for the incredibly close relationship he had with him. But, when the player shared his personal plans his father went ballistic. The father spewed disdain, disbelief and anger towards his son. I said to the father, his son was reluctant to mention this previously because he was afraid his father would flip out. The fact was the son was right, he did lose it. I reminded the father he was melting down with the knowledge his son had been accepted to one of the most elite law schools in the nation.

As a parent, it is your job to raise your child to be independent enough that they no longer need you. That might sound abrupt or sad but it is the job of every parent. That does not mean the young adult will always make the best choices but he is responsible for his choices. Parents are to instill their value system, provide opportunities and love him throughout his development. The parent's mission is to be there for him and give him every advantage possible along with your guidance and beliefs.

The great youth golf teacher, Michael Hebron (Youth Golf, powerpoint online live, 2017) encourages parents and coaches to, "promote without pressure, support without stress, interest without intimidation, and care without confrontation." He offers three comments parents can say to their athlete before competition, "Have fun. Play hard.

I love you" and then after competition, "Did you have fun? I'm proud of you. I love you."

Parents of Elite Athletes have Three Jobs

I have often been asked by coaches to help them out by addressing the parents of their athletes. Too often parents feel it is their job to re-coach their child/athlete. Some parents become loud and obnoxious at practice or during game competition. Occasionally parents has been ejected from the competitive arena by officials because of their over-the-top antics.

In many cases, the parents have never achieved the level of success experienced by their child, yet they feel it necessary to share their lack of wisdom or "vomit" their emotions. One athlete I worked with was referred to me by his Pediatrician with the diagnosis of Post-Traumatic Stress Disorder (PTSD) based upon the years of verbal and physical assaults from his father. The father had an explanation for why he treated his son the way he did. He felt his son was not applying himself, and not living up to his potential. His way of informing his son was to blow a gasket.

As a parent, ask yourself these questions: Has an adult told you to "calm down" or "watch your mouth around kids"? How much better does your child perform when you are not in attendance? Am I the only person who doesn't seem to understand how inappropriate my behavior is? If your answers are yes, you're that overly involved and hyper-reactive parent who may need to be asked to avoid attending a match or tournament.

As a parent, ask yourself, "What are the reasons I want my child to play sports?" How do you handle your child's losses? Do you publicly declare how important you have been in your child's development? Does your child avoid you after a game due to fear of judgment, embarrassment or worse? Are you coaching from the bleachers? Do you ever go "nuts" at a referee? Do you ever taunt your child's opponents?

Some parents are insightful enough to know they have a problem, and wish they could control their reaction while maintaining high standards and expectations for their child. As we Psychologists like to say, 1) insight is the first step. Without insight, there is no identifiable behavior that needs to be addressed, and 2) behavioral change is the second step. If the parent is motivated to acknowledge his behavior and participate in his individual therapy, gaining insight on how his contributes to his child's struggles.

There are four (4) roles during competition: the Parent/Spectator, the Competitor, the Official, and the Coach. If you are a parent/spectator, then accept that role. Be your child's parent offering support and love after competition, is not conditional based on performance.

When signing your child up with an elite program, be aware second-guessing the coach's strategy or technique teaches your child to question the coach and discounts lessons.

I tell parents of elite athletes they have three (3) jobs.

1. Provide unconditional love and support
2. Transportation
3. Write a check

Ten Keys to Being a Supportive Parent

Remember as a parent you are the most significant influence in your child's life. Even when they become a teen, elite athlete and start to detach from the family with a focus predominantly on their peer group, you are still the most significant influence in their lives.

To be a supportive parent with all the distractions in the 21st century, you need to;

1. Display healthy sportsmanship when winning and losing.
2. Show your child how to manage him emotions by keeping your emotions in check. Teach poise and controlled emotional reactions.

3. When things don't go as planned, help your child develop the mindset to learn from the loss. Find the positives from the experience. Learn and improve from the negatives.

4. Help your child understand that he will react, but the key is how fast he will bounce back and respond in a productive manner.

5. Reinforce the coach's messages and coaching. Encourage the mindset of one instructional voice.

6. Encourage the love of playing, learning and applying his talent to his sport.

7. Teach good habits, dietary requirements, sleep habits, respect, long-term goal-setting and short-term strategic steps.

8. Keeping life in perspective by having a healthy balance in your life.

9. Teach the capacity to stay focused on doing his best in the moment, and to not solely be focused on the outcome. Life in the 21st century offers many distractions.

10. Be a healthy role model by providing unconditional love.

Take Away for Step Fourteen:

You can add stress or support as parent. If you are emotionally reactive you need to address your own behaviors. Remember the 4 A's of Love. Be a role model and supportive.

Step Fifteen: **Being a Coach of a Champion**

Outline:

1. **Coaches are supposed Coach**
    Criteria that determines an elite coach
2. **Secret Agents**
    Criteria used to determine the professional representing you

Coaches are supposed Coach: How to Recognize a Good Coach

If your only tool is a hammer, you must force everyone to becoming a nail. A teacher is supposed to teach the student. As a faculty member at Johns Hopkins School of Medicine, my job was to communicate clearly the educational points. For years I have said, "Just because someone is a professor doesn't mean they know how to teach." The most stimulating conversations of my three-hour lecture was always the additional hour after class when a half-dozen students would be inquisitive for further information.

Good communication is not the words that just came out of your mouth, but rather how the recipient understands your message. As the sender of information, it is truly my responsibility to discover what facilitates this student, athlete, recipient towards fully understanding the lessons, information and material I am providing.

How to recognize a "bad" coach:

1. Some coaches don't understand the detail required to be a great leader of athletes. They do not know how to motivate a range of personalities and don't understand the importance of establishing a relationship with the athlete.
2. The Tampa Bay Buccaneers were once coached by John McKay. This was an example of an emotional driven coach. He didn't think. In one game, the kicker, Alan

Levett missed a 50-yard kick. The coach said, sarcastically "Nice Kick Alan" which was devastating to him. The coach blamed him for the miss. The coach knew better but was emotional and sarcastic.

3. Some coaches use the Hammer approach. They are harsh without offering details to improve performance. They can be mean and say offensive, belittling comments. There was a coach that was so mean-spirited, he would verbally and publicly say the most hurtful comments to the top national athletes.

4. Coaches that become too emotional overwhelmed by their emotions or say/do something they later regret. They don't display emotion management, impulse control or judgement.

5. A team of coaches asked me to meet with their nationally-ranked top athletes and discuss the reasons for their recent lack of effort. The athletes shared one of their coaches believed he was being helpful, but tended to overreact, publicly embarrass them, and use sarcasm at their expense. The athletes told me that this pattern had been going on for a long period of time. They had approached the coach and stated their concerns but his behavior only continued. By the time I met these athletes, they had decided to discontinue their relationship with this coach and transferred to a different facility and work with another coach. When I spoke with the coach, he denied any possibility his behavior had contributed to their lack of motivation and their interest to move to a different facility. Denial is a powerful defense mechanism.

6. Some coaches have the "Clueless" approach. They seem friendly enough but don't offer any advice of substance. They often provide nebulous, obtuse comments to players. I knew of a coach of a youth lacrosse team who would

consistently tell a player that he was good enough to start and yet never put him in the games. The coach offered no helpful advice or suggestions on how to improve, he simply told the athlete, "Just give it time." There is nothing wrong with a coach that puts a roster together that fields the best skilled or experienced athletes for the games. Yet, every time the athlete approached his coach he received no direction, advice or game plan. The subsequent season, this young athlete switched to another team that was higher ranked and was immediately selected as a starter.

7. The Non-Leader Coach. I observed a basketball coach who told a player that he "wouldn't" start him. It is certainly reasonable for a coach to select certain players for specific positions which might preclude a player from starting. However, this player was the only one on his team that played on the far more competitive AAU travelling team that represented the major city where he lived. The reality was the coach "couldn't" start him because there were several seniors on the high school team that threatened to quit if their senior friend was benched allowing the freshman to start. This loss of power and impotence prevented him from taking charge, and not making the best decisions for the team and players.

8. The Democratic Coach. This coach wants everyone to like him. He never takes a stance. Decisions are never declared. He always wants input. And his eventual decision might not be in the best interest of the team, but rather to placate certain members of the team. This coach needs to be more empowered to make the decisions and feel secure that his decisions are based on experience, knowledge and feedback.

Let's now talk about how to recognize a "good" coach.

The great Morgan Wootten delineated the distinction between good and bad coaches. "True basketball coaches are great teachers. You do not humiliate. You don't physically go after. You do not push or shove. You do not berate or curse if you are a true coach...They are really not coaches." (Wootten, 1994). Having a great impact on the lives of young men is a part of coaching. What works in sports works in life. Coach Wootten use to say, "You have to be willing to park your ego at the door in order to be part of something bigger than yourself. That's what makes basketball work, that's what makes business work."

Bottom line to be an exceptional coach you need to discover what motivates individual players and how he best learns.

As an athlete, your progression depends on many variables. Just because you believe you are awesome and amazing does not mean you have the physical strength, stamina, coordination, size, etc. to compete at the level your coach believes is necessary to be victorious. Yet, your coach should be able to give you helpful feedback, accurate observations and detailed plans to foster your growth, advancement and proper game plans.

The following is a checklist of 10 Criteria of an exceptional coach. It will help determine if you have the right coach for your child. He/She:

1) Helps young athletes learn life lessons from sport
2) Develops a positive rapport with athletes
3) Understands there is more to a sport than winning
4) Supports, encourages, motivates and inspires
5) Wins and loses graciously
6) Is the first and last person at training and games
7) Works together with athletes to set team and individual goals
8) Listens to player's thoughts and opinions
9) Doesn't interfere with referees
10) Understand the research Three Key Characteristics of the World's Best Coaches or "Serial Winners." This research shows

multinational sporting bodies and conducted intensive interviews.
https://playerdevelopmentproject.com/key-characteristics-of-the-worlds-best-coaches/?utm_source=hootsuite

Results:

a. Coaches read a lot
b. Coaches know themselves well and continue to personal/professional grow and are open to change
c. Coaches aim is always to get to know the athletes better

Coach Jim Harbaugh of the University of Michigan is a coaches' coach. When he speaks people listen. His wisdom comes from a long and successful career as a player, a coach in the NFL and a coach of one of the NCAA most revered institutions. He encourages his athletes to be their best saying, "Realistic expectations for life are that we are going to be better today than we were yesterday, be better tomorrow than we were today. That's a plan for success. So the key is simple: just work."

Secret Agents

Prior to reaching the pro ranks, athletes are not allowed to work with an Agent. The reason is the amateur athlete is supposed to be focusing on a well-balanced life (school, social, physical development) as well as preventing exploitation or violating/child-labor laws. Most agents do an exceptional job representing their client. However, there are a few unscrupulous agents who will over-sell and under-perform. They will promise the world and deliver empty promises.

It is important to discuss the reasons for having 1) an agent, 2) the credentials of a credible agent and 3) what to expect from this relationship. Initially, I would suggest all athletes and their families look for someone they really feel comfortable with, and then consider following these six key characteristics before committing to any representative, including a family friend or inexperienced lay person.

1) **Accessibility.** Open and honest communication should be provided in a responsive manner. Access to the agent or the office is vital and they should respond to the athlete or their representative in a reasonable time frame.

2) **Authenticity.** Don't look for someone who just makes "promises", but for someone who has taken the time to get to know who you are and what a realistic blue print is for your career. They should manage expectations, not promise the world.

3) **Experience.** It is not about the number of years the agent has been in practice, but rather the specific expertise the agent has developed. References are always good to ask for and contact in order to gain perspective on this professional.

4) **Leverage.** It's not about having the most well-known agent, but it is about having the best agent who has connections, influence and the ability to represent you during all negotiations, legal, media, and public opportunities. A clear conversation and written commitment regarding all of these should occur before signing any contracts with the agent. Your agent needs to have leverage with General Mangers (GM's), teams and sponsors.

5) **Respect.** This is similar to Trust and it must exist. Without the ability to feel respect the relationship will invariably fail. You should feel the agent is representing your best interests. The way

they communicate in a written form and when speaking on your behalf should present the best possible image.

6) **Trust**. The "Feeling of confidence and integrity" of someone who has your best interest in mind, and with whom you want to work. It's a relationship you want for life, so it's important to have chemistry. You should want to talk and, be with them. They should feel like a "family." That may not happen right away, but go slowly with your gut while assessing their history, experience and reputation will prevail. The player-agent relationship is one of trust. The athlete ultimately needs to trust the agent is doing everything they can for them. Does the athlete have that deep trust that his agent is capable and aggressively helping him to get the best deal to get ahead?

Here are a few more points the athlete should assess before hiring an agent/agency.

What makes up a management team?

Ideally your agent is a lawyer. That's all you need at first. If you need legal advice in addition to your agent, they can QB it for you. I would prefer your agent have his/her law degree because he is "negotiating" on your behalf and should be an expert. He should be able to help with legal matters or have people on his team that can help with common legal matters. He can QB if you need something more specific (like a real estate attorney, or a copyright attorney, etc). The ability to successfully represent a Major League Baseball player comes in large part from a thorough understand of the rights, benefits, and obligations spelled out in the very lengthy and legal Collective Bargaining Agreement. Your agent needs to understand the collective bargaining agreement of your sport.

Depending on the level of the athlete, I don't think it's necessary to hire an outside publicist or marketing team. Find an agency that has those capabilities in-house. There are plenty who have it and you will

ALWAYS get the best service if one team is managing your brand. The right hand and left hand need to know what's going on and work on the same program/plan.

You do not want your business manager or financial person working in house with your agent. This could lead to a potential conflict of interest. However, he should have a close relationship with the business person. Your agent can help vet or introduce you to the right person.

Every sport or league is different and is governed by their own players' union or players' association. The State Bar Association governs licensed attorneys. In baseball, the Major League Baseball Players Association controls who can represent their players. Only certified agents can represent MLB players.

What should an athlete expect from an Agent/Agency?

A skilled sports management Agent should be attentive, honest, offer guidance, provide structure, organize the process. Your agent needs to be proactive. Years of experience should offer wisdom regarding the logical steps to anticipate, and your agent needs to be there with you through the process and provide assistance to you or your family whenever necessary.

Communications: The skilled agent stays in contact with the player wanting to know how they are doing in their journey, and wanting to help them along the way.

The skilled agent is passionate about representing you. It is easy to be excited about representing someone who is a 1st Round pick or is in the Big Leagues, but real passion is representing every client no matter where they are at or at what level. An agent must be passionate about the game of baseball, and about representing baseball players. Of course, if the agent is representing a player in a different sport it is the same. Baseball is an all-encompassing sport. Through research and conversation with the prospective agent, the athlete should seek an agent with a deep love of the sport and and a successful record of representing baseball players.

What will the Agent/Agency expect from the athlete?

As the client/athlete you will need to be honest, trustworthy, and responsive. This relationship needs to be a 2-way street. If the athlete isn't honest about his/her opinions, thoughts, needs – how can an agent help guide? If an athlete isn't responsive, trusting, how can an agent adequately leverage his negotiations with a team?

Agents look for athletes that have a passion to be successful at the big-league level. The athlete needs to have a very strong work ethic and the perseverance to tough it out. Agents expect their athletes to be responsive in communicating with them and appreciative of the process.

What should an athlete expect from an Agent/Agency to achieve his optimal physical abilities to compete at the highest levels?

As the athlete, you should expect to discuss and received a plan. There needs to be a review of both long-term and short-term goals. You should anticipate your agent has access to the highest-level trainers, conditioning teams, and facilities. Your agent should possess the know-how of what you NEED to be at your best and have the ability to get everything organized. Also, your agent should have the leverage with the athlete's team to ensure what they ask for is in the athlete's best interest, not the team's best interest.

What Red Flags should an athlete be aware of regarding the Agent/Agency?

When looking to the agent or agency to be your public representative, find the retention rate with the athletes they represent. If athletes don't leave – that's a good sign. If there is a high turnover – that is NOT a good sign. Long-term relationships speak volumes. Get as many references as possible. This is a decision which should not be taken lightly.

Google them! Check for any negative press. Not just one comment but a pattern. One of my colleagues is head of a significantly large outpatient clinical practice. He has won numerous professional awards. However, not one patient rated him above 3 out of 5. As a matter of fact, several former patients dissuaded other people from using his clinical services.

A good agent doesn't often appear in the media. The athlete does, not the agent.

Is the Agent/Agency upfront with ALL fees? There should be NO SURPRISES. There should be no nickel and diming tactics.

The agent should always meet with the athlete not with the recruiter. If you meet only with the recruiter that could indicate the agent does not value direct communications with the athlete or the agency is too big and relies only on the use of recruiters to try to get athletes. I think it best to have at least a few conversations with any potential agent. If the agent talks more about themselves and makes grandiose promises, that may not be the right person. The key factor is, 'who is going to be represent me?' Often the athlete/family will meet a 'recruiter' type of person first. That person may have good communication and sales skills to try to get the player on board, but he will not be the one doing the real work of representing the athlete.

You still see some unbelievable things in the news regarding agents/advisors, including financial advisors who are stealing players' money. Though I think that has been greatly reduced over the years due to good enforcement and prosecution.

An agent that does not communicate directly and timely with the athlete is a big, red flag. It may be unfair to expect 24/7 access and response from an agent, but certainly responsive communications should be the norm. One of the biggest complaints from athletes who have had prior agents is the agent would not call or text them back in a timely manner, or the player was the one initiating the communications and the agent didn't seem to be that engaged with what was going on in the athlete's career.

This is a relationship which will hopefully bring much security and opportunity for both the athlete and the agent. If done correctly, this relationship could last a long time and provide everyone with numerous benefits. If your agent is more about his ego rather than putting your needs first, consider looking elsewhere. Again, trust, honesty, communication, leverage, and respect need to be the hallmark of this relationship.

Take Away for Step Fifteen:

Key people in an athlete's life can make a world of difference. Parents provide the foundation for a fantastic future. Supportive parents can be the difference between shining like a star or struggling. Coaches guide the development of each athlete and you should look for the qualities successful coaches possess. Lastly, the sports agent you select should have your best interest as their priority. You and your family should consider the questions provided as a road map to determining the best agent for your future.

Contributors

Thank you to Dr. Collins Medlin, Psy.D. for your input on concussion and superstitions. It was an honor to supervise you throughout your dissertation and help foster your development as a professional in the field of neuropsychology. Your literature review was helpful and an exceptional method to help further your own career interests in neuropsychology.

Some individuals are self-driven and possess intrinsic motivation. Blair Zuck is just that individual. Thank you for your literature review in the area of injury rehabilitation and athletes. This area has become a complex topic because psychologist have become an integral part of the medical/physical therapy rehab team.

Thank you to my friend, Attorney Ed Kravitz, J.D. for assisting me on the topic of sports agents. He provides exceptional legal guidance and personal services to his clients. Mr. Kravitz prioritizes his clients and addresses their individual needs from start to finish. His 20 years of litigation experience helping athletes and their families understand the business of baseball proved very insightful.

When you have reached the pinnacle of your profession you offer insights and wisdom that benefit those seeking answers to vital questions. Thank you to Jaymee Messler for her succinct steps and exceptional points on the topic of sports agents. Her expertise in this area is merely a drop in the bucket compared to her leadership and entrepreneurial creativity.

Thank you to Rachel Waag for her assistance in the area of perceived stress. Our conversations pertaining to the Laws of Physics sparked your interest to pursue more research in this dynamic are which emphasizes that stress is not based on reality by perception.

Blair Zuck as a student contributing to this manuscript in the areas of injury, visualization and more you were responsible, thorough and capable. I am grateful for your willingness to summarize the literature.

Thank you, Dr. Zack Isoma, for your contributions on the topic of Acceptance and Commitment Theory (ACT). Your descriptions and summary of the ACT material reveal an exceptional depth of knowledge in this area. I am grateful for your willingness to participate as a contributor on this developing area of the profession.

Thank you to Dr. Herb Goldstein, my colleague and friend. Your willingness to share your wisdom, personal experiences and helpful stories expanded key points throughout this book. I am grateful for your encouragement and motivation which brought life to my material with additional clinical examples.

A good editor is hard to find but a good editor who has lived the competitive life of an athlete is rare. Rich Libero is just that person. I am grateful to have your personal experience as a competitive athlete coupled with your wordsmithing acumen during the editing process of my book.

Thank you to my buddy, Brad Mount. Your ability to spot grammatical errors or problems with sentence structure are unequalled. The limitations of time were the unfortunate reality, yet your input is greatly appreciated.

I am grateful for the wisdom and critical eye offered by my friends who volunteered to review my manuscript during the development phase, Dr. Andy Hicks and Marcus Lee.

The final editorial, "icing on the cake", was graciously provided by Jamie Mayo. Your consultative analysis on editing, formatting and content polished my manuscript into the best-selling book that you see in front of you now.

"Less is More" is best illustrated by the wonderful editing provided by Gail Prince or as I say, Mom. Your clarity and conviction to simplicity helped tighten my book. Your loving support was ever-present.

A big thank you to the Honorable Edwin Shinitzky or as I prefer to call him, Pops. My father has been my role model and rock. He is a never-ending source of motivation to reach for the stars, live by a higher moral code and to do the right thing. Your input both as editor and content reviewer immensely helpful. You always encouraged me to be a competitive individual both in sport and in life and strive to always do my best.

One of my mentors from The Johns Hopkins University School of Medicine, Dr. Adger encouraged the staff and residence by saying, "If you possess some knowledge that you're not using, and it could benefit another individual, but you don't share it, then it does neither of you any good. So, share your knowledge." Sharing my professional lessons with each athlete, presenting to teams or writing this book is my way of giving back, paying it forward and displaying gratitude to my mentors. If I am tall it is because I stand on the shoulders of giants. Thank you Drs. Adger, Schretlen, Silberstein, Edwin, Snyder, McKusick, McHugh, Oski, Walker, Wilson, Brandt - a veritable list of champions.

Lastly, for nearly thirty years I have been fortunate to work with some of the most elite athletes and coaches representing every sport. I hope the journey has been mutually rewarding for my athletes as it has been for me. I can never thank all the individuals for the incredible lessons they have taught me. It has been an honor to collaborate with each of you. The journey has been thrilling as we worked together to reach your personal best. Thank you.

References

Step One: Master the Sport Psychology Triangle

NinjaInfographic

Ford, Henry

Step Two: Managing Stress

profootballhof.com, Sports Illustrated, Rick Rielly

sports.espn.go.com

Shinitzky, H.E. & Cortman, C. (2009), Your Mind: An Owner's Manual for a Better Life, Career Press

Yerkes, R.M. & Dodson, J.D. (1908), The relation of strength of stimulus to rapidity of habit-formation. Journal of Comparative Neurology and Psychology, 18, 459-482.

https://adaa.org/about-adaa/press-room/facts-statistics#

https://www.theplayerstribune.com/kevin-love-everyone-is-going-through-something/

https://www.theplayerstribune.com/mardy-fish-us-open/

Step Three: Mental Toughness

Zig Ziglar quote, Success is the doing, not the getting; in the trying, not the triumph. Success is a personal standard, reaching for the highest that is in us, becoming all that we can be. If we do our best, we are a success.

Step Four: Emotions Out, Information In

Dr. Herb Goldstein consultation 2016

A League of Their Own Tom Hanks quote, "There's no crying in Baseball

Zig Ziglar quote, failure is an event, not a person

Ross, JS et al. The Mind's Eye: Functional MR Imaging Evaluation of Golf Motor Imagery. AJNR Am J Neuroradiol. 2003 Jun-Jul;24(6):1036-44)

Milton, John et al. The Mind of Expert Motor Performance is Cool and Focused. Elsevier Inc. NeuroImage 35 (2007) 804-813)

Bernardi G et al. (2013) How Skill Expertise Shapes the Brain Functional Architecture: An fMRI Study of Visuo-Spatial and Motor Processing in Professional Racing-Car and Naïve Drivers. PLoS ONE 8(10)

Jacini WF, et al. J Sci Med Sport. (2009). Can exercise shape your brain? Cortical differences associated with judo practice. J Sci Med Sport. 2009 Nov;12(6):688-90. doi: 10.1016/j.jsams.2008.11.004. Epub 2009 Jan 14

Di Paola M, et. al., Prolonged rock climbing activity induces structural changes in cerebellum and parietal lobe. Hum Brain Mapp. (2013) Oct;34(10):2707-14. doi: 10.1002/hbm.22095. Epub 2012 Apr 21.

W.C. Fields quote, "It ain't what they call you, it's what you answer to."

Michael J. Fox quote, "What other people think about me is none of my business".

Step Five: Manage Your Thoughts and Emotions

Csikszentmihalyi, M, 1990, Flow: The Psychology of Optimal Experience.   Harper & Row, New York, NY. USA Jacobson Progressive Muscle Relaxation Training" approach

Short, S. E., Afremow, J., & Overby, L. (2001). Using Mental Imagery to Enhance Children's Motor Performance. JOPERD— The Journal of Physical Education, Recreation & Dance, 72(2), 19.

Retrieved April 2, 2006, from Questia database: http://www.questia.com/PM.qst?a=o&d=5002388782

Zig Ziglar quote, "You've got to 'be' before you can 'do', and you've got to 'do' before you can 'have

Mousavi, SH. and Meshkini, A. (2011), The Effect of Mental Imagery upon the Reduction of Athletes' Anxiety during Sport Performance, International Journal of Academic Research in Business and Social Sciences, October 2011, Vol. 1, No. 3, pp. 342-345.

Munroe, K. J., Giacobbi, P. R., Hall, C., & Weinberg, R. (2000). The four Ws of imagery: Where, when, why, and what. The Sport Psychologist, 14, 119-137.

Hall, C. (2001). Imagery in sport and exercise. In R. Singer, H. Hausenblas, & C. Janelle (Eds.), Handbook of Sport Psychology (pp. 529 – 549). New York, NY: John Wiley & Sons, Inc

Zig Ziglar, quote, "If you want to reach a goal, you must 'see the reaching' in your mind before you actually arrive at your goal

Ranganathan V.K. (2004) From mental power to muscle power – gaining strength using the mind. Neuropsychologia, 42(7) 944-56).

Jones, M. V., Bray, S. R., Mace, R. D., Macrae, A. W., & Stockbridge, C. (2002). The Impact of Motivational Imagery on the Emotional State and Self-Efficacy Levels of Novice Climbers. Journal of Sport Behavior, 25(1), 57+. Retrieved April 2, 2006, from Questia database: http://www.questia.com/PM.qst?a=o&d=5002456546

Wolpe of Temple University, who uses the combination of Progressive Relaxation and Systematic Desensitization

Hayes, S. C., Strosahl, K., & Wilson, K. G. (1999). Acceptance and Commitment Therapy: An experiential approach to behavior change. New York: Guilford Press.

Harris, R. (2009). ACT Made Simple: An Easy-To-Read Primer on Acceptance and Commitment Therapy.Oakland, CA: New Harbinger.

A-Tjak, J. G., Davis, M. L., Morina, N., Powers, M. B., Smits, J. A., & Emmelkamp P. M., (2015) A meta-analysis of the efficacy of acceptance and commitment therapy for clinically relevant mental and physical health problems. Psychotherapy & Psychosomatics, 84(30), 30-36.

DOI: 10.1159/000365764

Hayes, S.C, Strosahl, K.D., & Wilson, K.G. (2012). Acceptance and commitment therapy: The process and practice of mindful change (2nd edition). New York, NY: The Guilford Press.

Moore, Z. E. (2009). Theoretical and empirical developments of the Mindfulness-Acceptance-Commitment (MAC) approach to performance enhancement. Journal of Clinical Sport Psychology, 3(4), 291-302.

Bernier, Marjorie & Thienot, Emilie & Codron, Romain & Fournier, Jean. (2009). Mindfulness and Acceptance Approaches in Sport Performance. Journal of Clinical Sport Psychology. 4. 10.1123/jcsp.3.4.320.

Gustafsson, H., Davis, P., Skoog, T., Kenttä, G., Haberl, P. (2015) Mindfulness and its Relationship with Perceived Stress, Affect and Burnout in Elite Junior Athletes. Journal of Clinical Sport Psychology, 9(3): 263-281\

Kabat-Zinn, Jon. Mindfulness for Beginners: Reclaiming the Present Moment--and Your Life. Sounds True, 2012.

https://contextualscience.org/Talladega Nights "Second Place is First Loser

Step Six: Strive for Excellence, Not Perfection

Sara Yoheved Rigler proverb If you are not a better person tomorrow than you are today, what need have you for a tomorrow?" The purpose of human life is to improve one's character traits, by working on oneself every day. That's why God gives us today – and tomorrow.

Voltaire, 1700, quote, Don't let perfect be the enemy of good

Alexander Pope, quote, To err is human, to forgive divine.

Zig Ziglar, quote, "If you learn from defeat, you haven't really lost".

Step Seven: Increase Your Probability of Success

Charles Swindel or Lou Holtz, "Life is 10% what happens, and 90% how you react to it."

Albert Einstein Insanity is doing the same thing over and over again and expecting a different result.

Young, A. et. al. Alcohol-Related Sexual Assault Victimization Among Adolescents: Prevalence, Characteristics, and Correlates* Journal of Studies Alcohol and Drugs. 2008 January ; 69(1): 39–48

NIDA. (2017, July 18). College-Age & Young Adults. Retrieved from https://www.drugabuse.gov/related-topics/college-age-young-adults on 2017, August 17

Fact Sheet Underage Drinking, https://www.cdc.gov/alcohol/fact-sheets/underage-drinking.htm

Schulenberg, JE., Johnston, LD, O'Malley, PM, Backman, JG, Miech, RA, and Patrick, ME, (2016), Monitoring the Future National Survey Results on Drug Use, 1975-2016. Vol. II, College Students and Adults Ages 19-55.

Abbey, A, (2002), Alcohol-Related Sexual Assault: A Common Problem among College Students, Journal of Study of Alcohol, Supplement No. 14: 118-128.

Wechsler, H, Davenport, A, Dowdall, G., Moeykens, B., and Castillo, S. (1994), Health and Behavioral Consequences of Binge Drinking in College: A National Survey of Students at 140 Campuses. The Journal of American Medical Association, Dec. 7, Vol. 272

Powell, LM, Ciecierski, C, Chaloupka, FJ, Wechsler, H., (2002), Binge Drinking and Violence among College Students: Sensitivity to Correlationin the Unobservables, ImpacTeen, Bridging the Gap Initiative, Research Paper Series, No. 20.

Ansari, WE, Stock, C and Mills, C. (2013), Is Alcohol Consumption Associated with Poor Academic Achievement in University Students?, International Journal of Preventive Medicine, Oct: 4(10): 1175-1188.

White, A & Hingson, R, The Burden of Alcohol Use: Excessive Alcohol Consumption and Related Consequences Among College Students, https://pubs.niaaa.nih.gov/publications/arcr352/201-218.htm

Roehrs, T & Roth, T., Sleep, Sleepiness, and Alcohol Use, https://pubs.niaaa.nih.gov/publications/arh25-2/101-109.htm

Dr. Randy Pausch (2008), The Last Lecture: Achieving Your Childhood Dreams, https://www.youtube.com/watch?v=ji5_MqicxSo

Michael Jordan, quote

Wootten, 1994, http://www.usatoday.com/story/sports/preps/basketball/2013/05/01/morgan-wootten-dematha-basketball-coach-innovators-icons/2124931/

http://articles.latimes.com/1986-01-06/sports/sp-13578_1_adrian-dantley

Mark Twain quote The greatest fears in my life never happened.

President Roosevelt quote The only thing to fear, is fear itself

http://www.katinkahesselink.net/tibet/zen.html

Shinitzky, et. al. 2009, Your Mind: An Owner's Manual for a Better Life, Career Press

Arnold, R., & Sarkar, M. (2014). Preparing athletes and teams for the Olympic games: Experiences and lessons learned from the world's best sport psychologists. International Journal of Sport and Exercise Psychology, 13(1), 4–20. doi:10.1080/1612197x.2014.932827

Cheng, W.-N. K., & Hardy, L. (2016). Three-dimensional model of performance anxiety: Tests of the adaptive potential of the regulatory dimension of anxiety. Psychology of Sport and Exercise, 22, 255–263. doi:10.1016/j.psychsport.2015.07.006

Hodge, K., & Smith, W. (2014). Public Expectation, Pressure, and Avoiding the Choke. The Sport Psychologist TSP, 28(4), 375-389. doi:10.1123/tsp.2014-0005

Hodge, K., et. al. 2014, A Case Study of Excellence in Elite Sport: Motivational Climate in a World Champion Team, The Sport Psychologist, 2014, 28, 60-74, http://dx.doi.org/10.1123/tsp.2013-0037, 2014 Human Kinetics, Inc.

Kent, R. (2016, June 10). Great British Athletes' Perceptions of Competing at the London 2012 Olympic Games. U.S. Sports Academy - The Sports Journal.

Oudejans, R. R. D., Kuijpers, W., Kooijman, C. C., & Bakker, F. C. (2011). Thoughts and attention of athletes under pressure: Skill-focus or performance worries? Journal of Anxiety, Stress & Coping, 24(1), 59–73. doi:10.1080/10615806.2010.481331

Doran, G, Miller, A, and Cunningham, J. (1981) There's a S.M.A.R.T. Way to Write Management's Goals and Objectives.(vol. 70, issue 11)

Hebron, Michael (Youth Golf, powerpoint online live via Steven Guilano, 2017)

Step Eight: Develop an Optimistic Attitude

Muhammed Ali, quote

Zig Ziglar, quote

King Solomon, Proverbs, 24:16., quote

Dr. Randy Pausch, (2008), The Last Lecture: Achieving Your Childhood Dreams, quote

Prochaska, J. O., & DiClemente, C. C. (1982). Transtheoretical therapy: Toward a more integrative model of change. Psychotherapy: Theory, Research and Practice, 19, 276–278.

Step Nine: Establish Realistic Goals

Putting Averages - https://thesandtrap.com/forums/topic/51757-pga-tour-putts-gainedmake -percentage-stats/

http://www.better-golf-by-putting-better.com/putting-expectations.html

Derek Jeter, http://bleacherreport.com/articles/2190547-refelcting-on-all-that-derek-jeter-was

Zig Ziglar, quote

Dr. Randy Pausch, (2008), The Last Lecture: Achieving Your Childhood Dreams, quote

Step Ten: Finish Strong

https://youtu.be/BqhK55JVEd8

Step Eleven: The Unmentionables

Laird Hamilton, quote

photo from The Daily News front page October 21, 2004

Wang, J., Marchant, D., & Morris, T. (2004). Coping style and susceptibility to choking. Journal of Sport Behavior, 27(1), 75-92

Sampras, (2000). Historic win for Sampras, The Advertiser, July II, pp. 68.

Dr. Sian Beilock (Professor of Psychology at University of Chicago, wrote Choke: What the Secrets of the Brain Reveal About Getting it Right When You Have To (https://www.youtube.com/watch?v=zcr4ZD-Vrsg)

Caddyshack, 1980

O'Neill, Brian. "Finding Joy in Life Cured his Steve Blass Disease." Pittsburgh Post-Gazette. July 3, 2012. (Aug. 8, 2012) http://www.post-gazette.com/stories/opinion/brian-oneill/finding-joy-in-life-cured-his-steve-blass-disease-641744/

Philippen, P., & Lobinger, B.H. (2012). Understanding the Yips in Golf: Thoughts, Feelings, and Focus of Attention in Yips-Affected Golfers. Sport Psychologist, 26(3), 325-340

Stinear, CM, Coxon, JPl, Fleming, MK, Lim, VK, Prapavessis, H, Byblow, WD, (2006), The Yips in Golf: Multimodal Evidence for Two Subtypes., Medicine & Science in Sports & Exercise, 0195-9131/06/3811-1980/0

Priori, A.A., Presenti, A., Cappellari, G., Scarlato and Barbieri, (2001), Limb immobilization for the treatment of focal occupational dystonia. Neurology 57:405–409, 2001.

Zeuner, KE., Shill, HA, Sohn, H, et. al. (2005), Motor training as treatment in focal hand dystonia. Mov. Disord. 20:335–341.

Zeuner, K.E., W. Bara-Jimenez, P.S. Noguchi, S.R. Goldstein, J.M. Dambrosia, and M. Hallett. Sensory training for patients with focal hand dystonia. Ann. Neurol. 51:593–598, 2002).

Palle-Rosted, A., (2005), Acupuncture for treatment of the yips?, Acupuncture Medicine, 23: 188-189

Bell, RJ. And Thomson, CL. Solution-Focused Guided Imagery for a Golfer Experiencing the Yips: A Case Study. www.athleticinsight.com/Vol91ss1/Golfimagery.htm

Step Twelve: Recovery from Injury

Dr. Charles Silberstein personal communication January, 1989.

Dr. John Andrews, USA Today, January 6, 2013, interview with Klemko, Robert

Hamson, J. The Effects of Mental Imagery on Recovery Time and Adherence to Sport-injury Rehabilitation Programs of College Athletes. American Alliance for Health, Physical Education, Recreation and Dance, Salt Lake City, Utah, April 2006

Andrews, J.R., Harrelson, G.L. (1991), Physical Saunders Company

Shuer, M.L. & Dietrich, M.F., (1997), Psychological Effects of Chronic Injury in the Elite Athlete, Western Journal of Medicine, Sub; 166: 104-109.

Granito, Jr., V.J., (2002), Psychological Response to Athletic Injury: Gender Differences. Journal of Sports Behavior, 25(3), 242-260.

Storch, E.A., Storch, J.B., Killiany, E.M. and Jonathan, W.,(2005), Self-Reported Psychopathology in Athletes: A Comparison of Intercollegiate Student-Athletes and Non-Athletes. Journal of Sports Behavior, 28(1) 86-96.

Wiechman, S.A. and Williams, J. (1997), Relation of Athletic Identity to Injury and Mood Disturbance. Journal of Sports Behavior, 20. 199-210.

Manuel, J.C., (2002), Coping with Sport Injuries. An Examination of the Adolescent Athlete, Journal of Adolescent Health, 31, 391-393.

San Jose, A., (2003), Injury of Elite Athletes: Sport and Gender-Related Representations. International Journal of Sport and Exercise Psychology, I, 434-459.

Tracey, J., (2003), Emotional Response to the Injury and Rehabilitation Process., Journal of Applied Sport Psychology, 15:4, 279-293.

Weiss, M.R. and Troxel, R.K., (1986), Psychology and the Impaired Athlete: Athletic Training, Kinesiology, 21, 104-109.

Caine, C & Garrick, J. (1996), Dance, In: Caine, D., Caine, C., Linder, K (Eds): Epidemiology of Sport Injuries. Champaign, IL. Human Kinetics, pp. 124-160.

Kerr, G., Krasnow D, and Mainwaring L., (1992), The Nature of Dance Injuries. Medical Problem Performance Art, 7:25-29.

Liederbach, M. (2000), General Considerations for Guiding Dance Injury Rehabilitation. Journal of Dance Medical Science, 4(2): 54-56.

Flanigan, D.C., (2013), Fear of Re-injury (Kinesiophobia) and Persistent Knee Symptoms are Common Factors for Lack of Return to Sport After Anterior Cruciate Ligament Reconstruction, Journal of Arthroscopic and Related Surgery. 29.8: 1322-1329.

Kvist, J et al (2005), Fear of Reinjury: A Hindrance for Returning to Sports After Anterior Cruciate Ligament Reconstruction, Knee Surgery Sports Traumatology Arthroscopy, Jul: 13(15): 393-397.

Thomee, P. et. al. (2008), Self-Efficacy of Knee Function as a Pre-Operative Predictor of Outcome One Year After Anterior Cruciate Ligament Reconstruction. Knee Surgery Sports Traumatology Arthroscopy, 16(2), 118-127.

Barefield, S. and McCallister, S. (1997), Social Support in the Athletic Trianing Roo: Athletes' Expectations of staff and Student Athletic Trainers. Journal of Athletic Training, 32, 333-338

Green . S.L. and Weinberg, R.S. (2001), Relationship Among Athletic Identity, Coping Skills, Social Support and Psychological Impact of Injury in Recreational Participants. Journal of Applied Sport Psychology, 13, 40-59

Bandura, A. (1977). Self-efficacy: Toward a unifying theory of behavioral change. Psychological Review, 84(2), 191-215.

Ardern, C.L., Webster, K.E., Taylor, N.F. and Feller, J.A. (2011), Return to Sport Following Anterior Cruciate Ligament Reconstruction Surgery: A Systematic Review and Meta-Analysis of the State of Play. British Journal Sports Medicine, June: 45(7): 596-606.

Ardern, C.L., Taylor, N.F., Feller, J.A., and Webster, K.A.. (2013), A Systematic Review of the Psychological Factors Associated with Return to Sports Following Injury, British Journal of Sports Medicine, November; 47(17): 1120-6.

Driediger, M., Hall, C. and Callow, N. (2006), Imagery use by Injured Athletes: A Qualitative Analysis. Journal Sports Science, March; 24(3): 261-271.

Evans, L., Hare, R. and Mullen, R. (2006), Imagery Use During Rehabilitation from Injury. Journal of Imagery Research in Sport and Physical Activity. Vol 1, Issue 1(5).

Wiese-Bjornstal, D.M., (2010), Psychology and Socio-Culture Affect Injury Risk, Response, and Recovery in High-Intensity

Athletes: A Consensus Statement, Scandinavian Journal of Medicine and Science in Sports. Vol. 20, Supplement s2, Oct. pp. 103-111.

Williams, J.M. and Anderson, M.B. (1998), Psychological Antecedents of Sport Injury: Review and Critique of Stress and Injury Model, Journal of Applied Sport Psychology, Vol. 10, Issue 1, pp. 5-25.

http://www.stopsportsinjuries.org/media/statistics.aspx

https://www.safekids.org/search?search_api_views_fulltext=sports+injury

https://www.safekids.org/

Preserving the Future of Sport: From Prevention to Treatment of Youth Overuse Sports Injuries. AOSSM 2009 Annual Meeting Pre-Conference Program. Keystone, Colorado

Step Thirteen: Avoid These Roadblocks

Pavlov, I.P. (1927). Conditioned Reflexes: An investigation of the physiological activity of the cerebral cortex. Retrieved from http://psychclassics.yorku.ca/Pavlov/lecture6.htm.

Pavlov, I. P. (1928). Lectures on conditioned reflexes. (Translated by W.H. Gantt) London: Allen and Unwin.

Perry, B. W., & Kristi, J. E. (2008). Sport Superstition as a Function of Skill Level and Task Difficulty. Journal of Sport Behavior, 31(2), 187-199

Gmelch, G. (1974). Baseball magic. In J. Spradley & D. McCurdy (Eds.), Conformity and conflict (pp. 346–352). Boston: Little, Brown.

Bleak, J. L., & Frederick, C. M. (1998). Superstitious behavior in sport: Levels of effectiveness and determinants of use in three collegiate sports. Journal of Sport Behavior, 21(1), 1-15

https://en.wikipedia.org/wiki/List_of_professional_sportspeople_c onvicted_of_crimes

The National Eating Disorder Association (NEDA) website, www.NationalEatingDisorder.org

Williamson, et. al., (1995). Structural Equation Modeling of Risk Factors for the Development of Eating Disorder Symptoms in Female Athletes, International Journal of Eating Disorders. Vol. 17, No. 4, 387-393 (1995)

Managing   the   Female   Athlete   Triad (http://multimedia.olympic.org/pdf/en_report_517.pdf

The American College of Sports Medicine, The Female Athlete Triad Position Stand, www.acsm.com

Bachner-Melman, R., Zohar, A, Ebstein, R, et.al. 2006. How Anorexic-like are the Symptom and Personality Profiles of Aesthetic Athletes? Medicine & Science in Sports & Exercise 38 No 4. 628-636

Zucker NL, Womble LG, Williamson DA, et al. Protective factors for eating disorders in female college athletes. Eat Disorders 1999; 7: 207-218)

Hausenblas, H. and Carron, A,. (1999), Eating Disorder Indices and Athletes: An Integration,   Journal of Sport & Exercise Psychology, 21, 230-258.

Klock, S.C. & DeSouza, M.J. (1995) Eating disorder characteristics and psychiatric symptomatology of eumenorrheic and amenorrheic runners. International Journal of Eating Disorders. Mar;17(2):161-6.

Hulley A.J. & Hill, A.J., (2001), Eating Disorders and Health in Elite Women Distance Runners. International Journal of Eating Disorders 30, 312-317.

Lundholm, J. K., & Littrell, J. M. (1986). Desire for thinness among high school cheerleaders: Relationship to disordered eating and weight control behaviors. Adolescence, 21(83), 573-579

Szymanski, L. A., & Chrisler, J. C. (1990). Eating disorders, gender-role and athletic activity. Psychology: A Journal of Human Behavior, 27(4), 20-29.

Reel, J.J & Gill, D.L, (1996). Psychosocial Factors Related to Eating Disorders among High School and College Female Cheerleaders, The Sport Psychologist, Vol. 10(2), June 1996, pp. 195-206.

Blouin, A.G. and Goldfield, G.S. (1995), Body image and steroid use in male bodybuilders, The International Journal of Eating Disorders, Vol. 18(2), Sept. pp. 159-165.

Goldfield, G.S., Harper, D.W. & Blouin, A.G. (1998), Are Bodybuilders at Risk for an Eating Disorder, The Journal of Treatment and Prevention, Vol 6(2). pp. 133-151.

Klenk, Courtney A., "Psychological Response to Injury, Recovery, and Social Support: A Survey of Athletes at an NCAA Division I. University" (2006). Senior Honors Projects. Paper 9.

http://digitalcommons.uri.edu/srhonorsprog/9http://digitalcommons.uri.edu/srhonorsprog/9

Psychological Issues Related to Injury in Athletes and the Team Physician: A Consensus Statement. 2006, American College of Sports Medicine, 0195-9131/06/3811-2030/0,

https://www.sportmedicine.ru/recomendations/psychological_issues_related_to_injury_in_athletes_and_the_team_physician.pdf

Rodriguez, Carissa, 2005, Can Sport Psychology Help Athletic Performance By Increasing Mental Toughness Through Decreasing Anxiety?

http://healthpsych.psy.vanderbilt.edu/MentalTough.htm

Powell, JS and Barber Foss, KD, 1999. Injury Patterns in Selected High School Sports: A Review of the 1995-1997 Seasons. Journal Athletic Training. 34: 277-84

Photo from Why do football players keep dropping the ball before the end zone? www.sbnation.com

Dear Abbey, What is Class? Advice Column

Avatar, (2009), Lightstorm Entertainment Dune Entertainment Ingenious Media, 20th Century Fox

Lyndon Johnston, Canadian Pairs figure skating champion and Olympian, Coach US National Pairs Figure-Skating Teams, 2016, personal communication

Step Fourteen: Being a Parent of a Champion

Marx, Jeffrey, (2004), Season of Life: A Football Star, a Boy, a Journey to Manhood, Simon & Schuster,

Step Fifteen: Being a Coach of a Champion

Edwin, D. and Denckla, M. (1995), Parenting Children on the Autism Spectrum, Clinical Seminar Rounds Johns Hopkins Medical Institution, Department of Psychiatry, Baltimore, MD.

Morgan Wootten,

www.usatoday.com/story/sports/preps/basketball/2013/05/01/morgan-wootten-dematha-basketball-coach-innovators-icons/2124931/

https://playerdevelopmentproject.com/key-characteristics-of-the-worlds-best-coaches/?utm_source=hootsuite

Kravitz, Ed, J.D. (2016), Personal communication

Messler, Jaymee (2016), Personal communication

Additional Materials for further investigation:

Morgan, W, Brown, D, Raglin, J, O'Connor and Ellickson, K, 1987. Psychological Monitoring of Overtraining and Staleness. Britich Journal of Sports Medicine, 21: 107-114

Kentta, G., Hassmen, P., and Raglin, J. 2001, Training practices and overtraining syndrome in Swedish age-group athletes. International Jouranl of Sports Medicine 22: 460-465.

10-Minute Toughness by Jason Selk

Finding Your Zone by Michael Lardon and David Leadbetter

Mentally Tough Teens: Developing a Winning Mindset. (2014), Justin Su'a

Parent Pep Talks: The 10 Mental Skills Your Child Must Have to Succeed in School, Sports, and Life, (2013), Justin Su'a

An Athlete's Guide to Sport Psychology by Tony Reilly

Mind Gym: An Athlete's Guide to Inner Excellence by Gary Mack

Datameer biometric data analysis

Positive Coaching Alliance, http://www.positivecoach.org/

Coakley, Jay. 2006. The good father: Parental expectations and youth sports. Leisure Studies 25, 2: 153-164.

National Association for Sport and Physical Education. (1977). Bill of rights for young athletes. Reston, Va.

NASPE Bill of Rights for Young Athletes. http://www.aahperd.org/naspe/pdf_files/billofrightsforyoungathl etes.pdf

Moms Team.com: The Place for Moms With Children in Youth Sports, http://www.momsteam.com

Do's and Don'ts for Sport Parents, by Amy Wheeler (USA Gymnastics Online: Athlete Wellness) http://www.usa-gymnastics.org

Ten Commandments of Parental Behavior, http://www.ct-starters.org/tencommd.htm

College Athletes: Academic Performance: Behind the line on grades By Mike Knobler, The Atlanta Journal-Constitution, Sunday, December 28, 2008. SAT

Loss Aversion in Riskless Choice: A Reference-Dependent Model, Amos Tversky and Daniel Kahneman, The Quarterly Journal of Economics, Vol. 106, No. 4 (Nov., 1991), pp. 1039-1061, Published by: Oxford University Press

Additional publications and consultation services by Dr. Shinitzky

If you would like more information from Dr. Shinitzky, you would enjoy reading his previous books.

In Your Mind: An Owner's Manual for a Better Life (Career Press, 2010) you will read about the ten most common issues presented in his practice. Each issue will be discussed in real world, clinical examples and practical exercises are provided at the end each chapter for you to learn healthier coping skills to address and resolve these issues.

In Take Control of Your Anxiety: A Drug-Free Approach to Living a Happy, Healthy Life (Career Press, 2015) you will read valuable information regarding the most common mental health condition. You will learn the benefits anxiety/arousal provide by motivating you. Throughout the book you will discover helpful tools to resolve your anxiety symptoms.

Dr. Shinitzky conducts corporate training with a sports twist. This educational and entertaining approach, "edutainment" is the hallmark of Dr. Shinitzky's presentation style. The topics covered and skills developed through his training programs help top management achieve greater productivity from employees and foster the development of a more engaged workforce.

About the Author

Dr. Shinitzky has worked with Olympians (figure skating, diving, sailing, biathlon) and professional athletes from every major association (PGA, NFL, NBA, MLB, NHL, MLS, WTA) as well as nationally ranked junior athletes. He is a highly sought after motivational speaker for teams at all levels and applies his upbeat, engaging and entertaining presentation style when sharing mental conditioning steps and prevention principles to athletes, teams and coaches. He is a consulting Sport Psychologist for Athlete Connections Foundation, an educational life skills training program helping youth athletes, Division I university athletes and professionals.

Dr. Shinitzky has shared his insights on the NBC Today Show, MSNBC Last Word with Lawrence O'Donnell, Animal Planet's Fatal Attractions, Discovery ID, Radio Disney, ABC-Baltimore (Fast Forward) and ABC-Tampa (ABC's of Parenting), and FOX-Tampa (Your Turn, Good Day Tampa Bay).

Dr. Harold Shinitzky is a licensed psychologist with a specialty in sport psychology. He was on the faculty at the Johns Hopkins University, School of Medicine, Department of Pediatrics, Adolescent Clinic where he was the Director of the Assessment Intervention Team/Prevention Services and the Director of Communication Skills Training. He completed two 3-year fellowships while on faculty.

Dr. Shinitzky was the recipient of the 2015 Florida Psychological Association (FPA) Outstanding Contributions to Psychology in the Public Interest, recipient of the 2011 Outstanding Contributions to FPA Award, the recipient of the 2009 FPA Distinguished Psychologist Award, and the 2009 FPA Outstanding Contributions to Psychology in the Public Interest.

He was selected as the 2000 Martin Luther King, Jr. National Award for Community Service.

Dr. Shinitzky co-authored Your Mind: An Owner's Manual for a Better Life (Career Press, 2010) and Take Control of Your Anxiety: A Drug-Free Approach to Living a Happy, Healthy Life (Career Press, 2015). He co-authored The Game Plan: Athlete Connections Student-Athlete Workbook. He is the creator and developer of Project Champions: Youth Resiliency and Prevention Program. Project Champions integrates best practice, evidence-based research into a fun and interactive prevention curriculum to help youth develop social-intelligence, grit, healthy decision-making and leadership skills.

Dr. Shinitzky also consults with financial institutions and Fortune 500 corporations. He takes the traditional corporate training programs and adds the fun and entertaining aspects of sports along with real-life stories of athletes to elaborate each informative point. His highly entertaining corporate training programs address peak performance, empowering the entrepreneur and creating a psychologically healthy workplace.

www.drshinitzky.com

www.achampionsmindset.com

Printed in Great Britain
by Amazon